CW01476138

Transmissions in Dance

Lesley Main
Editor

Transmissions in Dance

Contemporary Staging Practices

palgrave
macmillan

Editor
Lesley Main
Department of Performing Arts
Middlesex University
London, UK

ISBN 978-3-319-64872-9   ISBN 978-3-319-64873-6   (eBook)
https://doi.org/10.1007/978-3-319-64873-6

Library of Congress Control Number: 2017949198

© The Editor(s) (if applicable) and The Author(s) 2017
This work is subject to copyright. All rights are solely and exclusively licensed by the
Publisher, whether the whole or part of the material is concerned, specifically the rights
of translation, reprinting, reuse of illustrations, recitation, broadcasting, reproduction
on microfilms or in any other physical way, and transmission or information storage and
retrieval, electronic adaptation, computer software, or by similar or dissimilar methodology
now known or hereafter developed.
The use of general descriptive names, registered names, trademarks, service marks, etc. in this
publication does not imply, even in the absence of a specific statement, that such names are
exempt from the relevant protective laws and regulations and therefore free for general use.
The publisher, the authors and the editors are safe to assume that the advice and
information in this book are believed to be true and accurate at the date of publication.
Neither the publisher nor the authors or the editors give a warranty, express or implied,
with respect to the material contained herein or for any errors or omissions that may have
been made. The publisher remains neutral with regard to jurisdictional claims in published
maps and institutional affiliations.

Cover illustration: Forest (1976) by Robert Cohan. Dancers: Darja Guzikova and Harshil
Chauhan. Photograph by Andrew Lang

Printed on acid-free paper

This Palgrave Macmillan imprint is published by Springer Nature
The registered company is Springer International Publishing AG
The registered company address is: Gewerbestrasse 11, 6330 Cham, Switzerland

Foreword

In the professional world of the repertory company, 'transmission' or teaching parts to either solo artists or individual dancers, or bringing back an entire dance is really common practice. The work is usually done by the rehearsal director, with of course help from dancers who originally danced the parts, or from the choreographer if available. Every attempt is used to repeat the same movement as was done in the original but sometimes there have to be major adjustments depending on the skill of the replacement or the ability. The rehearsal director is usually an ex-dancer but someone who retains movement pattern very skillfully. We depend on the rehearsal director to do this work but there is no training as such–so how do we train someone to do that? It may be someone who worked with the choreographer, and this in a way is the best rehearsal director because they know the choreographer's pattern of movement and creation and if something has to be changed they can speak for the choreographer in the changing of the movement.

In my personal experience of teaching parts I have no hesitation in changing the movement in order to keep the meaning of the dance moment intact. But I know other choreographers insist that every movement be exactly as it was. Of course now, that is very easy because of the widespread use of video/film during the rehearsal period and of the finished work. There are still several problems–the intention of the dance and the intention of each little part that is performed–usually a choreographer makes movement to further the meaning of the dance or the intention of the dance, and although not always narrative, it has a certain feeling and look for the choreographer that makes it appropriate. It is important, for instance, that if changes are made to the movement, people who 'know the dance' should not notice the changes because the intention or the feeling, the atmosphere, the meaning of the dance is still the same. Once a movement is performed, it loses its uniqueness and becomes part of the dance language, therefore in a way, it loses its original meaning and care must be taken to retain it.

There is obviously a lot to discuss about this topic and to delve into it—which I don't recall it being done before. I don't know of any other writing that exists like this, that talks about the individual tasked with bringing back a dance and also the role of the dancers who contribute to that process, so I welcome this book.

London, UK   Robert Cohan CBE
April 2017

ACKNOWLEDGEMENTS

Any artistic endeavor is reliant on collaboration and support. This project is no different and I would like to express the collective gratitude of the contributors to those individuals and organisations who supported the creation of this volume. I would especially like to acknowledge the generosity of the group of photographers whose artistry helps bring our dances to life within these pages: Henry Chan, Jeff Cravotta, Camilla Greenwell, Dieter Hartwig, Guy L'Heureux, Christophe Jeannot, Scott Klinger, Andrew Lang, Julie Lemberger, Jennifer W. Lester Pari Naderi, Rocco Redondo, Vitali Wagner, Sam Williams. Thanks also to Gail Corbin, Ann Dils, Anne Donnelly, Susan Melrose, Kim Shigo, Yolande Yorke-Edgell; to the National Resource Centre for Dance, the Martha Graham Center for Contemporary Dance and to Middlesex University for financial support and, most importantly, for fostering an environment where performance practice as research is highly valued.

Thanks to Victoria Peters and Victoria Bates at Palgrave whose support made this volume possible.

An ongoing thank you to the many dancers who appreciate the significance of these dances and others like them, and bring themselves wholeheartedly into the process of discovery and performance.

The last word of gratitude goes to Robert Cohan, who continues to inspire us all to do better work.

CONTENTS

1   Introductions   1
    Lesley Main

2   Transmission: From Archive to Production Re-imagining
    Laban—Contemporizing the Past, Envisioning the Future   11
    Alison Curtis-Jones

3   Impure Transmissions: Traditions of Modern Dance Across
    Historical and Geographical Boundaries   37
    Fabián Barba

4   Performing History: *Wind Tossed* (1936), Natural
    Movement and the Hyper-Historian   61
    Maria Salgado Llopis

5   The Transmission–Translation–Transformation of Doris
    Humphrey's *Two Ecstatic Themes* (1931)   85
    Lesley Main

6   Transmission as Process and Power in Graham's
    Chronicle (1936)   109
    Kim Jones

7   Transmitting *Trio A* (1966): The Relations and Sociality of
     an Unspectacular Dance   143
     Sara Wookey

8   Silent Transformations in Choreography—Making Over
     Time: Rosemary Butcher's Practice of 'Looking Back and
     Ahead'   163
     Stefanie Sachsenmaier

9   The Living Cultural Heritage of Robert Cohan   189
     Paul R. W. Jackson

Index   227

NOTES ON CONTRIBUTORS

Fabián Barba was born in Quito in 1982, where he studied dance, theater, and literature. In 2004 he moved to Brussels where he completed the training and research cycles at P.A.R.T.S. Since graduation he has worked as an independent dancer, choreographer and researcher. His articles have been published in *Dance Research Journal, NDD l'actualité en danse, Documenta* and *The Oxford Handbook of Dance and Reenactment* (Oxford University Press, 2017).

Robert Cohan CBE joined the Martha Graham Dance Company in 1946 and was invited to become the founder/Artistic Director of The Place, London Contemporary Dance School and London Contemporary Dance Theatre in 1967. He is widely regarded as the founder and mainstay of contemporary dance in the UK. Cohan has choreographed over fifty works for contemporary and ballet companies around the world, with his most recent dances choreographed for Yorke Dance Project and the Richard Alston Dance Company.

Alison Curtis-Jones is artistic director of **Summit Dance Theatre**, a contemporary dance company re-envisioning works choreographed by dance innovator, theorist and founder of German Expressionist dance, Rudolf Laban, (1879–1958). The company is currently funded by the Swiss Government to stage and tour *Drumstick* (1913) and *Journey into Hades,* (1913) which have not been re-created before. Summit Dance Theatre are also recent winners of the 'Dance as Cultural Heritage' award. Alison is on the teaching faculty at Trinity Laban.

Paul R.W. Jackson trained in both music and dance and has worked in both areas professionally and academically. He has written extensively on both subjects and won the Chris de Marigny Dance Writers Award in 1997. He is the biographer of two of the leading figures in 20th century art; Oscar winning composer Sir Malcolm Arnold CBE and the 'father' of contemporary dance in Britain Robert Cohan CBE. Until retiring in 2017 he was Reader in Choreography and Dance at the University of Winchester.

Kim Jones is Associate Professor of Dance at UNC Charlotte and a régisseur for the Martha Graham Resource Center. A former dancer with the Martha Graham Dance Company from 2002–2006, her research includes restaging, reconstructing, and reimagining historical American modern dance works. Among these are a restaging of Martha Graham's *Primitive Mysteries* (1931) and a reimagining of Martha Graham's *Imperial Gesture* (1935), as well as a commissioned reconstruction of Paul Taylor's *Tracer* (1962).

Maria Salgado Llopis has over 20 years of international experience in the dance field. As a dancer, she was first artist at the Thuringer Staatsballet and principal dancer at the Pfalztheater Kaiserslautern, performing leading roles in classical ballet repertoire and contemporary works by choreographers such as William Forsythe, Dietmar Seyffert, Nils Christie and Mario Schröder. Her doctoral research focuses in the history and revival of Natural Movement (1920–1939). Maria's most recent performance of Madge Atkinson's Wind tossed was in Ireland, in November 2015.

Lesley Main is Head of the Department of Performing Arts at Middlesex University, London. She danced in the United States with Ernestine Stodelle from 1985, is director of the Doris Humphrey Foundation UK, and stages Humphrey's dances for Arke Compagnia D'Arte (Italy) and MOMENTA Dance Company (Chicago). She is the author of *Directing the Dance Legacy of Doris Humphrey: the Creative Impulse of Reconstruction (2012)*.

Stefanie Sachsenmaier (Ph.D. Middlesex University, DEA Sorbonne Nlle, M.A. Goldsmiths College) is Senior Lecturer in Theatre Arts at Middlesex University, Programme Leader of B.A. Theatre Arts (Performance) and HEA Fellow. Her research interests and publications relate to the processual in creative practice. She has published several articles emerging from her long-term research with choreographer Rosemary Butcher and recently co-edited, together with Noyale Colin, *Collaboration in Performance Practice: Premises, Workings and Failures,* Palgrave Macmillan, 2016.

Sara Wookey is based in London on a Tier 1 Visa endorsed by Arts Council England. Sara has been a dancer for Siobhan Davies, Matthias Sperling and Yvonne Rainer. She has been recently published in *The Ethics of Art: Ecological Turns in the Performing Arts* (2014, Valiz Press) and co-edited *WHO CARES? Dance in the Gallery & Museum* with Siobhan Davies Dance, London (2015). Sara is a certified transmitter of Yvonne Rainer's repertoire and a lecturer at Trinity Laban Conservatoire of Music and Dance.

LIST OF FIGURES

Fig. 2.1   Summit Dance Theatre in *Drumstick*, Teatro Del Gatta,
            Switzerland, 2015. Choreography by Alison Curtis-Jones.
            Photograph by Paolo Tosi, Tosi photography   27
Fig. 2.2   Summit Dance Theatre in *Drumstick*, Teatro Del Gatta,
            Switzerland, 2015. Choreography by Alison Curtis-Jones.
            Photograph by Paolo Tosi, Tosi photography   29
Fig. 3.1   Fabián Barba in *Drehmonotonie* by Mary Wigman.
            Photograph by Dieter Hartwig   52
Fig. 4.1   Russian Album Vol. II: Miscellaneous compositions for piano
            (London: W. Paxton & Co., 1916, p. 34). From the National
            Resource Centre for Dance   75
Fig. 5.1   Gail Corbin in *Two Ecstatic Themes*, Circular Descent.
            Photograph by Jennifer W. Lester   90
Fig. 5.2   Gail Corbin in *Two Ecstatic Themes*, Circular Descent.
            Photograph by Jennifer W. Lester   95
Fig. 5.3   Gail Corbin in *Two Ecstatic Themes*, Circular Descent.
            Photograph by Jennifer W. Lester   98
Fig. 5.4   Gail Corbin in *Two Ecstatic Themes*, Pointed Ascent.
            Photograph by Jennifer W. Lester   104
Fig. 6.1   Author Kim Jones coaching the final dress rehearsal
            for the premiere of her reconstruction of *Tracer*
            with the Taylor 2 Company, September 30, 2016.
            Photograph by Jeff Cravotta   111

Fig. 6.2   Program for the Martha Graham and Dance Group
            premiere of *Chronicle* at the Guild Theatre, NYC,
            December 20, 1936. Program materials provided
            by Martha Graham Resources, a division of the Martha
            Graham Center for Contemporary Dance, Inc   113
Fig. 6.3   Principal dancer Terese Capucilli (red dress) in *Chronicle*'s
            "Prelude to Action" with dancer Virginie Mécène
            at the Joyce Theater, NYC, 1999. Photograph
            by Julie Lemberger   123
Fig. 6.4   Author Kim Jones (left) with Fang-Yi Sheu (center) in dress
            rehearsal for *Chronicle*'s "Prelude to Action," coached
            by Artistic Director Terese Capucilli, Joyce Theater, NYC,
            2003. Photograph by Christophe Jeannot   129
Fig. 6.5   Blakeley White-McGuire in rehearsal for the "pops" section
            of *Chronicle*'s "Steps in the Street," 2005. Photograph
            by Christophe Jeannot   131
Fig. 6.6   Author Kim Jones (right) with dancers Yuko Suzuki
            Giannakis (center) and Erica Dankmeyer (left) in dress
            rehearsal for *Chronicle*'s "Prelude to Action," Joyce Theater,
            NYC, 2003. Photograph by Christophe Jeannot   132
Fig. 6.7   Blakeley White-McGuire in Martha Graham's
            Imperial Gesture, reimagined by Kim Jones at the Knight
            Theater, Charlotte, North Carolina 2013. Photograph
            by Jeff Cravotta   135
Fig. 7.1   Sara Wookey performing *Trio A* (1966) at VIVA! Art
            Action Festival, Montreal. 2011. Photograph
            by Guy L'Heureux   144
Fig. 7.2   Sara Wookey notation of *Trio A*   150
Fig. 7.3   *Trio A* (1966) tune-up with Yvonne Rainer and Sara
            Wookey at FADO Performance Art Centre.
            March 22, 2015. Photograph by Henry Chan   152
Fig. 7.4   Sara Wookey co-teaching with Yvonne Rainer as part of
            Trio A in 10 Easy Lessons at University of California, Irvine.
            2010. Photograph by Scott Klinger   157
Fig. 8.1   Rosemary Butcher during rehearsals for *18 Happenings
            in 6 Parts 1959/2010*, Clore Ballroom, Royal Festival Hall,
            London, 2010. Photograph by Rocco Redondo   173
Fig. 8.2   Rosemary Butcher, *18 Happenings in 6 Parts 1959/2010*,
            Rehearsal Notes, Clore Ballroom, Royal Festival Hall,
            London, 2010. Photograph by Rocco Redondo   175
Fig. 8.3   Rosemary Butcher, *SCAN*, Tanz im August, Berlin, 2015.
            Photograph by Tanz im August—Vitali Wagner   180

Fig. 8.4   Rosemary Butcher, *The Test Pieces*—Munich 2014;
            Nottingham 2015, Berlin 2015. Photographs top
            and mid by Sam Williams; lower by Tanz im
            August—Vitali Wagner   182
Fig. 8.5   München Olympiastadion Station, 2014. Photographs
            by Sam Williams   183
Fig. 9.1   Darja Guzikova and Harshil Chauhan in *Forest*.
            Photograph by Andrew Lang   203
Fig. 9.2   Yolande Yorke-Edgell in *Canciones del Alma*.
            Photograph by Pari Naderi   210
Fig. 9.3   Yorke Dance Project (Yolande Yorke-Edgell,
            Laurel Dalley-Smith, Kieran Stoneley, Jonathan Goddard)
            in *Lingua Franca*. Photograph by Pari Naderi   214
Fig. 9.4   Liam Riddick in *Sigh*. Photograph by Camilla Greenwell   220

CHAPTER 1

Introductions

Lesley Main

Transmissions in Dance is a collection of essays that capture the artistic voices at play during a staging process. The primary focus of this volume is on a range of dance works that continue to be presented today. The writing is by dancer/directors, or close associates of the choreographers, who offer deep insights into selected dances from the performer's perspective. Familiar practices such as reimagining, reenactment and recreation are situated alongside the related and often intersecting processes of transmission, translation and transformation. The breadth of practice on offer illustrates the capacity of dance as a medium to adapt successfully to diverse approaches and, further, that there is a growing appetite amongst audiences for seeing dances from the near and far past. The time period of the featured works spans a century, from Rudolf Laban's *Dancing Drumstick* (1913) to Robert Cohan's *Sigh* (2015). In between come works by Mary Wigman, Madge Atkinson (Natural Movement), Doris Humphrey, Martha Graham, Yvonne Rainer and Rosemary Butcher—an eclectic mix that crosses time and borders.

A common thread that runs through each chapter is the dancing in terms of the physical, artistic, sensorial, historical (and other) considerations that dancers have to navigate in order to achieve the requisite

L. Main (✉)
Middlesex University, London, UK
e-mail: l.main@mdx.ac.uk

© The Author(s) 2017
L. Main (ed.), *Transmissions in Dance*,
https://doi.org/10.1007/978-3-319-64873-6_1

state for a particular choreographic context. In each instance, dancers are engaging with movement material created on different bodies and, in some cases, from decades previously when bodies simply moved differently because of the training regimes in place. The quest to make sense of these movement enigmas is articulated in these pages in as many ways as there are chapters, which is refreshing and a healthy state for an art form as elusive as dance can be. That said, these 'quests' are also firmly grounded and rooted in careful artistic and historical scholarship in order that the choreographer's intent remains at the heart of the process. The diverse range of theoretical positions employed by the contributors to locate these works illustrates the span of possibility.

A second thread is the engagement with and understanding of 'transmission', a term in its plural form that serves in an overarching capacity as title of this volume. It is a term that has been usefully embraced by the field because it adds a further layer to the ways in which we can think about and define dance performance practice. There has already been a significant shift since the early 2000s, when the predominant forms of staging practice were reconstruction or restaging. The myriad 're' descriptors that have emerged since have done so to accommodate forms of staging practice that required definition beyond the parameters of those established terms—'reimagining' and 'reenactment' are two that have gained particular prominence through the work of dance artists such as Kim Jones, with her reimagining of Martha Graham's 'lost' solo, *Imperial Gesture* (1935) in 2013 and Fabián Barba's reenactment project on Mary Wigman's solo dances from 1925 to 1929.

Each chapter is focused around a single work, or a small group of works, to provide the reader with deep insights into the connecting aspects that are involved in a staging process. The balance of these aspects alters within each narrative for a variety of reasons such as the amount and quality of evidence available, including literary and visual documentation, and oral recollection from former dancers and the choreographers themselves. A commonality is that each artist is engaged in a construction process, a bringing together of a series of variables out of which a 'new' form of the work will emerge. The approaches taken to these variables are what actually define the individual's process as recreation, reimagining and so on. I was especially interested in capturing the articulation of these approaches in book form following *Transmission—A Performance Symposium* in 2014.[1] The event included performances of dances by Robert Cohan (*Agora* 1984/*Lingua Franca* 2014), Martha

Graham (*Imperial Gesture* 1935) and Doris Humphrey (*Two Ecstatic Themes* 1931) alongside *Le Marbre Trembre* (1982/2014), originally conceived by Mark Franko in collaboration with photographer Ernestine Ruben and performed on this occasion by Franko and Fabián Barba.[2] It was clear from the exchanges on that occasion, performative and otherwise, that the notion of 'transmission' had currency across a wide array of work. This book, therefore, serves as a forum for the particular group of artistic voices represented here, to convey the approaches that underpin their respective practices so that we can see and understand the decision making involved.

The structure of the book is (nearly) chronological, with chapters on Laban, Wigman and Atkinson grouped together as representative of early European/British dance; Graham and Humphrey sit naturally alongside each other as pioneers of American modern dance; the chapters on Rainer, then Butcher and Cohan take us forward in time, spanning both sides of the Atlantic. By way of closer introduction, there follows a brief synopsis of each chapter:

In Chap. 2, 'Transmission: from to production. reimagining Laban—contemporizing the past, envisioning the future', Alison Curtis-Jones considers *Dancing Drumstick*, one of Laban's early compositions from 1913. Through a methodology developed from choreological roots, Curtis-Jones reimagined the dance as *Drumstick* (2015) for Summit Dance Theatre, a company for whom she's staged a number of Laban's works funded by the Swiss government, this point evidencing the public desire for sight of these historically significant dances. Curtis-Jones introduces the reader to the range of concepts/practices she employs, including the notion of 'material remains'. The chapter's principal focus is on the transmission process of *Dancing Drumstick* from archive to production. Key issues include identifying what the 'material remains' of Laban works are, how these elements are translated for production, and what the process is for the interpretation, transference, transmission of live archive/documents into practice. Curtis-Jones has devised a method to reimagine the works, bridging archival gaps to create what she defines as a new 'living archive'. In so doing, she articulates a transmission process from archive to production that uses performance as a tool for translation and transformation, and the dancer's body as archive and 'place' for creative exchange.

When I invited Fabián Barba to contribute a chapter, the spur was that I wanted to know more about how it felt to dance the Wigman

soli and the processes he undertook to accumulate that bodily knowledge, having had an enticing glimpse in a previous article.[3] In Chap. 3,
'Impure transmissions—traditions of modern dance across historical
and geographical boundaries', he does so by way of a detailed exposition on the influence of *Ausdruckstanz* in relation to the development
of modern dance in South America and, specifically, Ecuador. Barba
relates 'transmission' to the notion of '*mestizaje*' (mixing) as offered
by María Lugones in order to understand the dynamics between these
two dance traditions in their complex and conflictive relations as they
operate at the core of the reenactment of the Wigman dances. This
discussion is positioned alongside his account of rehearsing with former dancers who worked closely with Wigman—Katharine Sehnert,
Irene Sieben and Susanne Linke, and the impact their combined experiences had on his ability to embody Wigman's style of movement.
Barba contends that to fully understand the transmission processes
that occurred during the creation of the nine solo dances that became
A Mary Wigman Dance Evening, it was important to first understand
the ground on which the transmissions happened, meaning the work
involved in reenacting the dances and also the role of his training
within a dance culture in Ecuador that motivated and made possible
the reenactments.

In Chap. 4, 'Performing history: *Wind Tossed* (1936), Natural
Movement and the hyper-historian', Maria Salgado Llopis discusses the
navigational challenges she had to undergo to make sense of Madge
Atkinson's solo, *Wind Tossed*, from her ingrained corporeal experience
as a classical ballet dancer. Salgado Llopis defines her approach as 'performing history' within the domain of reenactment, and in so doing
articulates the process of the transmission of this work in the present
from the point of view of the dancer as a 'hyper-historian'. Ideas from
Michael de Certeau and Freddie Rokem are drawn on to underpin the
discussion on the role of the hyper-historian, with this role being seen as
pivotal because it establishes the idea of the dancer as a connecting link
between past and present in performance. In the course of her discussion, Salgado Llopis refers to locating the 'remains of the performance'
in the present. She further argues that both the archive and the repertoire as referential systems and systems of transfer have the body at the
heart of their operations. One aspect of the rehearsal process that recurs
in other chapters is the importance of grasping the idea of the dance as
much as having physical command of the movement vocabulary.

My own contribution, Chap. 5, 'The transmission–translation–transformation of Doris Humphrey's *Two Ecstatic Themes* (1931)', is sited around Humphrey's signature solo and explores the intersecting relationship of the three 't's. Alliteration neatness aside, I argue that these three positions are germane when staging existing work because of the distinctive but connecting facets each offers in relation to aspects of a staging process. The chapter draws on ideas from André Lepecki, Walter Benjamin and T.S. Eliot that resonate with the form of staging practice I choose to engage in. This group of ideas, when considered together, mesh with the notion of a work's capacity to grow in the present but with a continuing connection to and with the source, the choreographer and/or dance work. Accounts from former dancers provide important perspectives of the performer's experience of *Two Ecstatic Themes* and, collectively, allow insight of the thought and movement processes that are worked through by the individual in rehearsal and how these processes then come together in the moment of performance.

In Chap. 6, 'Transmission as process and power in Graham's *Chronicle* (1936)', Kim Jones explores the concept of transmission in two associated contexts as indicated by the title. The work is placed in a socio-historical framework that situates Graham's political leanings at the time of creation alongside her continuing development of the work during its early performances, as evidenced through contemporary reviews. The work's more recent history is detailed through a series of reconstruction/recreation processes that took place under the auspices of the Martha Graham Dance Company, including Jones' own engagement as both performer and director. In the course of her research, Jones has gathered previously undocumented testimony from key figures in the Graham community, including Yuriko and Terese Capucilli and other former dancers, that substantively extends the existing knowledge base on this important work from the perspective of the performer. Further, Jones articulates a clear distinction in terms of how she operates within the positions of reimagining, recreation and restaging. In so doing, she asks a series of critical questions that include identifying 'what' is being captured and conveyed, and how to present historical movement practices, images, and ideas in ways that can be understood as history but also as contemporary performance.

The core proposition in Chap. 7, 'Transmitting *Trio A* (1966): the relations and sociality of an unspectacular dance' by Sara Wookey, centers on the role of the artist practitioner through whom the work is conveyed to performers. It was Yvonne Rainer herself who introduced the title, 'Transmitter of Trio A' some years previously to identify the group of artists who are approved by her to transmit the work to others. Wookey holds a role that brings with it both privilege and responsibility as one of this select group of five. She views her role as transmitter as moving beyond the transfer of physical memory and knowledge and onto a platform of exchange that includes her own experiences and interactions with Rainer. Wookey refers to the collaborative mix of movements, memory and anecdotes that make up an exchange across generations and keeps dances alive. For her, a crucial aspect within the process is the 'passing on' of an idea, in much the same way as has been identified in other chapters. Beyond the work itself, Wookey further prompts us to look past nostalgia for the dance product and into what are still gaps in the area of critical thinking in dance about relations and intersubjectivity. Such a view, Wookey suggests, may open up possibilities not only for the exchanges between the unique relationships between dancer and choreographer but also offer insight into the world of an artist who lived and worked during a different socio-economic time. In turn, this might tell us what making dance means at different periods; how different historic moments allow or hinder dance making and how dance reflects the times.

Chapter 8, 'Silent transformations in choreography-making over time: Rosemary Butcher's practice of "looking back and ahead"', is contributed by Stefanie Sachsenmaier, long-time associate of Butcher. This chapter explores the complex ways in which Butcher engaged with the past in three selected creative processes between 2010 and 2015, and how the idea of transmission was manifest in each instance. The first is Butcher's 'reinvention' of American artist Allan Kaprow's seminal first Happening from 1959, entitled *18 Happenings in 6 Parts*, that was commissioned in 2010 by the South Bank Centre, London. Butcher engaged for the only time in her choreographic career in a creative process that was instigated through a direct engagement with another artist's completed work. Here, Butcher explored how aspects of Kaprow's work can be 'passed on' into her own piece—*18 Happenings in 6 Parts 1959/2010*. The second work considered is Butcher's *SCAN* (1999), which was presented again in 2015 as part of a retrospective event in Berlin. On this occasion, Butcher refrained from making choreographic changes to the work and reassembled most of the original cast. What changed, however, was the framework through which the dance was viewed, with the structures of retrospective and memory creating new ways of seeing and experiencing the work. A third example addresses what was to be Butcher's final live choreographic work, entitled *The Test Pieces* (2015). Butcher developed three versions of *The Test Pieces* with different casts, with the final version presented as part of the aforementioned retrospective event in Berlin. Sachsenmaier outlines how the new work was created alongside Butcher's active engagement with her own archive, and how the past was addressed in Butcher's creative focus and through her interest in modern architectural ruins. She further addresses the concept of transmission specifically in relation to Butcher's investment in times past through her consideration of what 'remains'—both in the form of past works, her wider archive and her interest in architectural ruins, as well as how what remains is processed and presented in the present.

Chapter 9, 'The living cultural heritage of Robert Cohan' by Paul R. W. Jackson, is an extended narrative that spans four works, four decades and is told through four principal voices—Robert Cohan CBE, choreographer and founder/artistic director of London Contemporary Dance Theatre (LCDT); Anne Donnelly (Went), former dancer with LCDT; Yolande Yorke-Edgell, director of Yorke Dance Project; and Jackson himself who, as Cohan's biographer,[4] has worked closely with the choreographer in recent years. The works considered are a restaging of Forest (1977) by Donnelly; Cohan's own translation of his solo work, Canciones del Alma (1978, 2013) and the transformation of *Lingua Franca* (1984, 2014) for Yorke Dance Project; and Sigh (2015) a new work created for Liam Riddick of the Richard Alston Dance Company in which Cohan transmits his legacy to a new generation. Jackson foregrounds the discussion on the dances with an intriguing perspective on 'intangible cultural heritage' that he illustrates by way of the UNESCO 1972 *Convention Concerning the Protection of the World Cultural, Natural Heritage* (World Heritage Convention), the revisions to which in 2003 added arts and performing traditions including dance. A further aspect is the impact that technological advances can have on revisited work. Such advances proved influential to Cohan's rethinking of his own lighting design for *Forest* in 2014, as one example, to take advantage of LED lighting and projection that did not exist when the work was previously performed.

In addition to the two core themes, noteworthy subthemes emerge across chapters. Curtis-Jones, Salgado-Llopis and Sachsenmaier refer explicitly to the 'remains' of a work/performance; for Barba, Jones and Wookey, inter-generational transmission features as crucial in their own bodily understanding of the particular movement material they are engaging with; Jackson, Salgado-Llopis, Wookey and myself comment on the significance of performers understanding the 'idea' of a work and, linked to this, the performer's overt awareness of environment, as stressed by Barba and Curtis-Jones.

An invigorating aspect of this project was the discovery of the unexpected. At the outset I was clear in myself about the kinds of writing I wanted to include and that the focus should be firmly on the dancing, the 'how it feels' to engage with movement from the past and make sense of it in the present. I was also clear that I wanted the writing to be undertaken by those engaged in the dancing, or close to, in order to draw forth the internal facets of a work from the performer's perspective. The theme of 'transmission' held meaning for all of the contributors but I hadn't fully anticipated the wealth and scope of ideas and narratives that were forthcoming. The array of historical and philosophical positions that underpin the practice and the resulting performances provide a welcome indication of the fluid capacities of the art form. As a field, we can be excited about the ever-expanding means through which current work can be conveyed at a future point in time, and reassured because the careful artistic scholarship demonstrated here, on both contextual and physicalized levels, is becoming a matter of course when dance artists engage with the work of another.

NOTES

1. *Transmission—A Performance Symposium* took place at Middlesex University, London on December 13, 2014. Available at https://transmissionperformancesymposium.wordpress.com (Accessed July 26, 2017).
2. Program note, *Transmission—A Performance Symposium*, 2014 (Franko, Mark): *Le Marbre Tremble* was at its inception a collaboration between Mark Franko and photographer Ernestine Ruben. The dance used Ruben's large-scale photographic projections of the caryatids sculpted in the seventeenth century by Pierre Puget. These two figures (Puget used galley slaves in the port of Marseille as models), one old and one young, were the pretext for the piece, which premiered at the Toulon Art Museum (France) in 1988 as part of a photography exhibit—*Le corps/la galère: noir et blanc* (*The body and suffering: black and white*). This dance was also performed in Berlin and New York. *Le Marbre Tremble* was danced again in 2014, this time as the product of the collaboration between Mark Franko and Fabián

Barba. Fabián started learning the solo, originally performed by Mark, as a way to conjointly investigate the process of transmission of a dance, the relation of that dance to the context in which it was created and in which it is performed and the personal stories mobilized in this operation. The memories, reflections and sensations that constitute the dance will be called onto the stage as an accompaniment to it.

3. Barba, Fabián. 2011. "A Dancer Writes: Fabián Barba on Mary Wigman's Solos". *Dance Research Journal* 43 (1) Summer: 81–89.
4. Jackson, Paul R. W. 2013. *The Last Guru: Robert Cohan's Life in Dance from Martha Graham to London Contemporary Dance Theatre*. London: Dance Books.

CHAPTER 2

Transmission: From Archive to Production Re-imagining Laban—Contemporizing the Past, Envisioning the Future

Alison Curtis-Jones

Rudolf Laban (1879–1958), thinker, artist, innovator and fundamental in the rise of Central European Modern Dance, is well known for his dance notation system but less so for his dance theatre works. Over the course of two years, I researched two 'lost' works, *Ishtar's Journey into Hades* and *Dancing Drumstick*, choreographed by Laban in Monte Verita, Switzerland, in 1913. Following a 'Dance as Cultural Heritage' award from the Swiss Federal Office of Culture in 2014,[1] my company, *Summit Dance Theatre*,[2] mounted these two works for performances in Switzerland. The reimagined dances, *Drumstick* and *Ishtar's Journey into Hades* were premiered in Teatro Del Gatta, Ascona, October 2015, as part of *Laban Event*, an international conference, in Monte Verita, Ascona, overlooking Lake Maggiore, in the Italian region of Switzerland where Laban first conceived the works and established his dance school.

A. Curtis-Jones (✉)
The Coach House, Hampshire, UK
e-mail: alisoncurtisjones@virginmedia.com

© The Author(s) 2017
L. Main (ed.), *Transmissions in Dance*,
https://doi.org/10.1007/978-3-319-64873-6_2

This discussion outlines the archeochoreological methods devised and used in practice to draw Laban's early choreographic work *Dancing Drumstick* (1913) out of the archives and into the theatre. I define archeochoreology as a method of searching for 'lost' dances, using choreological principles and contemporary developments of Laban's principles of space and dynamics. The process involving the examination of the material remains of the work, including archive documents and the transmission of these in studio practice to reimagine the work for contemporary dance audiences, creates a new 'living archive' and potentially changes perceptions of existing documentary archives through embodied experience and observation of the work in practice.

In this chapter, I focus primarily on the transmission process of *Dancing Drumstick* from archive to production, and discuss key issues in relation to the staging process including: identifying what the 'material remains' of Laban works are and how these elements are translated for production; what the process is for interpreting, transferring, transmission of live archive/documents into practice; how specifically interpretation is used; what archeochoreological methods are used to 'reimagine' the work; and the notion of the 'body as archive' and embodied knowing. My work is not about exhuming relics. It uses live arts practice to draw attention to significant historic work which would otherwise be forgotten. I have devised a method to reimagine the Laban works—bridging archival gaps to create what I call a new 'living archive'. This transmission process from archive to production uses performance as a tool for translation and transformation and the dancer's body as archive and 'place' for creative exchange.

My role in reimagining these works requires a certain amount of detective work, of finding evidential remains, then deciding how I will use this information to discover and understand the works further through interrogation of practice. It is this theoretically informed and embodied practice that creates a deeper understanding of the possibilities and potential of the work. My understanding of *Dancing Drumstick* is formed through different sources including engagement with historic references, cultural contexts and use of archives. How archives are defined and used is a source of debate, with Lepecki claiming archives can place works under 'house arrest' (2010, 35). Foucault's proposal on the other hand, that the archive 'does not constitute the library of all libraries' (1972, 130) and Lepecki's view suggest that using archives as a way to find, foreground and produce (or invent or 'make', as Foucault proposed) difference (2010, 46) encourages newness and moves away from sameness. Lepecki's metaphor of archives where work is kept inside confines, preserved and held in its original form, not deviating from the source material suggests that evidential remains can limit the work. Foucault's ideas of invention and difference resulting in newness, and Lepecki's proposal of 'virtual inventiveness' (2010, 46) suggest creative approaches, such that material evidence does not have to limit, but that limits can be used to facilitate, much like the parameters set up in an improvisation task.

Providing structures for movement responses through improvising facilitates the discovery of new or different movement possibilities. Sameness suggests a dull reworking of something already in existence. A contrary view could question the necessity for newness, calling instead for the reliance of sameness. So how, as an artist, do I use material remains? For me, the function of material remains is not to capture and hold; their very existence, rather, encourages interpretation. My approach also experiments with creative responses resulting from the converse situation; the absence of material remains. The boundaries are absent but there if I choose to define them, and at the same time, limitless. I am, however, somewhat bound by the context of the original work, the choreographer's intention and ideas. Creative/interpretive thought processes begin as a result of discerning what the archival evidence or material remains might be. This virtual inventiveness comes through a combination of the practice of making and the intangible thought processes existing in the mind of the creator. The process of how this is transmitted to the dancer to activate or facilitate the translation of ideas in embodied practice creates a new form. The use of choreographic activation of the dancer's body as an endlessly creative, transformational archive provides limitless opportunities to access new modes of working (see Franko 1993). My work aligns with the view that archives are a place of creative exchange, and the involvement of the dancer as a means to experiment with and facilitate movement language correlates with the view shared by Foucault and Franko of the body as a creative, transformational archive and Lepecki's view of transformations and transmutations which take place through the bodies of new performers (Lepecki 2010, 35).

I draw as closely as possible from available sources and use Laban's known methodologies: improvisation, space harmony and effort. The translation of ideas and distance from the time the works were created, along with my contemporary development of Laban principles to create a methodology to reimagine, and my interpretation of sources suggest the work materializes in a new form. So what is this form and why is it significant? Dance historian Lesley-Anne Sayers states, "at issue here is not the simple case of one work being inspired by an earlier one, but a more complex one in which a new work emerges from a close analysis and creative dialogue with an earlier work and its contexts" (Preston-Dunlop and Sayers 2011, 30). This emergence of the 'new' from existing materials has led me to examine my process of creative interpretation in this context.

Gathering material remains for Laban's *Dancing Drumstick* was an extensive process, leading me to UK archives including the National Resource Centre for Dance, Surrey and Trinity Laban Conservatoire of Music and Dance, London, the second Dalcroze International Conference in Vienna, and the Kunsthaus in Zurich. Documents and letters written by Laban to Suzanne Perrottet (1889–1993) between 1910 and 1914 were translated for me by Laban's great granddaughter, Miriam Perrottet, at the Kunsthaus in 2014.[3] Detective work was all the more difficult because material remains of Laban's dance works are scarce. Despite being well known for his Labanotation system, published in 1928 to document movement, few of Laban's choreographic works are notated, if at all.[4] Laban eventually moved away from notation because he felt it did not adequately record or reflect the qualitative content of movement. His belief in moving ideas forward rather than fixing them is evident in works such as *Die Grunen Clowns* (1928), which appeared in various forms with different numbers of dancers. It was not notated, aligning with his view that works did not necessarily need to remain the same. I was researching Laban works from 1913, before his notation system existed and prior to his publishing of *Effort* with F. C. Lawrence (1947)[5] and *Choreutics* (1966), the principles of which I use retrospectively to reimagine his works. Letters written to Suzanne Perrottet expose Laban's thinking about the culture and his ideas at that time, but there are few actual, that is, tangible, remains of Dancing Drumstick to draw from. With such limited resources, how is it possible to mount the work for performance? 'A complete exhumation' of a work where little evidence of the original surface form exists is almost 'impossible' (Hodson and Archer 1987).

I have devised a method of practice using choreology to mount the Laban works, one that I established through my previous recreations of

Green Clowns (1928) and *Nacht* (1927).[6] I have also drawn from my embodied research and previous collaborations with former student of Rudolf Laban, Valerie Preston-Dunlop, as 'living archive'.[7] Reimagining uses my approach of contemporary developments of Laban's principles of *Choreutics* (1966) and *Effort* (1947) to make and shape the work. Laban's theories of choreutics and movement as living architecture are significant in my practice because this work provides a direct link to the artist and creates a foundation from which to operate in the present. I propose this process of reimagining as a form of contemporary practice.

REIMAGINING

Much has been written about Laban's theatre practice (for example, Preston-Dunlop 1998, 2013; Bergsohn and Bergsohn 2003; Doerr 2008; Bradley 2009; McCaw 2011; Preston-Dunlop and Sayers 2011) but embodied practical recreations of Laban works are rare. Views on Laban's way of life, the vegetarian colony in Monte Verita and the emerging philosophies evident in the work he did there are documented in a number of sources (for example, Preston-Dunlop 1998; Doerr 2008), and it is this context that provides much of the inspiration for my reimagining of *Dancing Drumstick*. The terms used here to describe the process of mounting Laban works can be ambiguous. I use the term reimagine or (re)creation to imply a creative process which generates a new form. The tension here is the wider issue of identity, which goes beyond the parameters of this chapter. I will, however discuss the terms used in relation to my work.

The wider contextual issues that surround the reimagining of Laban works draw from Lepecki's notion of 'returning' as a method of experimentation. Choreographically experimenting by turning back, or looking to the dance past, without what Lepecki describes as "Orpheus's curse of being frozen in time" (2010, 29), but is it possible to be frozen in time? Dancers move differently from era to era. Training programs have different demands today and dancers are informed through their experience of current practice, cultural and political contexts and thus cannot really be frozen. Dancers themselves are living archives, embodying their own training practices, influences and experiences. Embodied archives are particularly relevant when contemporary dancers contribute to the choreographic process, rather than being taught specific steps, and improvisation is used when generating and shaping movement material.

These dancers are not pretending to be dancers from 1913 and I am not imitating Laban's 1913 approach, but I am influenced by my understanding of it. My dancers are also influenced by my artistic practice and approach. What, then, is this process of reimagining another's work?

The Notion of the 're'

The proposal of reimagining, actualizing or reviving archives creates an interesting tension: are they at odds? The debate around the notion of the 're', of restaging in particular, is relevant in today's dance practice. Very little 'actual' evidence of *Dancing Drumstick* exists, so according to categories of 're', it is not possible to reproduce, remake or restage as there are too few sources to draw from. Nor could I stage a reconstruction, restoration or reenactment because there is little documentary evidence to rely on. My work aligns with the category of reimagining or reenvisioning, where an artist has less constraint and more freedom to explore and develop their own view of the work and how the work might be. Preston-Dunlop's view is that "[r]e-creation of any sort begs the question: is the new production sufficiently imbued with the originator's style to warrant his or her name being attached to it?" (Preston-Dunlop and Sayers 2011, 23). Contrary to Preston-Dunlop's view, I am not imbuing Laban's style. The question of a choreographer's 'style' is debatable, particularly in this case, when no footage of *Dancing Drumstick* exists. I am more concerned with the spirit of the work, Laban's intention and what he was trying to portray in his works.

By placing these reimagined works in the public domain, could they be viewed as revivals, where works come back into focus? Other terms, such as review, research, reevaluate, rethink, respond, which could be linked to this process of looking back and re-presenting work are also interesting, each posing a different perspective.

The 're' and Significance of Interpretation

Reimagining, where a lack of 'actual' evidence exists, means there are fewer tangible reference points for interpretation than with reconstruction. The approach I take, therefore, is to provide 'virtual' evidence through engagement with contextual sources and create my own virtual material remains through interpreting archival gaps, coupled with the interpretation of visual evidence such as documents and photographs.

Scores are documents, actual, tangible evidence of the previous existence of a work, although how one reads a document is as diverse as the creative processes used to make that work. Dance scores need interpreting and they are themselves an interpretation, recorded in the most part, by a specialist notator who is unlikely to be the choreographer him/herself (Pakes 2017, 7).

The challenge of recreating lost works includes interpreting the work's performance potential (Pakes 2017; Jordan 1987). Lesley Main discusses the extent to which creative imagination should be employed and the notion of contemporary interpretation in her stagings of Doris Humphrey's work (Main 2012), but the absence of identifiable steps from a score provides a different challenge. Pakes refers to the retrievability or irretrievability of 'lost' dances and asks whether performance is repeatable and to what extent dances can persist through time (2017). Pakes illustrates the point that embodied interpretation is significant in the process of revival to understand the appropriate style of the movement, giving the example of the Balanchine Foundation, which employs former dancers to direct or contribute to the process. This approach suggests that dancers can contribute insight into the qualitative content of movement, dynamic phrasing and rhythmic nuance, and the intention and motivation for movement that are not evident or recorded in notated scores. I would suggest that these dancers as living archives can store and transmit that valuable information, but their personal interpretations of felt embodied experience will influence the outcome. In the mounting of Doris Humphrey's works, Main is not engaged with reconstruction but with interpretation. Main refers to processes of interpretive and creative intervention in her use of a notation score (2012, 23). A notation score implies that steps are set and can be reconstructed or reproduced, which in itself is widely debated. What happens when, as with Laban works, there is no score and no dancers to refer to? In contrast to Main's processes, my work is not derived from the actual evidence of a score, it comes from limited archive remains and virtual, potential evidence facilitated by archival gaps. The lack of 'actual' or 'tangible' evidence encourages my thought processes to 'fill in' the archival voids, thereby creating virtual evidence through creative interpretation, and thoughts or visions in my mind, of what the work might be. These virtual thought processes become potential evidence through my actual creative practice of dance making, through trying out ideas in the studio with dancers and musicians. Like Main, I am aiming towards interpretive freedom by creatively engaging with the past but not intending (or able) to bring the past back to the present in its original form. Main refers to R. G. Collingwood's idea of the 'living past' by illuminating what we think happened through present knowledge (2012, 25) and of using detective work to interpret as a creative artist (Main 2012). This implies that the translation of knowing to telling through the interpretation of evidence is a constantly evolving process, informed by newly acquired knowledge.

Franko refers to construction as opposed to reconstruction which implies the making of, or the building of structure (1993, 135). The way one builds, constructs, the interpretive choices and decision making will determine the outcome. Through bridging archival gaps and staging for contemporary audiences, my process of reimagining is not replicating a work but rather aligns with the "live re-working of past creations rather than a backward-looking exhibition of what has passed" (Pakes 2017, 2). I am not reenacting or being historic(al) with this work. Dance critic Graham Watts, as an example, refers to my work as a resuscitation of ideas rather than the resuscitation of a work (personal correspondence 2016). Mine is an established personal practice of reimagining, a methodology devised using specific Laban principles and an embodied understanding of Laban's practice. However, I battle with intuitive (known knowledge) and cerebral responses in the studio, and the ontological concerns of what 'it' was/is.

LABAN'S INFLUENCES

The creative processes I use when reimagining, are informed by extensive research of Laban's history. I refer now to the period just before *Dancing Drumstick* was created in order to highlight the importance of knowing the context of Laban's work.

Laban moved to Munich in 1910, which at that time was a centre of artistic activity and philosophical thought. There he began to explore his ideas about the nature of bodily rhythm through the separation of movement from music. Laban's movement influences during this period also included the body-culture approaches of Bess Mensendieck (1866–1959), Rudolf Bode (1881–1970) and Emile Jaques-Dalcroze (1865–1950), all of whom were part of the physical, spiritual and expressive culture that was prominent in Munich at that time. Bradley and Preston-Dunlop write that Laban's approach was in contrast to the music-centric theories and practices of Dalcroze's Eurhythmics work and moved beyond the unrestrained, free flowing movement that dancer Isadora Duncan performed to Chopin and Beethoven (Bradley 2009; Preston-Dunlop and Purkiss 1989). Laban, it seems, was searching for something more specific. Dalcroze based his method on his observation that the body was inclined to respond to music by moving and, in his early work, taught movement as the externalization of the form inspired by sound. Laban, however, was interested in the movement itself, its content, meaning and relationship to the human spirit. Despite what might seem to be similar philosophies regarding sensory experiences of the body (Greenhead and Habron 2015), Laban was not concerned with the embodiment of music or a particular aesthetic ideal; he preferred movement that was expressive of itself. Dalcroze's method for him, it seems, did not allow for the body's expressiveness.

In 1912, Marie Steiner proposed a new prayerful movement art, Eurythmie, in which vowel and consonant sounds are translated into a series of gestures so that poetry or biblical stories could be 'danced' as 'visible speech, visible song' (Preston-Dunlop and Purkiss 1989). For Laban, according to Preston-Dunlop, this was derivative. Following Laban's viewing of Dalcroze's production of *Orfeo and Euridice* and the accompanying published paper 'How to Revive Dance', in which Dalcroze proposed a way forward for dance through 'music visualization', Laban's view of movement for its own sake was solidified (Preston-Dunlop 1998).

Preston-Dunlop and Selma Odom write about Laban's meeting with Suzanne Perrottet in 1912. Perrottet, a trained pupil and teacher of Dalcroze's method, abandoned the 'music-bound' Dalcroze method in order to pursue more radical movement experiments with Laban. According to Odom, Perrottet reflected that after working with Dalcroze "she could not move for a long time" because she had been formed by set gestures and exercises that now seemed false to her (2002, 8). She found interesting Laban's ideas about the body in space, how the parts of the body function, how their range of motion relates to geometric form, how exploring through improvization can lead to movement invention. Like Laban, she was fascinated with musical dissonance and percussion, areas that, at the time, did not interest Dalcroze.

It could be said that Perrottet was able to convey firsthand understanding of Dalcroze's work, methods and theories and was thus instrumental in helping inspire and solidify Laban's thinking in relation to movement, rhythm and sound. My research of archive documents including Perrottet's letters at Kunsthaus, Zurich, reveal how she used her newfound method pedagogically to challenge dancers' rhythm and develop skills, technically and creatively. These letters were crucial to my research, including one in which Laban asked Perrottet, 'what if I take music away from dance?' Through examples such as this, I was able to discern that Laban's intention at the time was primarily to experiment through improvization, to find an alternative way to challenge rhythmic phrasing in the body, which did not rely on musical phrasing.

Perrottet joined Laban's school in Monte Verita in 1913 along with Mary Wigman, (1886–1973), giving up her post at Dalcroze's school in Hellerau where she had been a pupil. Wigman went on to establish 'Absolute Dance' (autonomous expressive dance, independent of music and codified steps) and became an acclaimed figure in German Expressionist Dance, '*Ausdruckstanz*', following her choreography of *Witch Dance* in 1914. This era included the premiere of Stravinsky's *Le Sacre du Printemps* (1913) in collaboration with Valsav Nijinsky and Nicholas Roerich, along with Dalcroze's student Marie Rambert who served as both performer and dance mistress. Laban, it seems, was affected by seeing Le *Sacre du Printemps*, which may have led to the experiments in Ascona in 1913 which included at least two choreographic works, *Dancing Drumstick* and *Ishtar's Journey into Hades*. *Dancing Drumstick* was 'the rhythm of the body made audible', 'dance as a visible language' and is Laban's attempt to shift dance away from what he referred to as the 'constraints of music' (Laban 1975, 87). The counterpoint of movement and sound proved interesting for Laban and he moved away from set codified steps to reveal its potential, exploring how rhythm and patterns of the mind and spirit manifest in movement. Laban used the term 'Free Dance' (*der Freie Tanz*), meaning free from musical constraints, from dramatic narrative and set steps, therefore the dance material was made up of freely juxtaposed rhythms and forms. His thinking in relation to the rhythmic, dynamic body was revealed in the year before, when he stated that the division of time in the natural movements of the human being "has nothing to do with metric rhythmic systems…they follow another law" (Preston-Dunlop and Purkiss 1989, 15).

Further evidence of Laban's shift away from Dalcroze is seen in 1915, in Laban's publicity material for his summer school Tanz-Ton-Wort (Dance-Sound-Word) which explains how his approach to movement education is through the individual finding his own movement rhythms—through the principles of swing, tempo, beat, order, structure—and is quite different from Dalcroze's early eurhythmics, in which the body submits to musical rhythms. *"Dance has things to say and express that cannot be said through music or acting, and in a deep way. It is the music of the limbs."* (Laban 1926) This idea, arguably, is suggestive of movement expressivity being made visible through the body's rhythmic phrasing and spatial articulation. Our body is in constant flux and its dynamic phrasing communicates through its own chordic system, creating harmony and discord through spatial form. Laban referred to this organization of the body as "limb correlation" or "limb organisation" (1926, 86–87), or "sequencing" (1926, 14) relating to the action of fingers playing the piano.

Laban's Movement Principles

Laban's former career as an architect influenced his thinking in relation to space and is revealed in his work exploring geometric form and spatial scales. His principles of space harmony include the balance of opposites, a system of harmonic relationships in movement and the art of dance. How we use space as we move is expressed through spatial forms, governed by harmonic laws. The balance of opposites includes basic rules of harmony built into the human psyche and can be understood in relation to the harmonic laws of movement including body, action, space, and relationships, dynamics which are inextricably linked. Our body is structured in a particular way and movement is therefore intrinsically structured. Harmonic opposition is evident in spatial form such as the three-dimensional cross—by moving from open to closed, forward/back, up/down—and work in relation to laws of gravity. The harmonic laws of movement can be related to mathematical ratio and harmonic proportion, the Fibonacci scale, Pythagoras, Plato's *Timaeus* and constructs in nature, art, architecture, music and cosmology. Laban used geometric forms such as spatial planes, the cube and icosahedron to establish spatial scales, (Laban 1966) which I use with dancers to help them embody and understand their relationship in and with space, intention and expressivity.[8]

The laws of nature and geometric form also inform our perception of what is harmonic, and can be viewed in relation to principles of architecture and our built environment. The body in dynamic flux manifests in what Laban refers to as the architecture of the dynamic body with "space as the hidden feature of movement and movement a visible aspect of space" (Laban 1966, 4). Together with F. C. Lawrence, Laban's observation of factory workers in 1947 led to the development of his 'Effort' system, which identifies four motion factors—time, weight, space and flow—with polar opposites of sudden/sustained, light/strong, direct/flexible, free/bound. The embodiment of these extremes and their variations challenges dancers to broaden their dynamic range and understand the efficiency of movement according to natural affinities. Dancers become aware of their habitual preferences dynamically and can choose to adhere to or go against their affinities to extend qualitative nuance. In my work, dancers experiment with varying amounts of force, degrees of tension and release, acceleration and deceleration, rupturing affinities and creating inorganic movement choices. The motion factor of weight, which Laban identifies as light or strong, relates to the observation of factory workers and the muscular tension required to move objects efficiently. The notion of weight in Laban's effort graph does not consider the weight of the body itself. Dancers often question how the effort graph addresses 'heavy'. For Laban, heavy does not apply to muscular tension and release, or force, it indicates an absence of tension, leading to inertia. The potential of 'heavy' as an additional quality can change how we view the effort graph in relation to today's practice, particularly with regard to release technique. This system can be used in a number of contexts, not only dance, but also in movement therapy and actor training. Variations in our embodiment of harmonic principles create meaning, expression and intention. Similarly, variations in intention and motivation result in differences of movement in time and space.

It is important to point out that these methods were not yet established by Laban in 1913. I used these methods retrospectively as I reimagined *Dancing Drumstick*, and I have developed the principles in a way that is relevant to my practice today as a contemporary dance artist. My research suggests that the established principles that Laban published in 1947 and 1966 are evident in his early works as a way of experimenting to define his thinking of space and time. I have the advantage of looking back to these early works with an in-depth understanding both theoretically and corporeally of choreutics and effort today, and have developed the theories further for the contemporary practice of reimagining. I work with dancers to facilitate an embodied understanding of spatial principles and the significance of dynamic phrasing in movement. I use affinities creatively, rupturing the order of what might be considered to be 'organic'. Dancers work within an improvisational framework to create interpretations of the dance works originally created by Laban based on my interpretations of available sources. Responses from dancers to my improvisational tasks are influenced by my method of technical training, the warm-up activities and movement vocabulary I use when teaching technique classes. I attempt to challenge dancers with the use of rhythmic phrasing and such embodied experiences influence their responses by creating an embodied impression, an imprint which becomes evident in their practice and improvised responses.

DANCING LABAN'S MOVEMENT IN THE TWENTY-FIRST CENTURY

Dalcroze' eurythmics and Laban's principles of choreutics and eukinetics are associated with a number of different fields including health, well-being, therapy, arts and education. Laban's work continues to evolve in a number of disciplines including theatre and dance practice. I have drawn from these principles to establish a practice to train contemporary dance artists in contemporary dance technique. My practice encourages dancers to embody movement corporeally, referring to the multi-sensory body rather than taught steps which are given counts. Imagery is used throughout my rehearsal process to facilitate sensory awareness, to explore, identify and establish dynamic nuance in movement and to clarify intention. Choreological practice engages with the grammar and syntax of movement, the outward manifestation of inner feeling; what Laban refers to as 'drives' and 'states' (Hackney 2002), identifying the significance of human movement in functional and expressive forms. "Movement is first and fundamental in what comes forth from a human being as an expression of his intentions and experiences." (Laban 1975, 87) Laban refers to 'inner attitude' and connection with this inner sense or intention encourages expressivity.

My approach to technique is physically demanding. Training is a tool, to sculpt dance artistry, to encounter and embody the discipline of muscular strength and to experience the full spectrum of dynamic variation. The process is not only about what I teach, but how. My method of constructing classes and rehearsals allows me to create a conduit, to transfer a physical dialogue and understanding of corporeality and artistry through a choreological lens. My work involves the embodiment of Laban's theories of Space Harmony. Exploring dancers' relationships in and with space—the potential of spatial scales and rings, kinesphere, lability, superzone and harmonic opposition—enhances dancers' spatial awareness and understanding of choreutic form. Complex rhythmic choices encourage a wide dynamic range and use of effort qualities. Because there is no 'codified' 'Laban technique', I established a mode of training to teach movement principles for professional training to challenge the dancers. My approach also includes choreological perspectives and contemporary developments of Laban's principles in practice. I developed a movement base using 'swings' in the vertical, horizontal and sagittal planes, working with and from 'center', "concern with the centre of energy resonates with the Rosicrucian practice of locating and sensitising centres both within and outside the body" (Preston-Dunlop 1998, 11), use of the lemniscate, the 'A' Scale, three-dimensional cross and icosahedron. The technical base consists of intense commitment to the movement, deeply felt performance, a high level of group sensitivity and adaptability, labile forms, isolations and gestures. Unusual dynamic/spatial form combinations are deliberately included.

The embodiment of choreutics, not just as designs and shapes in space, but how it is to feel spatial form is important in my practice.[9] I draw attention to 'back space', so that dancers are more aware of their sensorial three-dimensional body, and to the resonance of stillness and how dancers engage physically and emotionally, projecting energy to keep stillness active. William Forsythe, for example, has developed an approach to encourage acute understanding of spatial articulation through his investigations of Laban's A Scale and specific locations in space. Forsythe's rupturing of Laban's choreutic laws, in 'superzoning' (first mentioned in Laban's *Choreutics* 1966), by crossing over the center line of the body, and questioning where 'center' is, or using multiple 'centers', has created a new living architecture (Forsythe 1994, 2009). Forsythe's experimentation and questioning of Laban's structures, and his use of algorithms and software to transform modalities, highlight the possibilities for an artist to adhere to or to rupture the traditions he/she inherits. I inherited Laban's themes and had to decide what I would adhere to and what I would rupture, giving the dancers and myself the responsibility of contributing to the process and thereby changing the form. Laban's way of working embraced this; if the process is a true reflection of his approach, then the form will change with each mounting.

I avoid the use of the mirror in rehearsal so that dancers become mindful of bodily sensation and feel the movement first, before it is given shape or form. Group cohesion is practiced through proprioception; raised consciousness and sensorial awareness of the ensemble, moving together with organic solidarity in shared space, facilitating a collective consciousness, so that unison work is felt and sensed corporeally, rather than seen objectively from the outside or by adding counts. When dancers engage in decision making—'where shall we go next in the space, who's leading?'—or they begin counting, movement becomes mechanical rather than organic, and cerebral rather than corporeal.

Envisioning the Future: Practice and Process

An important aspect of my process was contextual research of the era of *Dancing Drumstick*. It informed my view and perception of the reimagined work, which I entitled *Drumstick*.[10] The title differentiates the work from the original but refers directly to it, acknowledging that it has acquired a new form in the present. Main refers to how the arrival of a new work affects existing work (2012, 26). In my case, there is no other form, only an absence of existing work, until now. My reimagined *Drumstick* is an attempt to show Laban's shift to arbitrary rhythm—a materialization of extreme and subtle dynamic changes in which dancers establish their own felt rhythms and work together in unity without sound and make stillness resonate. Musicians accompany the dancers, playing in response to what they see as opposed to dancers responding to what they hear. This is not radical today, but it was in Europe in 1913! This work was a radical departure at the time, and I believe, was a direct result of the rebellion against the established method of Jacques Dalcroze, his music visualization and music-inspired movement at the time.

My reimagined *Drumstick*, similarly, rejects the Dalcroze method of music visualization by replacing the reliance on music, meter and sound cues for the dancers with sensed group rhythmic changes in the body and general space. Composers and musicians James Keane and Oli Newman follow the dancers with sections of live improvisation in performance, responding to the dancers' movement in real time. During the reimagining process, I challenged dancers and musicians with complex non-metric, arbitrary rhythmic phrases, which are sensed and not counted, encouraging group cohesion through acute sensory awareness and phenomenological responses. Dancers improvise with different rhythms and actively sense when to initiate the movement together. An impulse, for example, creates an accent suddenly somewhere in the body; it starts strongly, becomes lighter and decelerates. Where the initiation begins in the body and whether the pathway of deceleration is direct or flexible is spontaneous and not fixed and varies for each performer. The duration of each movement is also not fixed therefore dancers need to be highly attuned with each other to generate the rhythmic impulse and to determine its duration together. Inner sensation of the qualitative content manifests in a different outward form each time for each individual dancer and creates variations in geometric group form, which I term *morphing*. This is not a cerebral decision-making process, it is a sensory felt experience in the lived moment. Experiencing the resonance of the movement's sensation results in what I call *active stillness*. The duration of the stillness varies each time the dancers perform the work, keeping a sense of aliveness through using what I have termed, *kinesthetic listening*.

Dancers' embodied knowing of dynamic rhythmic phrasing and effort qualities requires in-depth training. To encourage this understanding, I refrain from using counts in rehearsals and when setting technical warm-up exercises, so that the dancers did not rely on numbers, experiencing the movement phrasing corporeally instead. Dancers use breath and vocals to create a cacophony of sound, juxtaposing with the dynamic resonance of the body to create inorganic forms. Musicians work with polyrhythms as a way of contrasting what they see with what the performers and audience hear. This internal recognition and awareness of sensation is important to me, and my work requires outward expression of these experiences. Laban refers to the movement's impression which allows for expression and proposes that we understand movement through "continuous creation of spatial impressions through the experience of movement" (Laban 1966, 4). In my work, dancers feel the movement and the resulting shape and form manifest because of the felt experience rather than them creating shapes. "Space is a hidden feature of movement and movement is a visible aspect of space" (ibid., 4). The contribution of the dancers is central to the investigative process, so realizing and appreciating the training practices of current dance artists and the notion of habitus in generating material for the work are essential. Dancers establish dynamic and spatial skills through embodied knowing and movement literacy—a shared choreological language, a common terminology for movement principles introduced through my approach to technical training which is transferred to the studio, then ultimately the theatre, for further choreographic and performance investigation (Fig. 2.1).

Fig. 2.1 Summit Dance Theatre in *Drumstick*, Teatro Del Gatta, Switzerland, 2015. Choreography by Alison Curtis-Jones. Photograph by Paolo Tosi, Tosi photography

INSIGHT: HOW PERCEPTION AND IMAGINATION INFORMED *DRUMSTICK*

As part of the research process, I looked closely at photographic images of dancers in Monte Verita and Hamburg in the early 1900s, which informed my perspective of the physicality of the movement. Many images showed men and women jumping outdoors. To me, they appeared to be jumping high. The images are snapshots of a moment in time and it is impossible to know what movements came immediately before and after, but they were inspiring nonetheless, and allowed me to imagine, envisage and create. I wanted to capture what I perceived to be the spirit of abandon and liberation in the images and Laban's experiments to free the body from the restraints of sound and clothing. The still photographic images produced thoughts of virtual movement in my mind which I communicated to the dancers. I also shared the images with the dancers. The transmission process allowed them to express the visual stimuli, my perceptions, and subsequently their perceptions, through movement. A photograph of men outdoors in Hamburg in 1920 influenced my experiments with strength. The image was not directly related to the work but was interesting, along with other images from the era showing semi-naked, or in some cases, naked images of the dynamic body in motion. This particular photograph shows men pulling a rope in a 'tug of war'. The muscularity of the body is visible. In rehearsal, I worked with alternations of tension and release and variations of strength with the dancers, contrasting extreme and subtle dynamic changes in rhythmic phrasing. To help dancers embody the strength evident in the photograph, we used a rope in rehearsal and divided into two teams to pull. The degree of strength needed to sustain the tension in the rope and to hold one's ground was revealing. The strength was not only located in the centre of the body, it came from every sinew, from the feet into the ground, through the legs, gut, back, chest, arms, hands. Muscular tension was also reflected in the grimacing of the face. Interestingly, most dancers held their breath as they pulled. It appears the degree of muscular tension and force interfered with their 'natural' breath rhythm. We worked with this level of power in rehearsal to generate challenging levels of strength in movement. The 'tug of war' diagonal line appears in my reimagined *Drumstick* without the rope. Dancers find the power from their embodied knowing of the felt experience of a counter-tension pull, their focus projected on a direct pathway to illustrate the virtual spatial tension between them (Fig. 2.2).

I also saw photographs of dancers in different spatial formations, reaching downward, outward, upward, relating to Laban's explorations of low, medium, high; the earth, the horizon and the sky, and groups in spatial formation. The more I studied these photographs, the connection with the outdoors, the concern for freedom of movement, the more I connected with Laban's fear of the loss of the soul:

> I saw with growing clarity how man will come under domination of the machine. The soul-less steel oz, the locomotive is only the beginning. Thrilling as the power of conquest over air and sea may be, man will surely have to pay dearly for it. The whirring and clanking of thousands of wheels and chains is infectious: soon man himself will become a whirring of wheels and chains; soon he will see in life, in the whole of nature, and in himself nothing but the machine, and the soul will be forgotten. (Laban 1975, 48)

My concern with the multi-sensory body in *Drumstick* is especially relevant in today's digital world and our culture of technological connection

Fig. 2.2 Summit Dance Theatre in *Drumstick*, Teatro Del Gatta, Switzerland, 2015. Choreography by Alison Curtis-Jones. Photograph by Paolo Tosi, Tosi photography

mediated through a screen. In *Drumstick* the dancers have to be connected actually, not virtually. I used live sound, of dancers' breath, feet and drums. Laban refers to "the spiritual character of primitive music and especially of rhythm" (1975, 87). Initially, I chose not to use technology in the work, not even to amplify the sound; I wanted the work to be raw and visceral to reflect the soul. In my reimagined *Drumstick* I stripped back everything to reveal the body, including the costumes, inspired by Laban's references to 'primitive' (1975, 87) and photographs of the time. To experience the sensory responses of the body outdoors, we danced on the same ground in Monte Verita that Laban began his experiments. It had rained the day before we arrived and it was slightly chilly on that October day in Monte Verita, but we removed our shoes and outer layers of clothing. Feeling our feet in the earth, cold, soft but firm, the height of the trees around us, the fresh air, the cool temperature gave us an immediate shift in our relationship to space/place. The scale, the openness, the power of nature—it felt like sacred ground—the power in the earth as we jumped and ran, changed orientation, the environment transformed our experience of the movement. We did these movements repetitively to find a common rhythm, to communicate, referring directly to Laban's idea of our bodies as "morse-code apparatus" (1975, 87), and more importantly to experience the sensation of the dynamic body in space. Laban's interest in engaging with the body's resident sensations as sensory perception and experiential rather than cognitive is suggested here: "To primitive man the language of the drum seems nothing other than the rhythm of his body made audible. Therefore, as long as the European tries to investigate it with his intellect it will always remain a mystery to him" (1975, 87). This experience of dancing outside in Monte Verita was fundamental in capturing the *spirit* of the work then and now.

> The dancer of our cultural era...possesses the same sensitivity to the meaning of visible and audible body movements. For this reason, he understands rhythms and sounds as a kind of audible gesture and dance as a visible language. (Laban 1975, 87)

How Reimagining Contributes New Archival Evidence Through Performance Ephemera

These 'new' works become fragments of performance ephemera which, in turn, create new archival traces in the bodies of the dancers and in the minds of the viewer. Actual evidence, that is, tangible material, remains available in archives and its subsequent translation through interpretation leads to the provision of new images of the work, creating associations with Laban's work that potentially, along with seeing the live works, add 'being' to Laban. By sharing photographic images of my reimagining(s) of *Green Clowns, Nacht, Drumstick* and *Ishtar's Journey into Hades*, I am providing new images which are associated with the original work, thereby establishing a particular perspective of the work in the mind of the viewer. Can seeing reimagined Laban works live in performance also potentially change perceptions of existing archive materials and perceptions of Laban's work as an artist?

This work therefore, does not simply aim to restore Laban's choreography but to engage with finding his intention and meaning of the works through reimagining his work as contemporary dance practice. Reimagining past dances with embodied corporeal knowledge in practice provides a different insight to the work for dancers and audiences in a way that studying materials alone cannot provide. Using the body-as-archive (Lepecki 2010), dancers become the work, they provide a 'place' for it, the work lives in their continuing state of transformation as beings. Working with dancers and collaborators to actualize my (and their) interpretations, reimagining is not about the past that was, which is impossible to retrieve, it is about the present that is.

NOTES

1. The commission from the Swiss Federal Office was awarded following performances by Summit Dance Theatre, of my reimagined *Nacht* and *Suite'24*, at Teatro San Materno as part of The Laban Event International Conference, 2013.
2. Summit Dance Theatre is made up of professional dancers Robert Keates, Charlotte Pook, Claire Victoria Lambert, Ellen Jeffrey, James Kay, Andrew Race, Fred Gehrig, Ingvild Olsen, Verena Schneider, taught through my method of technical training at Trinity Laban Conservatoire of Music and Dance. Composers Oli Newman and James Keane play live. Costumes designed by Mary Fisher of The Royal Opera House, London. Producer and curator of Laban Event, Nunzia Tirelli, Switzerland. Filmmaker Giona Beltrametti and dance artist Nunzia Tirelli have supported this work from archive to production.
3. Nunzia Tirelli and Giona Beltrametti were also present at this meeting in the Kunsthaus, Zurich.
4. Laban's *Schwingende Tempel* (1923) has incomplete sections of notation. *Titan* is notated by Knust after the 1928/9 performances directed by him. The premiere was 1927, before Laban's notation system was published. The CNN Paris has details of scores written by Knust.
5. The word 'effort' was used by Laban to reflect the war effort. It is interesting to note the significance of the cultural context of the time. Following two World Wars when industrialization was needed to restore and to manufacture, Laban and Lawrence's observations of production line workers such as the female factory workers in Pilkinson Tile Factory resulted in their publication of the Effort Graph. This was to encourage movement efficiency and resulted in 8 basic 'effort actions'. Preston-Dunlop states that Laban observed how women would use flow to do men's work. Women would swing heavy objects whereas men would carry. Laban later considered the word 'exertion'. Both words

are unsatisfactory in describing the qualitative nuance of movement and human expression, whether movement is consciously controlled for performance or emerges subconsciously in behavior. Words are inadequate when attempting to capture the dynamics of the body.

6. *Die Nacht (1927)* is a political satire, exposing the underbelly of the Weimar Period—a tumultuous period in history. Laban refers to his distaste for "dollars, deceit and depravity" (Laban 1975). My reimagined *Nacht* is a response to one original photograph, drawings of costumes by Hans Blank, and Laban's choreographic notes. I write about my influences, including contextual sources such as the Fritz Lang's film *Metropolis* (1927) and George Grotz's artwork *Arbieter*, cabaret song lyrics and Berthold Brecht's perceptions of Berlin, in *Rudolf Laban: Man of Theatre*, Preston-Dunlop, V. (2014) Dance Books, London. My reimagined *Nacht* was performed at The Bonnie Bird Theatre, London in 2010, 2011 and 2014 with Trinity Laban Dancers, with Summit Dance Theatre in Teatro San Materno, Ascona, Switzerland 2014 and The Ivy Theatre, Surrey 2017. My reimagined *Nacht* has four sections and examines the superficialities of social etiquette in Smart Set, the greed of Stockbrokers, the way Tanz Bars were used for political propaganda, and the Monotony of work and labour. I collaborated with composer Oli Newman who plays live.

7. *Die Grunen Clowns* (1928) is Laban's anti-war piece dealing with the dehumanization of the body through repetitive work and industrial machine-like imagery, the horrors of war, the fragility of relationships, the humor and mindlessness of following political leaders. This work was the precursor to Kurt Jooss' *Green Table* (1932). My re-creations of this work are based on research by Preston-Dunlop. A draft of practical ideas were in place, based on Preston-Dunlop's practical experiments in the 1980s. Following Preston-Dunlop's research, I developed these ideas and mounted the work in its entirety using my methodology for the first time in 2008 with Trinity Laban dancers and again in 2009 in The Bonnie Bird Theatre, London. I recreated *Green Clowns* with Transitions Dance Company in 2008 for performances in Manchester and Dartington to commemorate 50 years since Laban's death. I was commissioned in 2014 to recreate *Green Clowns* with Centre of Advanced Training students to commemorate the centenary of World War I and in 2015 with Trinity Laban dancers for the Brighton Festival. The BBC filmed a section of my recreation of *Green Clowns* for a documentary program on modern dance, 'Dance Rebels' screened in the UK, 2015.

8. My research with Preston-Dunlop spans 15 years and is ongoing. I refer to Preston-Dunlop as a 'living archive'. Personal recollections of working with Laban, his approaches and ideas, from her perspective, have been

invaluable in my research. Preston-Dunlop's in-depth research of Laban's history and her writings are significant resources.

9. See Jeffrey Scott Longstaff's work. *Reevaluating Rudolf Laban's Choreutics. Perceptual and Motor Skills*, 2000, 191–210. Laban Centre London, City University London.

10. I propose that *Dancing Drumstick* (1913) is a significant historic work and *Drumstick* pays tribute to Laban's extensive experiments with the dynamic body in motion. *Drumstick* was performed by Summit Dance Theatre in Teatra del Gatta, Ascona 2015, and outside in Monte Verita. The work was filmed by the German TV company ARTE on the site where Laban's early dance experiments took place. The Swiss film company RSI captured the process and performance of *Drumstick* and *Ishtar's Journey into Hades* in 2015. A documentary film is available.

BIBLIOGRAPHY

Archer, Kenneth, and Millicent Hodson. 1987. Confronting Oblivion. In *Preservation Politics: Dance Revived Reconstructed Remade*, ed. Stephanie Jordan. London: Dance Books.

Bal, Mieke. 1989. *Quoting Caravaggio: Contemporary Art, Preposterous History*. Chicago: University of Chicago Press.

Barba, Fabián. 2011. A Dancer Writes: Fabián Barba on Mary Wigman's Solos. *Dance Research Journal* 43 (1) Summer: 81–89.

Bergsohn, Isa P., and Harold Bergsohn. 2003. *The Makers of Modern Dance in Germany: Rudolf Laban, Mary Wigman, Kurt Jooss*. New Jersey: Princeton Book Company Publishers.

Bradley, Karen. 2009. *Rudolf Laban*. Abingdon: Routledge.

Bullock, Alan, and Stephen Trombley. 1988. *Fontana Dictionary of Modern Thought*. London: Fontana Press.

Burt, Ramsay. 2003. Memory, Repetition and Critical Intervention: The Politics of Historical Reference in Recent European Dance Performance. *Performance Research* 8 (2): 34–41.

Doerr, Evelyn. 2008. *Rudolf Laban: The Dancer of the Crystal*. Plymouth: Scarecrow Press.

Foucault, Michel. 1972. *The Archaeology of Knowledge*. Tavistock: Routledge.

Forsythe, William. 1994. *Improvisation Technologies. A Tool for the Analytical Dance Eye*. CD-Rom.

Franko, Mark. 1993. Epilogue: Repeatability, Reconstruction and Beyond. In *Dance as Text: Ideologies of the Baroque Body*. Cambridge: Cambridge University Press.

———. 2011. Writing for the Body: Notation, Reconstruction, and Reinvention. *Common Knowledge* 17 (2): 321–334.

————. 2017. Epilogue to an Epilogue: Historicizing the Re- in Danced Reenactment. In *The Oxford Handbook of Dance and Reenactment*, ed. Mark Franko. New York: Oxford University Press.

————. 2009. *Synchronous Objects*. Ohio State University. Available at www.synchronousobjects.osu.edu. Accessed 2 Aug 2017.

Friedman, Jeff. 2011. Archive/Practice. *Dance Chronicle* 34 (1): 138–145.

Greenhead, Karin, and John Habron. 2015. The Touch of Sound: Dalcroze Eurhythmics as Somatic Practice. *Journal of Dance & Somatic Practices* 7 (1): 93–112.

Hackney, Peggy. 2002. *Making Connections: Total Body Integration* Through Bartenieff *Fundamentals*. New York: Routledge.

Hutchinson Guest, Ann. 1983. *Your Move: A New Approach to the Study of Movement and Dance*. Philadelphia, PA: Gordon and Breach Science Publishers.

Jordan, Stephanie (ed.). 1987. *Preservation Politics, Dance Revived Reconstructed Remade*. London: Dance Books.

Laban, Rudolf. 1926. *Choreographie*. Jena: Eugen Diederichs.

————. 1966. *Choreutics*. London: Macdonald & Evans.

————. 1971. *The Mastery of Movement*. London: Macdonald & Evans.

————. 1975. *A Life for Dance*. London: Macdonald & Evans.

Laban, Rudolf, and F. C. Lawrence. 1947. *Effort*. London: Macdonald & Evans.

Lepecki, André. 2007. Choreography as Apparatus of Capture. *The Drama Review* 51 (2): 119–123.

————. 2010. The Body as Archive: Will to Re-Enact and the Afterlives of Dances. *Dance Research Journal* 42 (2): 28–48.

Main, Lesley. 2012. *Directing the Dance Legacy of Doris Humphrey: The Creative Impulse of Reconstruction*. Madison, WI: University of Wisconsin Press.

McCaw, Dick (ed.). 2011. *The Laban Sourcebook*. New York: Routledge.

Odom, Selma L. 2002. Writings on Dalcroze Eurythmics and Hellerau. *American Dalcroze Journal* 28 (3) Spring/Summer.

Pakes, Anna. 2017. Reenactment, Reconstruction and Dance Historical Fictions. In *The Oxford Handbook of Dance and Reenactment*, ed. Mark Franko. New York: Oxford University Press.

Preston-Dunlop, Valerie. 1998. *Rudolf Laban. An Extraordinary Life*. London: Dance Books.

————. 2013. *Rudolf Laban. Man of Theatre*. Alton: Dance Books.

Preston-Dunlop, Valerie, and Charlotte Purkiss. 1989–1993. Rudolf Laban: The Making of Modern Dance. The Seminal Years in Munich 1910–1914, Part 1. *Dance Theatre Journal* 7 (3) Winter: 11–15.

————. 1989–1993. Rudolf Laban: The Making of Modern Dance. The Seminal Years in Munich 1910–1914, Part 2. *Dance Theatre Journal* 7 (4) February: 10–13.

Preston-Dunlop, Valerie, and Lesley-Anne Sayers. 2011. Gained in Translation: Recreation as Creative Practice. *Dance Chronicle* 34 (1): 5–43.

Rubidge, Sarah. 2000. *Identity in Flux: A Theoretical and Choreographic Enquiry into the Identity of the Open Dance Work*. Unpublished Doctoral thesis. Trinity Laban London.

Schneider, Rebecca. 2001. Archives Performance Remains. *Performance Research* 6 (2): 100–108.

———. 2011. *Performing Remains: Art and War in Times of Theatrical Reenactment*. London: Routledge.

Stalpaert, Christel. 2011. Reenacting Modernity: Fabian Barba's A Mary Wigman Dance Evening (2009). *Dance Research Journal* 43 (1): 90–95.

Thomas, Helen. 2003. *The Body, Dance and Cultural Theory*. New York: Macmillan.

Whatley, Sarah. 2013. Recovering and Reanimating 'Lost' Traces: The Digital Archiving of the Rehearsal Process in Siobhan Davies Replay. *Dance Research* 31 (2): 144–156.

CHAPTER 3

Impure Transmissions: Traditions of Modern Dance Across Historical and Geographical Boundaries

Fabián Barba

> *Mestizaje defies control through simultaneously asserting the impure, curdled multiple state and rejecting fragmentation into pure parts.* (Lugones 2003, 123)

In 2009 I created the performance *A Mary Wigman Dance Evening* (AMWDE) as a dance recital composed of the reenactment of nine short soli originally choreographed and danced by Mary Wigman between 1925 and 1929. These soli were part of her first tour through the United States in 1929–1930 and popularized *Ausdruckstanz*, a new form of dance emerging in Germany at that time, through large audiences across the country. I became interested in her work after seeing some of the few videos where she appears dancing. Viewing those dances was an uncanny experience: despite the perceived strangeness of the movement, I could sense a certain familiarity. To try and understand this ambiguity became the main motivation behind my work to reenact those dances.

F. Barba (✉)
Rue de La Tulipe 33, 1050 Brussels, Belgium
e-mail: barba.fabian@gmail.com

© The Author(s) 2017
L. Main (ed.), *Transmissions in Dance*,
https://doi.org/10.1007/978-3-319-64873-6_3

My first hypothesis, that I still maintain, is that the sense of familiarity with *Ausdruckstanz* was prompted by my early training in modern dance in Quito (Ecuador).

I should note that before I started working on the performance AMWDE, I did not have any close relation to the work of Wigman or *Ausdruckstanz*. It was only after watching the videos of Wigman that I sought to become acquainted with her dancing. Over a three-year period I endeavored to learn about and become familiar with this dance tradition. During this process I visited the Mary Wigman archives in the Akademie der Künsten in Berlin where I found many pictures of her dances, all the press reviews of her tour in the United States and the music scores for some of the dances I wanted to work with. I also read an important part of the literature in English about her work and her own translated texts. I talked and interviewed people who were knowledgeable about her career. I also read as many studies as I could about modern dance in Europe and the United States, and about Germany's social and cultural context from the 1900s to the mid-1930s. Hedwig Müller, Wigman's biographer, mentioned that her pillow books were Goethe's *The Sorrows of Young Werther* and Nietzsche's *Thus Spoke Zarathustra*, so I read those books too, trying to imagine the intimate horizon of her aesthetic and philosophical interests. Finally, I had the privilege of meeting and working with three exceptional women and dancers who studied in the Wigman School in Berlin in the 1950s and 1960s: Katharine Sehnert, Irene Sieben and Susanne Linke. Working with them was an invaluable experience and a gift, both personally and professionally.

From the beginning of the process and alongside the sources referred to above, I knew that my modern dance training in Quito was also an important source. Its significance was corroborated and became evident to me when I started working with Katharine, Irene and Susanne. The time I had to work with them in the studio was extremely short; I didn't work for more than 15 days with any one of them.[1] Yet, from the outset I had a predisposition that allowed me to enter into Wigman's physical aesthetic universe with relative ease. This allowed me to make the most of that short time in relation to learning and understanding the embodied knowledge these three mentors were imparting. If my already acquired bodily knowledge in Ecuador paved the way for my understanding of *Ausdruckstanz*, that is due precisely to the familiarity I perceive between them.

The transmission processes at work in the creation of AMWDE sprang from at least two dance traditions, and yet the final work cannot be said to be one *or* the other, nor can it be said to be one *and* the other, as if it was the product of a conflation or synthesis. This quality of being in the middle of *neither/nor* is approached by María Lugones (2003) in her discussion of *mestizaje* as impurity, as the resistance to homogenization and its corresponding treatment of difference by means of dichotomization, 'this *or* that'. Lugones makes a distinction between split separation and curdled separation. The first is the product of an archetypal modern imagination directed to segment reality into clearly defined and homogenous, that is, pure, units that lend themselves to hierarchical classification. The second is the product of *mestizaje* as the experience of the impossibility of pure separation and the impossibility of conflation or synthesis. It is a separation that pays attention to the unresolvable tension produced by heterogeneity and impurity; it resists classification and control as its complex and multiple constitutions cannot be reduced to simple units (2003, 121–123).

The dichotomous separation between West/non-West, relevant for this discussion, is similarly critiqued by Coronil (1996). For him, this split construction is the product of representational practices that "participate in the production of conceptions of the world, which (1) separate the world's components into bounded units; (2) disaggregate their relational histories; (3) turn difference into hierarchy; (4) naturalize these representations; and thus (5) intervene, however unwittingly, in the reproduction of existing asymmetrical power relations" (Coronil 1996, 57).

Both Lugones and Coronil stress the importance of embracing complexity and heterogeneity to understand the concreteness of peoples' experiences through distinct though related cultural histories. They do so by critiquing the unequal relations of power that categorize, separate and order hierarchically those related cultural genealogies and practices. Their thinking and perspective have been central to shape my account of the transmission processes across (fictitious[2] yet effective) geographic, cultural and historical boundaries. My aim is to try and understand the dynamics between these two dance traditions in their complex and conflictive relations as they operate at the core of the reenactment of the Wigman dances.

To fully understand the transmission processes during the creation of AMWDE, it is important to first understand the ground on which these transmissions happened. That is to say, the work involved in reenacting the dances and also the role of my training within a dance culture in Ecuador that motivated and made possible those reenactments. Furthermore, we need to understand the familiarity I had perceived between these two traditions and their related histories. The processes of transmission that made possible the creation of AMWDE go beyond the actual working period leading to the performance. Schematically, there are at least four processes that need to be considered conjointly: (1) the work with the three ex-students of Wigman which rested on (2) the embodied knowledge I had acquired during my training in Ecuador which channeled (3) an influence of modern dance as practiced in Europe and the United States alongside (4) an inherited Andean experience.

To pursue this question, I will start by outlining the influence of *Ausdruckstanz* in the formation of modern dance in South America. Then I will discuss how modern dance in Quito relates to *Ausdruckstanz* and Mexican and US modern dance in the midst of an Andean cultural landscape. After this, I will engage in a technical discussion of *Ausdruckstanz* and how my training in modern dance in Quito was useful in reenacting the Wigman dances. I will conclude by presenting a hypothesis that attempts to understand the ground for the familiarity between these two dance traditions, and will explore the distinct basic premises of each one without conflating the two dance cultures but, rather, exploring their differences.

AUSDRUCKSTANZ AND SOUTH AMERICA

In the wake of World War II, the migration of *Ausdruckstanz*-trained dancers to South America had an important impact on the consolidation of modern dance in the continent. Just to mention a few examples: the first dance department in a University in Brazil, at the Federal University of Bahia, had Yanka Rudzka and Rolf Gelewski, two European dancers trained in *Ausdruckstanz*, as its first artistic directors from 1957 to 1965. Carmen Paternostro Schaffner (2012) argues that the influence of *Ausdruckstanz* can still be felt today in the dance generated in this school, alongside other influences, such as the dances and rhythms of Afro-Bahian cults.[3] Kurt Jooss' company toured through several countries in South America and had an important presence in Chile;

Ernst Uthoff, Rudolf Pescht and Lola Botka (dancers in Jooss' company) taught in the newly founded Dance School of the University of Chile, to students who had first studied with Andrée Haas and Ignacio del Pedregal, themselves students of Dalcroze and Wigman respectively (Universidad de Chile 2016). Whilst many German dancers came to South America fleeing from the Nazi regime, Manning suggests that, after 1945, dancers like Dore Hoyer may have come because *Ausdruckstanz* was falling out of favor in the eyes of the institutions, the public and the new generation of dancers in post-war Germany (2006, 226–228).

Having said this, the arrival of dancers trained in *Ausdruckstanz* cannot totally explain the ease with which this dance tradition became established in South America. There must have been something that made the continent a ground that could usefully accommodate this artistic practice. I would propose that there was a cultural climate that welcomed those dancers and eagerly took that dance tradition to develop it further as its own. Expressive dance was not simply imported into South America; it was an artistic form that, once it arrived, had the potential to tackle questions relevant to its new environment.[4] I will return to this question later in the chapter.

The transatlantic exchanges between modern dance traditions in the United States and Europe have been well documented and discussed (e.g. Manning 2007; Burt 1998). It is also possible to trace the influence of *Ausdruckstanz* in several countries in South America. These exchanges passed through personal encounters of dancers who worked and shared time in the dance studio and theaters. However, the possible interaction that dancers in Ecuador had with other modern dance traditions is much thinner and, as a result, difficult to grasp. Wilson Pico, one of the modern dance pioneers in Quito, has noted this sense of insularity. Introducing an exhibition of photographs of German dancers, he says:

> [Jooss' company in 1940] had been... in Rio de Janeiro, Montevideo, in Buenos Aires and several provinces of Argentina; then it went to Chile and towards December it was present in Peru. We have no news as to how the company of German dancers passed through or skipped Ecuador... The truth is that in January and February '41 they were already in Colombia, in March in Venezuela and from there they went ten weeks to New York. (Pico 1999, my translation)

MODERN DANCE IN ECUADOR

With a recently established presence of ballet in Ecuador from the 1930s on,[5] and some incipient efforts to accommodate that dance tradition into the local context,[6] in 1972 the *Ballet Experimental Moderno* (Experimental Modern Ballet, BEM by its initials in Spanish) was founded in Quito by Wilson Pico and the brothers, Diego and Romel Pérez. Also unofficially named *El Taller Coreográfico del Hambre* (The Choreographic Workshop of Hunger), it can be recognized as the first dance practice that later on would be identified as modern dance in the country. After the BEM was disbanded in 1974, Wilson continued to work as a soloist, creating what he used to call *crónicas danzadas* (danced chronicles). The terminology used suggests that this dance form, at the time of its inception, was not immediately linked to traditions of modern dance as had been constituted elsewhere.

To generate their dance practice, the members of the BEM had two direct influences alongside ballet. The first was the work with Pascal Monod, a disciple of Jerzy Grotowsky who, during his one-year stay in Quito, taught workshops to actors and several dancers, including the members of the BEM. The second influence was the presence of Germán Silva, a dancer from Chile who had a background in ballet and was familiar with the work of Jooss and Béjart (Mariño and Aguirre 1994, 315–316), and who became Wilson's privileged interlocutor during his early formative years. Taking from these three artistic influences, the BEM sought to devise a formal dance language to interpret and interact with the social context in which it worked. Most of the themes of the early works were drawn from popular situations, engaged in social problems and staged characters (*personajes*) that could be easily recognized by the public as corresponding to part of their daily life. This is how Wilson summarizes the work of these early years:

> Precisely when he [Germán Silva] arrived, this group of boys to which I belonged, we were leaving the security that classical ballet could offer us and started to invent a way of dancing based on the observation of people in the street and on paying attention to the social situation in which we were living…for this group it was painful to tamper with the forms of classical ballet that we had learned, because we loved that which we were transforming, but at the same time *this technic was not enough or did not fit to interpret a forgotten mandate of ancestral Andean communication*—to the little technical knowledge we had, the group learnt to add what every

pioneer possesses: passion, faith and authenticity. (Pico, archive material, FB's emphasis)

After establishing himself as a soloist in 1974, Wilson traveled north to confront his artistic proposal in other contexts, both eager to learn and to share what he had found. He passed through Colombia and Mexico, where he stayed for eight months, training at the ballet of Guillermina Bravo, before arriving in the United States. Once there, he took workshops with Martha Graham for 15 days and a one-month intensive workshop with Katherine Dunham (Salguero 2007, 70). Pico then returned to Quito to continue working and dancing, but repeated these trips north several times. During his maturation as a dancer, he created a personal dance vocabulary that allowed him to explore on stage the social reality in which he lived and for which he created his works.

Kléver Viera, another modern dance pioneer in Ecuador and my teacher, followed a similar path. After a first encounter with dance in 1974 in the newly founded *Instituto National de Danza* (National Dance Institute) in Quito, Kléver went to Mexico for three years to further his training. There he studied with Xavier Francis who, together with José Limón, had been a disciple of Doris Humphrey. After that period, Kléver went back to Ecuador and started creating dances that were heavily influenced by this formative experience while trying to address social issues of the Ecuadorean context with a clear leftist political inclination. Later on and highly affected by the work of Wilson Pico, he tried to distance himself from his training in Mexico. He looked for a way of dancing that would allow him to channel his memories and experience as someone who grew up in the midst of the Ecuadorean sierra, where he had a vivid and intimate contact with kichwa people.[7] The outcome of this paradigmatic shift from modern dance (in its western genealogy) to Andean reality was a cycle of dances called *Viaje a la memoria festiva* (Journey towards the festive memory). Not radically different to Wilson in this respect, from then on his work combined his acquired knowledge in modern dance with the social reality of Ecuador and with an Andean cultural background:

> The journey towards the festive memory is a journey towards my own interior, it is not an anthropological journey, it was a journey towards memory, where I perhaps come to terms with several things, the conflict of my identity... The journey towards the festive memory implies the beginning of

my most idiosyncratic dance (*mi danza más propia*), more personal, and I would like to believe and say that it also has to do with the fact that it is a dance that is born here, that is Ecuadorean, that is Andean, that is the paramo, that is indigenous without being folklore, but it is rather a profound feeling, my own, of my provenance. (Mora 2015, 17 (FB's translation))

The contact of Wilson and Kléver with Mexican and US modern dance was relatively brief, and though it cannot account totally for their respective development as dancers, it certainly left an important mark. Direct contact with dancers who could have transmitted a legacy of *Ausdruckstanz* was non-existent. However, in trying to devise their respective artistries, they did look for input from *Ausdruckstanz* through texts, photographs and videos. In conversation, Wilson told me he considers himself to be an unofficial heir of Mary Wigman. During one period in his career, he referred to his dances as dances of expression. Recalling this period he says: "I understood that what I was doing could be related to that which appeared in Germany in the thirties" (Salguero 2007, 46). In the 1990s, they organized a dance festival that was called *Jornadas de la danza Mary Wigman* (Mary Wigman's dance sessions[8]) which means that Wigman was not only known, but also that she was perceived as an appropriate and relevant figure under whose umbrella they could present their own creations.

I maintain that the modern dance Wilson and Kléver developed has a strong affinity with *Ausdruckstanz* because we can observe in their creative work an independence from a consolidated "formal dance vocabulary; the idea that each dancer has to find a personal way of expressing her/his inner self; and the possibility that individual dancers can become autonomous creators rather than company members copying the skills of the master" (Barba 2011, 87). In this respect, neither Wilson nor Kléver (until recently) have ever transmitted their solos to other dancers.

TRANSMISSIONS OF BODILY KNOWLEDGE

In order to discuss the multiple transmissions of bodily knowledge that allowed me to reenact the Mary Wigman dances, I would like to start by taking into account some preliminary considerations. As stated elsewhere (Barba 2017), an education in dance is not only a technical education, it is also a way of becoming a part of a dance culture. Furthermore, such a process entails the incorporation of that dance culture into the dancer's body. The dance culture and the dancer pass through a process of mutual interpenetration and constitution. I would like now to reflect on the ways this might happen by considering a dancer's training in relation to the acquisition of what Mario Biagioli calls 'tacit knowledge'.

Biagioli (1995) defines tacit knowledge as that kind of knowledge that cannot be totally spelled out, that cannot be apprehended through a complete description of rules of behavior. A skill is a corporeal kind of tacit knowledge, a knowledge that has been in-corporated (Biagioli 1995, 71). A technique can be defined and transmitted with the help of verbal language and exercises: "put first the balls of the feet on the floor, and then the heels." Skills however, as tacit knowledge, escape this kind of formulation and explicit transmission. In a dance education, it is not only the rules of behavior (a describable technique) but also the ostensions (that which escapes complete formalization) that play an important role in the mutual constitution of a dance culture and the dance student.

For Biagioli, a skill can be incorporated and reproduced through the disciplining of the body, through continuous practice and training. Moreover, the student can incorporate a skill through the observation of the teacher's body (as the holder of that skill) and the continuous attempt to reproduce that skill in his/her own body. In this process the teacher as a model (or demonstrative body) plays an important role in creating a relation between the dancer's body (the perceived body) and the skills the student should eventually acquire (the ideal body[9]). Skills are opaque even to their own holders (Biagioli 1995, 71) and, what's more, even if the teacher could completely spell out that knowledge to his/her students, this description would not suffice. The transmission and incorporation of skills require two main conditions: the body-to-body encounter between the teacher and the student, and the time necessary to observe and attempt to reproduce those skills. Perhaps the best example of a skill, in relation to the reenactment of Wigman's dances, is the production of a subtext.

The subtext is a central element in Wigman's dances that constantly refuses authoritative formulation. For Wigman, a dance needs to express or communicate something to the audience; this 'something' is the subtext of the dance. However, whatever the dance communicates cannot be translated or expressed in words. In this sense the sub*text* is not textual, but it can be understood as the intensity that brings coherence and 'substance' to the dance. I have come to understand the subtext as an intense subjective experience produced through the dancing. It is this intensity that can be perceived as the emotional dimension of *Ausdruckstanz*, yet reducing this dynamic, and to some extent unidentifiable, intensity to a well-defined emotion misses out the richness and the potential of this kind of dance.

As Katharine Sehnert and Irene Sieben[10] made clear, in the classes at the Wigman School they would hardly ever talk about the emotional character of a dance; they were never asked to try and address an emotion directly. "It is not *about* emotions. *There are* emotions. It is different what I think a feeling looks like to what the body is doing. [At the Wigman School] we didn't work on emotions" (Sieben 2016, interview, FB's emphases). "Each movement has its own expression. It doesn't need to have a subtext. It *is* a subtext" (Sehnert 2016, interview, FB's emphasis). The work was approached through the physicality of the dance, with the student finding through experience and repetition the way to fully inhabit that movement, to find him/herself through it. By practicing the exercises proposed in class, they would explore all the qualitative ranges of a movement and the feelings (as sensations) associated with them. Cultivating this sensibility might have been key to the production of a subtext, which required that the students be fully engaged during class, because Wigman would never let a movement be done absent-mindedly.

If the students at the Wigman School could not be directly taught how to produce a subtext, they could learn about, and practice, that specific physicality with its associated sensorial realm. That physicality is the product of the interconnection of different technical tools; learning to handle these tools in an interrelated way allows for the emergence of a subtext (as a skill). These technical tools are related to specific uses of the gaze, the breathing, muscular tones and movement patterns, among others.

To look more closely at the breathing, neither Sehnert nor Sieben recall having had specific classes or exercises focused exclusively on breathing. However, all the exercises they practiced included a specific (though not always verbalized) use of it. The use of the breathing is of central importance in several of Wigman's movement principles. In gliding forward[11] for example, there is the sensation of pressing the volume of air in front of oneself. The intention and action of compressing that volume of air demands a certain muscular tone and is helped by a rather forceful exhalation. The quality of gliding backwards is altogether different; it is as if a void opened up behind oneself and that void pulls the dancer in that direction. The sensation is that of yielding backwards while witnessing how the space in front opens up and grows. The muscular tone is much softer and the exhalation matches that tone. If in gliding there are long exhalations, either forceful or soft, in vibrato the exhalations are short and fast, matching the vibration of the body as it bounces up and down. Percussive sharp movements, like those of *Sturmlied*[12] are short and forceful. The explosive character of some of those movements is supported by a corresponding engagement of the breathing. In relation to the use of the breathing, Katharine comments:

> For her [Wigman] the breathing was the main point. The breathing... has three functions: it transports this special energy you are working on, it builds up the phrase and time and it gives a special color to the movement. If you breathe small or flat, the movement goes only like this [gestures a small movement of the arms]. If you breathe more, the movement gets bigger. If you breathe much more, then you can lift your arms, not before. And so, this body feeling comes from the breathing... The breathing belongs to the movement, it creates the movement.

To this, Katharine added: "Wigman wouldn't mention this, it would be something that came in your mind later on." Similarly, discussing the use of the breathing in vibrato, Irene remarked: "But it's not that she said 'breathing has to be like that', 'breathe here or...' no!" Working with Katharine, Irene and Susanne, I don't recall having received central verbal remarks about the use of the breathing either. However, talking recently with Katharine and Irene, we agreed on most of our understanding. I am sure that as I saw them demonstrate gliding and I tried to emulate what I had seen, I must have inadvertently started playing with my breathing as well. As they demonstrated the exercises and talked through them, I must have been able to perceive how their breathing was being differently compromised. This is actually something we can see happening in the reportage made for Cobra TV's program *Canvas* (Cobra.be 2016), where Katharine is working with me on some of Wigman's movement principles and dances. In minute 05:40, for the last movement of the solo *Drehmonotonie*,[13] Katharine actually holds her breath first and then says: "don't breathe!"

In that same part of the recorded rehearsal, we can see how Katharine *does* much more than she *says*. In *Ausdruckstanz* these technical elements could not be approached individually, but in their interrelation. Each movement principle practiced by Wigman already engages all those technical aspects in an interconnected way. It is not possible to work with the breathing as if it was something separate from the muscular tone, the movement principle, the subtext and the motif of the dance or improvisation. All these elements need to be interconnected and worked out simultaneously as part of one and the same dance. Learning to connect all these technical elements and use them to 'find oneself in the dance' is something that cannot be totally spelled out. It is something that each dancer, with the help of the teacher, has to 'discover' for her/himself via observation, emulation and repetition. This is the acquisition of a skill, of a tacit embodied knowledge.

MODERN DANCE IN QUITO AS A SOURCE IN THE CREATION OF AMWDE: THE GRAFT—*EL INJERTO*

As I mentioned at the beginning of this text, the short time I had with Katharine, Irene and Susanne in the studio cannot account for the acquisition of the skills I have described. I believe that my prior training in Ecuador allowed me to access this kind of physicality. Katharine and Irene share the same impression: when they started working with me, I already had 'something', a kind of understanding that helped us to work on Wigman's movement principles and dances. It was *through*, or thanks to, this previously acquired bodily knowledge that we worked on the technical and aesthetic specificities of Wigman's universe. Reenacting the Wigman dances was like grafting *Ausdruckstanz* onto an Ecuadorean modern dance base. Moreover, my understanding of *Ausdruckstanz* (which allowed me to reenact these dances) was informed not only by my research on it and the work with the three ex-students of Wigman, but also by my own experience as a dancer in Ecuador. *My understanding and performance of Ausdruckstanz, therefore, is a* mestizo, *impure understanding, a product of multiple and impure processes of transmission.*

We can understand the suitability of my training in modern dance in Quito as a source and a ground for these reenactments due to the similarities between these two dance traditions. Indeed, there are technical consonances between *Ausdruckstanz* and modern dance in Quito in relation to the use of the gaze, the breathing, the muscular tone, the importance of the subtext and the perception of the body as having a commanding center, even if this center might be placed differently.

In the work of Kléver and Wilson, as well as in Wigman's work, the performer is asked to have his or her body under full control. No gesture should be executed if it is not purposefully produced. Despite a demand for technical precision, the performers are not meant to move mechanically (this would be dismissed as mere gymnastics). Instead, the dancer is expected to recapture the lived experience of the dance each time it is performed. Ideally, the dancers should reach a heightened or ecstatic state of being, transcending the mere physicality of the gestures and expressing the inner self of the human being. The dialectical interplay between rigid technical control and transcendent expression is a structuring principle of both dance traditions.

The gaze also functions similarly in both traditions: it should be 'intense' and almost always directed toward a well-defined but empty point in space. The straight and sustained gaze helps to make present the transcendental: it suggests that there is more to discover beyond the visual boundaries of a given space. The staring dancer leads us into a 'present absence', into an invisibility that can be seen. This use of the gaze can be observed in many pictures of Wigman, perhaps especially in those of a 'demonic' character. But the expressive use of the gaze can also take on soft, internalized connotations: *Anruf* and *Pastorale*[14] are, for example, almost entirely danced with the eyes half-closed. In Kléver and Susanne's classes I have practiced this use of the gaze by looking at a point straight in front of me, taking care not to deviate my gaze elsewhere while the exercise is being executed.

The use of breathing also plays an important role in creating a specific movement quality. Control of the breath modifies the muscular tone and affects the perception a dancer has of her/his own body. Attaching movement to specific breaths can produce a holistic perception of movement and body, thus enhancing the ecstatic, heightened state a dancer is expected to achieve within these traditions.[15]

If this technical familiarity could be explained by the encounter of modern dancers in Ecuador with the modern dance traditions developed in Europe, Mexico and the United States, we still need to understand why these tools were thus appropriated. Why did Pico feel that ballet was not a suitable technique to interpret a "forgotten Andean mandate", but modern dance could be? As stated earlier, I do not think we have to deal with an importation of a dance form into Ecuador, but with a useful appropriation of that dance form and technical tools as a means to deal with local concerns. I would like to advance the hypothesis that one of the conditions of possibility for this acclimation was that the non-modernist dimension of *Ausdruckstanz* opened spaces for the survival and exploration of non-modern, non-western experiences of the world. The modernism of early modern dance has been largely discussed (e.g., Manning 1988; Burt 1998; Franko 1995). In relation to the work of Wigman, I recognize two antithetical positions that are not, and do not need to be, resolved.

The first one points towards a modernist intention in Wigman's proposal. In formal aspects, Wigman's idea of an *absoluter Tanz* (absolute dance)[16] was an attempt to differentiate this kind of dance from ballet and the institutions that supported it (Franco 2007, 81). As a strategy (and resonating *avant la lettre* with Greensberg's understanding of modernist art), *absoluter Tanz* sought to discover and rely exclusively on what was proper to the dance medium: there is an abandonment of narrativity, mimetic representation, costumes that would fulfill a decorative function and dependence from music, all of this counterpointed by an increasingly important reliance on the physicality of the dance and what it could convey. These formal innovations bespeak of a modernist dimension of *Ausdruckstanz*.

The second position points towards a non-modernist dimension of *Ausdruckstanz*. This art form emerged not only in opposition to the values and aesthetic categories of nineteenth-century bourgeois society, but also in opposition to the individualization, alienation and instrumentality of growing industrialization. Hellerau and Monte Veritá, the places where Wigman studied with Dalcroze and Laban respectively, sought to cultivate a healthy and harmonious relation with nature and the community as an oppositional and utopic response to what was perceived as the pernicious consequences of modernity. As I will argue, the embodied, ecstatic and 'irrational' dimension of *Ausdruckstanz* plays against the ideal of a universal, rational, fully conscious, disembodied and mature modern Self.

In this sense, *Ausdruckstanz* and other kinds of modern dance, conversely, could have served as a base to graft a living dimension of Andean experience. That is what both Kléver and Wilson have mentioned: how the technique they learnt had to be transformed in order to be able to express the social reality in which they worked and the Andean cultural background in which they lived. Let us explore this question further by revisiting the discussion on the subtext both in Wigman and Kléver.

Two Oppositional Responses to Modernism: *Ausdruckstanz* and Modern Dance in Quito

The physicality of *Ausdruckstanz* has a transformative character; it must convey a strong subjective experience. This physicality and the intensity (or subtext) that it materializes can be put in relation to the ecstatic quality of the Wigman dances. I do not understand ecstatic as being possessed or as being totally taken away by the dance. As Ramsay Burt (1998, 179–181) discusses in relation to Wigman's solo *Drehmonotonie*, the physicality of spinning (one of Wigman's movement principles)— with the head tilted to the side which changes the position of the gaze and the visual relation to the space altering thus the sense of balance— can be related to kinds of "auto-hypnotic ritual movement" (167). This half-controlled, half-ecstatic state is clearly described by Wigman:

> Fixed to the same spot and spinning in the monotony of the whirling movement, one lost oneself gradually in it until the turns seemed to detach themselves from the body, and the world around it started to turn. Not turning oneself, but being turned, being the centre, being the quiet pole in the vortex of rotation!
>
> ...
>
> A jerk pierces the body, compelling it to stand still at the moment of the fastest turn; now the body is stretching high, lifted on tiptoe, with the arms thrown up, grasping a non-existent support. A breathless pause, an eternity long, lasting only a few seconds. And then the sudden letting go, the fall of the relaxed body into the depth with only one sensation still alive: that of a complete incorporeal state. And in that state only one wish: never be forced to get up again, to be allowed to lie there just like this, through all eternity. (Wigman quoted in Burt 1998, 180, Fig. 3.1)

The ecstatic dimension of *Ausdruckstanz* has a non-mimetic character that is also present in the idea of the *Gestalt*. As Susan Manning (2006) tells us, the *Gestalt* cannot be understood as the representation of a character, it is rather the materialization of forces in the space through the body of the dancer. In *Sturmlied*, for example, the dancer shouldn't do *as if* she was the personification of a storm, she has to *embody* the qualities of the storm. The dancer needs to find a way of embodying those qualities and intensities and thus materialize them in the space.

Fig. 3.1 Fabián Barba in *Drehmonotonie* by Mary Wigman. Photograph by Dieter Hartwig

The percussive, sharp, short, forceful and whirling movements of this dance help in embodying a *Gestalt* that is both threatening and in full command of the space around. As Katharine put it: "You are this movement in this moment, you never want to show [something] to the outside, you *are* this movement."

I understand the subtext as intimately linked to the ecstatic quality of the Wigman dances and the non-mimetic embodiment of a *Gestalt*. We might miss a lot of our understanding of *Ausdruckstanz* if we consider them separately as distinct and independent units. It is in this realm of auto-hypnotic movement, in the blurring of "the distinction between consciousness and the unconscious" (Burt 1998, 181) and the central role of sensations and the body that I see *Ausdruckstanz*'s opposition to the modern ideal of a disembodied and fully rational subject.

As in the Wigman School, in the classes and choreographic workshops with Kléver, we never approached the work with emotions directly. We were always focused on the movement and yet, during the classes and rehearsals, I almost always reached a point of wandering through some sort of emotional realm (this is already an important difference to Katharine's and Irene's experience as students, for whom emotions found no place in their technical training). Kléver is a very passionate person and dancer and the particular way he has of giving himself to and through the movement must have come across to me as his student. Working with Kléver I discovered an intimate connection between the physicality and the sensorial/sensual/emotional intensity of the dance. Alfredo Espinoza, a journalist in Quito who is familiar with the work of Kléver, mentioned that there is a Dionysian dimension to him as a dancer.[17] I couldn't agree more: *Kléver se embriaga en su danza*—Kléver gets intoxicated while dancing. *Embriagarse* (to get intoxicated) is not the same as reaching an ecstatic state while dancing, but there is a partial and contained loss of control that sets both experiences as similar to each other.

Kléver is not interested in the danced representation of characters either. Even though he may talk of the *personajes* (characters) of his dances, the kernel of his artistic proposition is not directed at *representing* them, but is an exercise in *becoming*. The characters of his dances are ways for him to deal with his own identity questions. They are materializations of intimate and intense attempts to self-understanding and self-transformation. When I learnt to dance *La mujer de los fermentos* (the woman of the ferments),[18] I was not asked to represent a female character, I was given the space, through the sensuality of the dance, to explore my own sense of gender indetermination and sexual interrogation.

In a recent conversation, Kléver talked about his interest in becoming in relation to his reading of Gilles Deleuze. In that sense he was relating his artistic proposal to a European genealogy of thought. However, and I believe without contradiction, in another interview he recounts a different story on becoming:

> [N]onetheless, after having two drinks he [a kichwa-speaking person in a celebration] turns into a god, he stops being that wretched being and is a dancing god; how can that indigene, festive dancer, mutate the body... Well, there I manage to break down this formal language I had inherited in Mexico and my journey towards the festive memory starts, where I find the gesture and find, I think, that my true identity is that of the festive dancer, I find the mutation of the body, I find the importance of the weight, of relaxation, of breathing. (Mora 2015, 16)

In this passage, Kléver is talking about the turning point that the *viaje a la memoria festiva* represented for him. In these dances he questions his own sense of identity and the significance of his dancing by 'returning' to the Andean 'memory of my people' (Mora 2015, 16). It is important to say that Kléver was born and grew up in a small town with a large kichwa population. His mother had a *cantina de indios,* a tavern where kichwa people would go to get heavily drunk. Returning to the 'memory of my people' is not to be understood as a utopic and romantic return to an archaic past. It is a return to his own childhood memories and lived experience in a highly racialized, discriminatory and conflictual bi-cultural environment.

The choice of words in *viaje a la memoria festiva* is extremely significant. In the Andes, a festivity has an important ritual and religious dimension. As Estermann tells us, in the contemporary Andes "in and through the ceremonial rite, the divine and cosmic order is made 'present' in a symbolic form" (1998, 276). The symbols of the ritual do not *represent* the cosmic order, but that cosmic order *is present,* in a condensed fashion, in and through the symbols. There is no mimesis here, but symbolic efficacy insofar as the symbolic rite can transform the reality that contains it and is a part of. The dances of Kléver, through their intoxicated physicality and the space open for self-understanding and self-transformation, should not be understood as a mimetic operation, but as an exercise in becoming. Kléver, through his dancing, reenacts the potential of Andean rites not to represent, but *to make present* and transform the relations with our selves and our community.

From this account, we might be able to understand better the resemblance between *Ausdruckstanz*'s subtext, ecstatic dimension and the *Gestalt* and the intoxication and transformative character of Kléver's dancing. These two traditions meet in their oppositional stance against the modern ideal of a disembodied, rational and abstract Self. This might help us understand the useful acclimation of *Ausdruckstanz* and other forms of modern dance in Ecuador. Having said this, it must be added that the political commitment, the genealogy and the character of their oppositional stances are different. While the non-modernist dimension of *Ausdruckstanz* emerges as part of an avant-gardist opposition to certain features of modernity and it relies on European philosophy and psychoanalysis (Manning 2006, 57; Burt 1998, 125, 162, 168), the non-modernist, non-western dimension of modern dance in Ecuador emerges against a background of colonial history and is grounded in the experience and world view of the Andes.

Conclusions

When I started working on AMWDE I had a clear target audience and a clear intention. I wanted to get as close as I could to producing a living and moving image of Wigman as a way of disrupting the conventions and codes with which my classmates and I had become familiar at P.A.R.T.S.[19] I wanted to do so because I had the impression that *Ausdruckstanz* and modern dance in Quito did not have a place within the 'contemporary' dance world into which we were being educated. I thought that through achieving a convincing portrayal of Wigman, I would get the strongest effect of confrontation. Even though I knew I was not interested in or aiming at an authentic reproduction, I went to every length to produce an illusion of authenticity (Barba 2017).

For this reason, in the performance *A Mary Wigman Dance Evening*, I focused on bringing Wigman to the forefront and I did not try to signal the presence of my inherited and embodied knowledge of modern dance as it had developed in Quito. However, invited to think about the transmission processes that were enacted in the creation of AMWDE, I felt the need to bring under the spotlight that other genealogy that created the ground and the conditions of possibility to reenact the Wigman dances.

Nevertheless, during the performance and despite my confessed efforts, people could not help noticing my hairy legs, flat chest and the color of my skin. These signs became a constant reminder that it was not Wigman, but a young South American male onstage. My body continuously disrupted the illusion of authenticity I was trying to produce. As Timmy de Laet noted:

> Barba's *Dance Evening* provokes a double-sided vision [comparable to] Wittgenstein's drawing of the so-called 'Duck-Rabbit', in which both animals can be discerned, although taken together it represents a schematic creature "that 'looks like' *neither* a duck *nor* a rabbit" (Mitchell 1995, p. 50[20]; original emphasis). A similar characterisation might hold for Barba's *Dance Evening*, since the body we see appearing on stage 'looks like' *neither* Barba *nor* Wigman, but rather seems to be a shifting conflation of both figures. (De Laet 2013, 144)

The impurity of AMWDE has been continuously remarked by members of the audience: "But is it Wigman or not?" There is not a simple and quick answer to that question; ambiguity and *mestizaje* are its marks, in the middle of either/or...

NOTES

1. A constant reminder of the shortness of these working periods is my inability to fully 'master' the movement principles they taught me. When I see Irene, Katharine or Susanne glide through space, I marvel at the ease with which they move, I cannot see the action of their feet punctuating the movement, it is really as if their torsos were sliding through space, as if they were moving over an ice surface. When I glide through space, I cannot counteract the punctuating action of my feet, even after performing these dances for more than six years!
2. I say fictitious to signify that these boundaries, seemingly an external and natural reality, are the product of a historical and epistemological construction that nonetheless effectively shapes our (representation of) reality.
3. Afro-Brazilian religions have their roots in communities of enslaved Africans and their descendants. They emerged as a means for the people to make sense of their experience of uprooting by constructing systems of meaning and sociality in their new environment. Trance, dance and percussive music are constitutive elements of these religious practices. In Bahia the most prominent one is *Candomblé*.
4. I first formulated this hypothesis in Barba (2010 and 2011).
5. Maurice Maugé, a French ballet dancer trained in the Paris Opera, arrived in Ecuador in 1929. He is considered to be the initiator of the practice of ballet in the country (Mariño and Aguirre 1994, 87–124).

6. Noralma Vera studied ballet in Guayaquil (Ecuador) and further trained in England and performed in France and Cuba. In the mid-1960s, she was in charge of the school of dance in Quito—where Wilson Pico started his training—and founded the *Compañía experimental de danza y ballet* (Experimental dance and ballet company) (Mariño and Aguirre 1994, 190–191).
7. Kichwa is the most widely spoken language in Ecuador after Spanish. It defines an indigenous nation composed of different ethnic groups (*pueblos*) across the country. Nowadays in Ecuador 13 different nationalities are officially recognized.
8. The Spanish word *jornada* could also be translated as workday. It has the connotation of viewing dance as labor and thus it relates dance to the working class. The *Jornadas de la danza Mary Wigman* were organized by the *Frente de Danza Independiente* (The Independent Dance Front) founded by Wilson and Kléver, among others. This choice of words bespeaks of the leftist political alignment and social concern of their work.
9. The notions of demonstrative, perceived and ideal body are taken from Foster (1997).
10. All the following quotes and mentions to Katharine and Irene are taken from interviews with the author.
11. Gliding is one of the movement principles practiced by Wigman. Other movement principles are vibrato, spinning, circles, jumping, hands.
12. *Sturmlied* is the fifth dance I perform in AMWDE.
13. *Drehmonotonie* is the ninth and last dance of AMWDE.
14. *Pastorale* is the third and *Anruf* the fourth dance of AMWDE.
15. The last three paragraphs have been taken from Barba (2011, 88).
16. Before the generic name of *Ausdruckstanz* became established, several other names were adopted for this artistic practice: absolute dance, new dance, artistic dance, new German dance.
17. Personal conversation.
18. This solo was created and performed by Kléver in 2003. He taught it to Fausto Espinoza, another dancer studying with him, and to myself. This is one of the few dances Kléver has ever transmitted to somebody else.
19. P.A.R.T.S. is the school of contemporary dance directed by Anne Teresa de Keersmaeker in Brussels.
20. Mitchell, W.J.T. 1995. *Picture Theory. Essays on Verbal and Visual Representation.* Chicago: University of Chicago Press.

Bibliography

Barba, Fabián. 2010. Questions nées de la reconstruction de *A Mary Wigman Dance Evening*. *NDD L'actualité de la danse* 49: 11.
———. 2011. Research into Corporeality. *Dance Research Journal* 43/1: 83–89.

————. 2017. Quito-Brussels: A Dancer's Cultural Geography. In *The Oxford Handbook of Dance and Reenactment*, ed. Mark Franko. New York: Oxford University Press.

Biagioli, Mario. 1995. Tacit Knowledge, Courtliness, and the Scientist's Body. In *Choreographing History*, ed. Susan Leigh Foster, 69–81. Bloomington, IN: Indiana University Press.

Burt, Ramsay. 1998. *Alien Bodies: Representations of Modernity, 'Race' and Nation in Early Modern Dance*. New York: Routledge.

Cobra.be. 2016. *A Mary Wigman Dance Evening—Fabián Barba*. http://cobra.canvas.be/cm/cobra/videozone/archief/muziek/1.967860 (accessed November 18, 2016).

Coronil, Fernando. 1996. Beyond Occidentalism: Toward Nonimperial Geohistorical Categories. *Cultural Anthropology* 11 (1): 51–87.

De Laet, Timmy. 2013. Bodies With(out) Memories: Strategies of Re-enactment in Contemporary Dance. In *Performing Memory in Art and Popular Culture*, ed. Anneke Smelik and Liedeke Plate, 135–152. London and New York: Routledge.

Estermann, Josef. 1998. *Filosofía andina; estudio intercultural de la sabiduría autóctona andina*. Quito: Ediciones Abya-Yala.

Foster, Susan Leigh. 1997. Dancing Bodies. In *Meaning in Motion*, ed. Jane C. Desmond, 235–257. Durham, NC and London: Duke University Press.

Franco, Susanne. 2007. *Ausdruckstanz*: Traditions, Translation, Transmissions. In *Dance Discourses: Keywords for Dance Research*, ed. Susanne Franco and Marina Nordera in conjunction with the Centre National de la Danse, 80–98. Abingdon and New York: Routledge.

Franko, Mark. 1995. *Dancing Modernism/Performing Politics*. Bloomington, IN: Indiana University Press.

Lugones, María. 2003. *Pilgrimages/Peregrinajes: Theorizing Coalition Against Multiple Oppressions*. Lanham, Boulder, New York, Oxford: Rowman & Littelfield publishers Inc.

Manning, Susan. 1988. Modernist Dogma and Post-modern Rhetoric: A Response to Sally Banes' *Terpsichore in Sneakers*. *TDR* T-120: 32–38.

————. 2006. *Ecstasy and the Demon: The Dances of Mary Wigman*. Minneapolis, MN: University of Minneapolis Pres.

————. 2007. *Ausdruckstanz* across the Atlantic. In *Dance Discourses: Keywords for Dance Research*, ed. Susanne Franco and Marina Nordera in conjunction with the Centre National de la Danse, 46–60. Abingdon and New York: Routledge.

Mariño, Susana, and Mayra Aguirre. 1994. *Danzahistoria, Notas Sobre el Ballet y la Danza Contemporánea en el Ecuador*. Quito: Ministerio de Educación del Ecuador.

Mitchell, W.J.T. 1995. *Picture Theory: Essays on Verbal and Visual Representation.* Chicago: University of Chicago Press.

Mora, Genoveva (ed.). 2015. *Diálogos que Trazan la Historia de la Danza Moderna y Contemporánea del Ecuador.* Quito: El Apuntador.

Pico, Wilson. 1999. Presentation to the Photo Exhibition of German Dancers Organized by the Humboldt Association. Quito. Unpublished.

Salguero, Natasha (ed.). 2007. *Wilson Pico, 40 años en escena.* Quito: Casa de la Cultura Ecuatoriana.

Schaffner, Carmen Paternostro. 2012. A Danca Expressionista Alema. Paper presented at *Anais Do II Congresso Nacional De Pesquisadores Em Dança—Anda,* July.

Universidad de Chile. 2016. Reseña histórica. http://artes.uchile.cl/danza/departamento-de-danza/40933/resena-historica (accessed November 18, 2016).

Interviews

Irene Sieben—September 14, 2016.
Katharine Sehnert—September 15, 2016.

CHAPTER 4

Performing History: *Wind Tossed* (1936), Natural Movement and the Hyper-Historian

Maria Salgado Llopis

As a dancer and dance scholar my theoretical interest lies in the intersection between the body, history and performance. I see the liminal space between the body and the past, between past practices and current performances, and between the archive and the repertoire as fertile ground for the exploration of a difficult but intriguing proposition: that bodily practices can inform and be an integral part of historiography. This proposition is grounded in the idea that experience and physical explorations of the past have the potential to function epistemologically.

The idea that experience and movement can function epistemologically is not new. In 1999, Sheets-Johnstone proposed that cognition springs from movement, and positioned our kinesthetic and tactile bodies as epistemological gateways (Sheets-Johnstone 1999; Parviainen 1998; Spatz 2015). Post-phenomenological philosophy on embodiment echoes this idea in the works of Parviainen, who argues that the "gestures, postures, and bodily attitudes of others" can gradually shape and inhabit our bodies. In this manner, we absorb cultural values *through* and *on* our body (Parviainen 1998, 27). In the fields of History and

M. S. Llopis (✉)
Kingston University, London, UK
e-mail: contact@mariasalgadollopis.com

© The Author(s) 2017
L. Main (ed.), *Transmissions in Dance*,
https://doi.org/10.1007/978-3-319-64873-6_4

61

62   M. S. LLOPIS

Performance Studies we encounter similar approaches: Kirshenblatt-
Gimblett describes reenacting history as a "way of doing, which is a
way of knowing, in a performance" (Kirshenblatt-Gimblett 1998, 196).
Taylor confirms this view by asserting that we "learn and transmit knowledge through embodied actions"; but she goes further to claim that performance functions as an *episteme*, as "a way of knowing, not simply an
object of analysis" (Taylor 2003, xvi). Thus, for Taylor, performance is
both a lens through which to analyze and a subject of analysis.

If we embrace the ideas that performance can be a form of knowing
and that embodied actions can act as epistemological gateways, we can
contemplate the possibility that historical meaning can be created when
we embody past actions and perform dance works of the past. The creation of meaning I am referring to here does not spring from an affective
mode of inquiry but from one that examines the epistemological potentialities of the body in the transmission, incorporation and articulation
when we engage and perform works of the past.[1]

In order to examine the epistemological potentialities of the body
I will position my performance and investigation of *Wind Tossed* inside
the paradigm of *performing history*. As defined by Rokem (2000), performing history can create performances that move towards fictional
and allegorical extremes or can be close to historical accuracy. Michel
de Certeau's argument regarding the paradoxical nature of the historiographical operation serves as the backbone for Rokem's concept
of performing history. For de Certeau the term 'historiography' contains within its own name a paradox, that is, the relation between "two
antinomic terms, between the real and discourse"; the task of historiography is "one of connecting them and, at the point where this link
cannot be imagined, of working *as if* the two were being joined" (de
Certeau 1992, xxvii). Rokem argues that in performing history, theatre and performance are also constituted in this 'as if' situation, in the
connection between the real—events taking place in the past—and performance. In performance "what de Certeau calls the 'real' and the
'discourse' become blurred or obliterated in such 'as if' situations"
(Rokem 2000, 12).

The key point in Rokem's (2000) approach is the emphasis on the
idea that the actor (in our instance the dancer) becomes a witness of the
historical event by performing as a historical figure. It is in the position
of witness that the actor (or dancer) becomes a sort of historian, what
he calls a 'hyper-historian', someone "who makes it possible for us…

to recognize that the actor is 'redoing' or 'reappearing' as something/somebody that has actually existed in the past" (Rokem 2000, 13). As a *hyper-historian*, the actor (the dancer) is "the connecting link between the historical past and the 'fictional' performed here and now of the theatrical event" (ibid., 13). The term 'fictional' should not be understood as lacking historical rigor but instead is a term that encapsulates some key ideas embedded in performing history, such as acknowledging the modus operandi of the theatre. It is important to clarify here that, from a theatrical perspective, the performance we see on stage is something that is *shown again*, something that has taken its course long before the performance (Rokem 2000). It is fictional; nothing on stage is real but the 'presentness' of the performance as a live event is perceived by the spectator. It is in the research and rehearsal period that retrospective and prospective approaches are taken, and where the actor or dancer engages in the process of embodying the past, constituting her/himself through acts of repetition and 'indwelling'.

The notion of the *hyper-historian* is helpful here because it establishes the idea of the dancer as a connecting link between past and present in performance. At the heart of the hyper-historian's position as witness in the constitution of the performance is the idea that the body is the site where different kinds of transmission, inscription and embodiment take place. In a way, the performer enacts a kind of 'palimpsest history' when performing a dance work, and by doing so, dancing itself effectively becomes an embodiment of history (Dean et al. 2014, 5).

By positioning the *hyper-historian* at the center of my performative investigation of *Wind Tossed*, this chapter explores the potential modes of knowing embedded in the solo that emerged in the process of its transmission, incorporation and articulation. The chapter is divided into two sections. The first section—'Tossed by the wind: history, memory, the repertoire and the archive'—outlines the context of *Wind Tossed* in past performances and explores the 'remains' of this performance in the present. The second section articulates the process of transmission and articulation of this work in the present from the point of view of the dancer as a hyper-historian. Drawing upon Polanyi's (1966) concepts of tacit knowledge and focal and subsidiary awareness, '*Wind Tossed* (1936–2013): indwelling the past, tacit knowledge and the hyper-historian' then investigates the epistemological potentialities embedded in the performance of this solo that surfaced during the process of incorporation and performance of *Wind Tossed*.[2]

TOSSED BY THE WIND: HISTORY, MEMORY, THE REPERTOIRE AND THE ARCHIVE

Choreographed by Madge Atkinson and with music by Pachulski, *Wind Tossed* depicts a dancer tossed by the wind. Upstage and poised, the dancer initiates the movement with the music. Her traveling actions at the beginning of the dance seem to flow at a relatively slow pace but, as the solo progresses, the movement amalgamations gain speed and become vigorous. Enhanced by a blue cape worn by the dancer, the movement depicts different qualities of the wind: swift, flutter and gust translate into runs, double hops and legs unfolding in space. The crescendo of the music sees the dancer leap across the stage and, like a whirlwind, run in concentric circles. She poises on the balls of both feet with the head tossed back in a suspended pose, there is a pause in the music and then...she falls sideways to the floor.

It was in July 1938—two months before Neville Chamberlain, Hitler, Daladier and Mussolini signed the Munich Agreement and a year before Britain declared war against Germany—when a young dancer dressed in blue garb was running and leaping on the stage of the Rudolf Steiner Hall in London. Her name was Jean Rogerson and, as a pupil of Madge Atkinson's method of Natural Movement, she was part of Atkinson's group of dancers who performed at the Steiner Hall in a program titled 'Dance, Mime and Music'. The program consisted of thirteen choreographies offering a variety of group dances, solos and a choral ballet with music by Rutland Boughton. Rogerson's performance of Wind Tossed was placed in the first part of the program. An earlier performance in April earned her the silver medal in the 'Classical' category at the *Sunshine Dance Competition* in England (*The Dancing Times* 1938, 297). In the same year, Nancy Watson Morris performed *Wind Tossed* in a program entitled 'Movement and Music—Lecture Demonstration' in Cape Town, South Africa.[3] A critic reported how Watson Morris "wore an exquisite costume of chiffon in all shades from white to the deepest iris mauve. As she glided over the stage she reminded one of the English paintings of about 1900" (NRCD, NM/M/4).[4]

As a solo performance, *Wind Tossed* inhabited two spaces: it was an artistic performance within the theatrical dance genre and, at the same time, a solo performance that was part of the syllabus of an educational program. Its dual position followed the ideology in which dances were not learned solely for the purpose of theatrical display or artistic performance but, echoing concurrent practices at the time, envisioned dance as an educational practice and as a means to improve life.[5] It was its educational position that facilitated the transmission of the solo through time.

In fact, *Wind Tossed* was taught as part of the Natural Movement branch of the Imperial Society of Teachers of Dancing (ISTD) and, as part of formal education, it was taught at the society's congress. The dance score for the solo was disseminated at congress on July 22, 1936 and was also published in *Dance Journal*, the society's official publication (NRCD, NM/T/2/4/3/2).[6] The dissemination of the solo by the ISTD via the publication of the score and the provision of practice-based days at congress provided a platform for teachers and students to learn and appropriate *Wind Tossed*. Moreover, the fact that Natural Movement was part of the curriculum in dance colleges such as the London College of Dance and Bedford College favored the continuous transmission, incorporation and performance of this solo.[7]

The institutionalization of Natural Movement, and Atkinson's practice of writing scores, created a sort of cultural memory of the practice of Natural Movement.[8] As disembodied artifacts, the existing scores created a referential system of gestural vocabularies that, on the one hand, required institutions for its dissemination, preservation and reembodiment and, on the other hand, lived through acts of transfer: non-archival systems of transfer operating from body to body through reiterated behavior. More than 80 years after its creation, the remains of *Wind Tossed* are to be found in similar structures to those of the past, housed in institutions (i.e. the V&A and National Resource Centre for Dance (NRCD) archives) and in non-archival systems of transfer (i.e. the repertoire, body-to-body transmission). An important aspect of these structures/systems of transfer is that they constitute the epistemological basis of the conceptualization, documentation, interpretation and performance of this solo.

In the archives—under 'house arrest' as Derrida would have it—we find the traces of *Wind Tossed*, the disembodied remains of erstwhile existing corporealities. Three photographs of Rogerson introduce us to some movements and positions and capture the dynamic force and momentum of her performance (V&A, Natural movement catalogue, 003).[9] Her costume, housed in the V&A, reveals the size of her body as well as the intricate design and dyeing technique used to display a wide range of blue tonalities in a flowing silk garb. Watson

Morris is also present: the NRCD holds one photograph of her posing on a pedestal in a natural standing position with arms extended in an open diagonal. Artifacts such as the medal won by Rogerson at the Sunshine matinee competition and performance programs—some hand written by Atkinson and some printed—provide us with explicit information about the venues and occasions at which this solo was performed. Furthermore, the disembodied artifacts of the archive reveal the performance in 1948 of Barbara Turner at the London College of Educational Dance Training at Rawdon Hall in Maidenhead (NRCD, NM/T/1/25/7). In the NRCD, we also find the remains or traces of disappeared embodied actions, disembodied inscriptions of the solo in notation scores.[10]

As forms of explicit knowledge, textual representations, and recording tools, the scores function in a dual way. They inscribe and foreclose actions on the page and, by doing so, they perform acts of erasure. In its own act of inscription, the score for *Wind Tossed* erases the body as it speaks of disembodied actions in space: "step on L. foot into low 'Speed' position, with arms in _____" (NRCD, NM/T/2/4/3/2). There are other absences, such as the lack of information on aspects of the performance; for example, missing positions such as the dancer's position at the commencement of the solo, absence of information about the dynamic range and the transitions between different movements and arm positions. Atkinson's scores also provide abundant information about her practice; for example, the emphasis on musical bars (48 bars in total) and floor pattern drawings suggest the importance of spatio-temporal relations in Atkinson's work. The existence of three scores of the same solo, with hand-written notes and a slight variation in bars 27 and 28, tells us of a change of movement material suggesting adaptations of this solo through time. Moreover, the phrasing of the actions and the use of symbols indicate the existence of a particular focalized dance practice.

The scores conjure up a way of reading and understanding, and a community of practitioners following and sharing a set of rules and values. However, to acquire an understanding of the modus operandi of these scores, of a 'knowing how' as well as a 'knowing', archival research alone is insufficient. Acquiring such an understanding via a research process is instead an exercise in deduction based on previous knowledge and experiences (i.e. the syntax of an abstraction). In fact, the content only becomes fully intelligible if one is introduced to, or acquainted with, its terminology and operational mode, its practice. To become acquainted with this practice—rules, values, terminology, ways of doing and reading—one had to be part of the community of practitioners engaged in the practice of Natural Movement (1936–1970). One needed to be part of the community that shared the same codes, habits, abilities and performance of the effects produced by the modes of transmission embedded in the score, or to be taught by an expert who had learned and been part of the community of Natural Movement practitioners. My expert informant was Jacqueline Ferguson, who trained in Natural Movement at the London College of Dance in the late 1950s, and introduced me to the modus operandi of the score—its 'knowing how'—and to *Wind Tossed*.[11] Ferguson's firsthand experience of Natural Movement and of this solo—through a direct link to Madge Atkinson and Anita Heyworth—provided her not only with a direct referential link to Natural Movement and to *Wind Tossed* but also with the acumen and experience to rely on her body as a vehicle of memory and remembrance.

To access Ferguson's embodied knowledge, here understood as a 'knowledge and a remembering in the hands and in the body' (Connerton and Goody 1989, 95), required presence, it required being there, "being a part of the transmission" (Taylor 2003, 20). In the process of transmission the body becomes a vehicle for memory and remembrance by incorporating, indwelling and absorbing practices, embodied histories that, recorded in the body, defy the authority of the written record (Johnson 2015). In doing so, it challenges the prejudice and suspicion in academia of bodily forms of knowledge transmission and new forms of historical representation (Schneider 2011). In order to gain legitimacy, these new approaches and forms of historical representation need to ensure that their participants foreground their interests and disambiguate their experience and determine "the extent to which affect can be considered evidentiary" (Agnew 2007, 309). It is for this reason that, before engaging in a description of the transmission between Ferguson and myself in the studio, the interests underpinning the process of transmission will be described.

Ferguson's intention and approach to the solo originated from an interest in recording and documenting a work she had experienced in the past. Connerton indicates how our present experiences depend upon our knowledge of the past; that our experience of the present "is causally connected with past events and objects and hence with reference to events and objects which we are not experiencing when we are experiencing the present" (Connerton and Goody 1989, 2). The connection or reference point was Ferguson's memory and her personal experience of this solo in the 1950s. Ferguson's firsthand experience and embodied memory of the work somehow obscured the possibility of looking back to previous iterations or looking for archival artifacts outside the use of a particular score (NM/T/2/4/3/2d).[12]

The choice to record *Wind Tossed* was not an arbitrary one. Ferguson explains that the selection was based on whether there were reasonable scores available and on the fact that she felt that she could "remember it reasonably well" (Ferguson 2015, interview). At the same time, this solo had a special place in Ferguson's memory: "I loved it. It was my favourite dance, my most favourite dance. I have a feeling that I did not actually do it for my exam in the end but I did learn it and I thought it was a wonderful dance.... To me, when I hear that music now, I just think of Natural Movement when I was at college" (Ferguson 2015, interview). The memories recalled here show the affective imprint that *Wind Tossed* had in Ferguson's experience of Natural Movement and might explain her wish to work on and record this particular solo. Moreover, Ferguson's words highlight the interaction between affect, inscribed sources (i.e. scores) and memory, and the role that these play when works of the non-inscribed kind are recapitulated, transmitted and repeated off the page.

As a dancer and dance scholar my interest in working with Ferguson lies beyond the performance of this solo. My interest in Natural Movement was triggered in London, in the summer of 2003, when I first encountered the traces of Madge Atkinson's work. I had decided to end my performing career and enrolled into the Professional Dancers Teaching Diploma course held at the Royal Academy of Dance. One of the subjects embedded in the syllabus was Free Movement and it was whilst dancing, learning, taking part in a Free Movement class that I encountered traces of the past. These traces evoked a past way of moving, one that was pregnant with social constructs and cultural signifiers such as considering the act of skipping as a 'natural' action. One could argue that the act of skipping in childhood is culturally and historically situated, whether it is only an Anglo Saxon phenomenon is yet unclear.

At that point in time, the movement material, the sense of 'otherness' only raised questions about how something so heavily codified could be named and perceived as consisting of free or natural actions. During this time, I was just wrestling, or dwelling, in the collision between my classically trained body, my corporeality, and my performance of what I perceived to be a culturally situated practice. As a result of this encounter and the curiosity triggered by the sense of 'otherness', I decided to engage in research and in a quest to reembody this practice. Thus, I started the project to reconstruct the training method of Natural Movement.[13]

For me, *Wind Tossed* was a gateway to furthering my understanding of the practice of Natural Movement and Madge Atkinson's choreographic craft more generally. Thus, my interest in working with Ferguson on this solo departed from my understanding that any given performance embeds not only technical and choreographic information but also information about the use of the body at a particular point in time. I saw *Wind Tossed* as a distillation, a creative outcome stemming from Atkinson's method and practice.[14] Hence, my position in the acts of transmission—archival and embodied—entailed not only engaging in a performance, but also the thorough investigation of the structures and systems of transfer that, as the epistemological basis of this work, would inform my embodiment and performance.

It was in my position as a dancer and researcher, as a hyper-historian, as the connecting link between past and present in performance, that I realized my engagement in a dialectic between multiple temporalities. Thus, the process entailed the transmission of Ferguson's memory of the 1950s, the archival data from the 1930s onwards and my performance of this solo in the present. My body would be the catalyst at the center of a network of systems of transfer and the channel in the inter-articulation, integration and materialization of the multiple temporalities of *Wind Tossed* in the present. Thus, the process was grounded on this network of systems of transfer but it entailed the integration and incorporation of these through indwelling *Wind Tossed*'s tacit and explicit dimensions.

WIND TOSSED (1936–2015): INDWELLING THE PAST, TACIT KNOWLEDGE AND THE HYPER-HISTORIAN

Acts of transfer are mediated practices encompassing multiple systems of transmission that take place within "specific systems of re-representation" and in which embodied acts reconstitute themselves by transmitting "memories, histories and values from one generation to the next" (Taylor 2003, 21). The systems at work here—the repertoire and the archive—have "different discursive and performatic structures," are "not reducible to another" and should not be regarded as oppositional or antagonistic, but as complementary, each exceeding the limitations of the other (Taylor 2003, 32). What the archive and the repertoire as referential systems and systems of transfer have in common is that the body is at the heart of their operations. The body is the site of these systems and networks of transfer. It is in the body that the archive and the repertoire—memories, artifacts, discursive, performative and embodied traditions—will be incorporated, examined, and articulated.

One could argue that at stake here is the transmission and embodiment of two kinds of knowledge, or what Polanyi calls the tacit and explicit:

> what is usually described as knowledge, as set out in written words or maps, or mathematical formulae, is only one kind of knowledge; while unformulated knowledge, such as we have of something we are in the act of doing, is another form of knowledge. If we call the first kind explicit knowledge, and the second tacit knowledge, we may say that we always know tacitly that we are holding our explicit knowledge to be true. (Polanyi 1966, 12–13)

Polanyi's epistemological approach positions acts of doing and the body as "the ultimate instrument of all our external knowledge, whether intellectual or practical" (Polanyi 1966, 15). Thus, the body is not only the locus of systems of transfer but also the instrument where knowledge/knowing is rooted.

Under this premise, we can position Ferguson's embodied knowledge, practical and tacit, as a key aspect in the transmission of *Wind Tossed*. It would be through practice, through working in the studio that knowledge and memories would be transmitted from Ferguson's body to mine through acts of indwelling and reiterated behavior. Indwelling should, to a certain extent, be considered as an act of surrender. By indwelling in the knowledge and directions provided by Ferguson, one surrenders to the authority of a particular tradition or practice. One also surrenders the body to new ways of moving, a new movement language and kinesthetic experience. This act of surrender or indwelling does not imply a passive disposition to the process of transmission but, rather, it turns "the subject into a process of action", it reveals "a setting into motion with directional intent" (Ness 2008, 4). The directional intent in this instance should be understood as departing from the idea that any act of learning and knowing follows a *from–to* structure: from the body towards an object of inquiry; in this instance, the performance of *Wind Tossed*.

In the *from–to* structure, we attend from a proximal pole—the inner core of our being, our subsidiary knowledge—to a distal pole—the focal point of our attention. The subsidiary knowledge is interior to the body, it is what "relevantly to the present focal point of my attention, I have assimilated to my very self; it is what out of my being-in-the world I have interiorized to the point where I can rely on it to guide me towards a distally located goal" (Polanyi 1969, x). Extrapolating Polanyi's ideas in this instance means that I would rely on what I had assimilated through my career and training in classical ballet, what I had interiorized through my being in the world to guide me towards the focus or goal of my inquiry: *Wind Tossed*. The from–to structure of knowing inherently embeds the idea that meaning would arise from the integration of the subsidiary and focal aspects of the process in the body. It is by "integrating clues in our body or by integrating clues outside...we may be said to interiorize these things or to pour ourselves into them. It is by dwelling in them that we make them mean something on which we focus our attention" (Polanyi 1969, 183). The integration however takes time; from–to knowledge is not instantaneous, "it is a stretch, not only of attention, but of effort, effort must be lived, and living takes time... knowledge, therefore, is embedded both in living process and in...history" (Polanyi 1969, xi). I will argue in the following paragraphs that it is in the integration of these two elements that the epistemological potentialities of the body arise.

During early rehearsals of this process, the focus was on learning movement material. The intention was to grasp the solo as a whole, to get the idea. Thus, my awareness was directed to the solo as a unit, the focus was placed in learning the movement material and grasping its totality. There was no attention to detail, nor did I focus on how my body was engaging or dealing with the material. At this stage, no questions were raised. There was a natural surrender and submission to the authority of Ferguson's knowledge and experience of this solo. After several acts of repetition and indwelling I was able to identify, see and understand through my body aspects of the work: its overall structure and internal logic. *Wind Tossed* has a clear structure, one that seems to follow or be dictated by the musical structure. The movement material devised for a particular phrase would reappear in every repetition of the musical phrase: movement phrases mirror the music phrase/motif. In one example, bars 1&2 and 3&4, the music repeats and so does the movement material, although with a different spatial orientation.[15]

As seen in this example, the repetition of motifs does not translate always into a direct copy of the movement material; instead the repetition shows slightly different variations: like doing the same movement material on a different side or introducing a slight variation of the movement phrase associated with the motif.

The correlation between music and movement clashed with my previous training and embodied understanding/habitus of the relationship between music and dance. In my embodied practice, I developed a way to see musical phrases as giving weight to play and exploration: it was possible to play with phrasing, movement dynamics, the rhythm of the music and the movement. In *Wind Tossed* there was no room for playing with or around the music, it did not work. During the initial rehearsals, Ferguson would repeatedly tell me that I was not on the music or that I was behind the music. The discrepancy between my practice and Ferguson's directions meant that the relationship between music and dance in this solo, and in the practice of Natural Movement, was far more prescriptive than I had initially understood and envisioned: notes corresponded to movements, the phrasing was set, there was no room for play. It seems paradoxical that the performance that led a critic/spectator in 1938 to define the dancer as gliding over the stage—a work that to the audience may appear as flowing and fluid—could feel constrained and fixed during performance.

The feeling of constraint or tension sensed during the rehearsal process should by no means be understood as bearing evidential value in historiographical terms, even if it does reflect particular qualities of *Wind Tossed* itself. This feeling responds to a clash between my embodied knowledge encountering a different way of moving, a different modus operandi. One could argue that encountering a new way of moving raised issues because by attending to the solo itself, in directing my attention to the movement and the music, I was relying on my existing embodied knowledge, memories, skills and hunches, or in other words, on my subsidiary knowledge and awareness to guide me "from proximal, interiorized particulars to the integration of a coherent, distal whole" (Polanyi 1969, xiv). The feelings of constraint, resistance or tension are present in the process of encounter and appropriation of new ways of doing. One could argue that it is the felt tension that triggers the kind of groping that constitutes the recognition of a problem, what leads us to seek for answers to the challenges faced in the transmission and integration of a new embodied practice. I would argue that it is in the sensed tension, between what we know, what we are and what we seek and try to comprehend that the potentiality of the body as a gate to knowledge resides.

Thus, what initially was felt as unfamiliar and uncomfortable not only triggered further investigation into the newly encountered movement–music relationship but, somehow, it also encapsulated traces of Atkinson's approach to music ideas. The new way of 'doing' signalled a clear progression between movements as they mirrored the music score and brought light to Atkinson's relationship between movement and music. The precision and sophisticated use of the music in this solo can be explained when researching Atkinson's approach to music. For Atkinson, the relationship between music and movement learning was inspired by Jaques-Dalcroze's ideas and it embedded the subordination of the movement to the music in terms of the use of rhythm and beats: "as a child learns her alphabet with single letters, so do we learn to control separately each limb, to move in unison with the music, to step each note" (Atkinson 1926b, 27). One could argue that rhythm and musical time would penetrate and discipline the body and as a result, "anatomo-chronological schema of behaviour" was defined (Foucault 1991, 152). Each gesture would be correlated to a note, music controlled the form and bodily time became synonymous with musical time. Moreover, among the aims of the method was the idea of creating "beauty of movement in the rhythm of the dance, to move in perfect harmony with music...and to have the will and power to express the inspiration derived from music" through dance (Atkinson 1926a, 297).

In *Wind Tossed*, these ideas manifest in the direct correlation between walks and the beats of the music. The sophistication of Atkinson's engagement with Pachulski's score can be seen for example, when the music motif in bars 5 and 6 repeats in bars 7 and 8 but an octave higher. One would think that a repetition of the same motif an octave higher would imply a movement or bodily action linked to rising or lifting. Instead, the choreographic relationship between the motif that repeats an octave higher and the movement is one of juxtaposition. The movement does not rise or lift but it goes downwards (in bar 7) to a 'low speed position', a position that holds the body in a parallel line to the floor whilst the leg is extended backwards.

What initially my body felt as an adherence to Dalcroze's methods and ideas would be challenged later by archival findings. Hidden in the archival catalogue of the NRCD, under the section 'music scores'

I found Atkinson's copy of Pachulski's music score (NM/T/1/25/7). The music score was filled with Atkinson's notes. These bring light to two aspects of her work. On the one hand, the correlation between movements, notes and bars that I had felt during rehearsal were explicitly represented (i.e. clear correlation between music structure and movement structure, relation between movements and notes). On the other hand, the score also shows Atkinson's moving away from the directions dictated by the score; there was room for interpretation in Atkinson's artistic approach to music. Notes made in the score under some bars indicate Atkinson's directions to alter the speed/tempo stipulated by the composer (i.e. allegro giusto) in order to slow down the movement. Furthermore, Atkinson had written the name of Jean Rogerson on top of the music score suggesting that this solo was initially choreographed for Jean. Whether the idea of slowing down some sections responded to Atkinson's choreographic intention or it was influenced by Jean's physicality and performance will remain unclear. Nevertheless, the importance of Atkinson's notes is that these allowed us to have a glimpse, or idea of the use of tempo in Jean Rogerson's performance (Fig. 4.1).

Atkinson's notes in the music score show a difference between the score that was used in the rehearsals with Ferguson and Atkinson's hand written notes. The slight variation in bars 27 and 28 in the annotated music score speak of a different performance. Atkinson's version for Rogerson is coherent with the overall musical structure of the piece: the music motif of bar 27 repeats in bar 28 and so does the movement material, bar 28 is a repetition of the same movement phrase in a different spatial orientation. From a historiographic point of view, an annotated music score delineating Jean Rogerson's performance should be regarded as a salient primary source. Moreover, photographs archived at the V&A showing Rogerson performing this solo reinforce this point. What is of interest here is not the fact that one could 'validate' one approach/version over the other but the ideas behind these differences.

According to Ferguson, to alter Atkinson's work to suit the dancer performing was a common practice among Natural Movement practitioners: somewhat minimal alterations were permitted. Paradoxically, we worked with the score published by *Dance Journal* (ISTD), which corresponded to the solo Ferguson had learned at the London College of Dance. She was familiar with it, and in our process there was no room for alterations. Thus it became clear that Atkinson's choreographic work performed by Jean Rogerson, what would later remain as 'living'

Fig. 4.1 Russian Album Vol. II: Miscellaneous compositions for piano (London: W. Paxton & Co., 1916, p. 34). From the National Resource Centre for Dance

repertoire of the Natural Movement practitioners engaged in educational programs, and the idea that minimal alterations to the solo were allowed, does highlight the multiplicity of incarnations and corporealities that coexisted in the transmission of *Wind Tossed* throughout time, as well as the different approaches to Atkinson's choreography by Natural Movement practitioners. Note that, during the transmission of the repertoire, I performed the score preferred by Ferguson but after recording the solo I changed my performance to reflect the outcome of my research, giving priority to Jean Rogerson's version. The rationale for this decision was not based on ideas of authenticity but by following the internal logic of the piece.[16]

The way Atkinson used and choreographed to the music came to the fore at the beginning of the process, but new meanings surrounding the use of the body emerged when the focus shifted from learning movement material to my body and performance. Having learned the overall structure and movement sequences of this solo; the focus of my attention was now directed to the body and to the way in which it reached certain positions, moved through space or attended to particular stimuli. During this phase of the process, Ferguson noticed my incisive questioning and stressed that in her times at London College, students did not ask so many questions, nor did they analyze movements so closely: "we just did it" (Ferguson 2015, interview). Ferguson's response brings attention to the ways of knowing that a community of practitioners share by engaging in the daily practice of the technique of Natural Movement and its tacit dimension. Connerton argues that the "appropriate performance of the movements contained in the repertoire of the group" commits to memory the "systems of classification which the group holds to be important" and at the same time that it requires "the exercise of habit-memory" (Connerton and Goody 1989, 88). What is relevant in Connerton's argument is that the rules, systems of classification and ways of knowing are then taken for granted by the performers in a group because these have been remembered as habits. Habit should be understood as bearing the "sense of operativeness, of a continuously practiced activity. It conveys the fact of exercise, the reinforcing effect of repeated acts" (Connerton and Goody 1989, 94). The fact that there is no longer the community of practice in which to build a habit and habitus, to embody and interiorize, the practice of Natural Movement meant that I relied on Ferguson's responses to my questions regarding all the details embedded in the solo. My approach was not only to learn and perform this solo but to gain a more in-depth understanding: one that moved beyond imitating and executing movements and movement patterns in space towards an in-depth engagement with the body and its ways of knowing.

Turning the focus of my attention towards the body allowed me to identify Atkinson's approach to the use and movement of the torso. Certain positions such as 'the backward expression, knee straight', 'backwards expression of rock', or movements like the 'quick turn' required a strong use of the center of the body. The oppositional force between the hip position and the rotation of the shoulders—a torque action—required the activation and strong use of the abdominal muscles. Embodying the torque of the torso increased my awareness of my previous training and bodily schema. My focal attention was placed in reaching the correct bodily position at the same time that I relied on, or recalled, the aesthetic outcome of this type of bodily position in images of Nijinsky in *L'Après-midi d'un Faune* (1912) and his two-dimensional position of the torso. It is possible to argue that Atkinson's approach seemed not to be based on an aesthetic idea. The fact that torque positions and actions were not prevalent and only occurred in specific movements suggests that the torque action of the torso was not only linked to an aesthetic choice in Atkinson's practice. To investigate and look for answers about Atkinson's ideas and approach to the use of the torso meant leaving the studio and heading back to the archive.

In the NRCD archive, a copy of Johnstone's (1924) book *The Physical Training of Girls* examined a range of physical training methods and provided an overview, description and evaluation of the merits embedded in each system. In her appraisal of the practice of Natural Movement, a particular movement caught Johnstone's attention. This action seemed to be central to the development of the muscles of the lower part of the abdomen: "In doing it, feet are placed together and shoulders straightened, then as the right foot moves forward, the left shoulder and arm also move forward, the bigger and greater the step, the greater the swing forward of the shoulder" (Johnstone 1924, 65). This action, Johnstone asserted, resulted in the activation of the abdominal muscles, would create a muscular corset and confer a fitness of the body that would be beneficial for childbirth and motherhood. Johnstone's argument is rooted in the discourses of the period regarding concerns about national health and child bearing and brings light to Parviainen's ideas regarding how we absorb cultural values *through* and *on* our body

(Parviainen 1998). Thus, the use of opposition and torque experienced when performing *Wind Tossed* did not only respond to an aesthetic idea but to one linked with physical culture and the development of the abdominal region of the body.

Engaging with the network of system of transfer, the repertoire and archival research resulted in a complex process in which differences between the performance of *Wind Tossed* in the 1950s and that of Jean Rogerson in 1938 became apparent. The transmission of the repertoire facilitated my understanding of the practice, reading the scores and receiving from Ferguson invaluable information about some of the principles embedded in this practice. The fact that Ferguson learned the solo in an educational context did have an impact in the staging of the work. For example, because at that time the solo was part of a particular curriculum by an examining body, Ferguson had no reference to the original costume and decided that we would use a plain silk tunic for the performance. When looking at Jean Rogerson's costume, and after having embodied the work, it became apparent that the original costume had not only being created to a particular aesthetic effect but it was part of the performance. The costume required the dancer to move in a particular way. One could argue that, as well as providing a particular aesthetic, the costume served as a prop. The original costume was part of the performance in the sense that it required a particular effort in the way the dancer initiated and used the arms during performance.

Crafted from Ferguson's approach to the score and her memories of the solo, the first performance reflected the way in which this solo was taught and practiced in educational institutions during the 1950s. Whilst I had embodied the movement material and come to a greater understanding of Atkinson's technique and choreographic practice, I struggled with embodying the aesthetic qualities of her work. That is, the execution of the solo was accurate but I felt the outcome was not representing the aesthetic qualities embedded in the practice of Natural Movement. I knew what to strive for; Ferguson's directions and the archival research had provided me with images of this work. However, I felt that I needed more time to integrate and embody in my performance the subtle aesthetic qualities of Atkinson's work. The idea of fully integrating the movement material to my way of being in the world together with the fact that I wanted to implement my archival research to the performance meant that, as in the past, this would be one incarnation of *Wind Tossed*, the first of many more to come in the future.

CONCLUSION

Through the tacit dimension and the tensions felt during the integration of the clues embedded in the network of system of transfer—the archive and the repertoire—I was able to discover and further my understanding of the cultural, aesthetic and choreographic aspects embedded in this solo and the practice of Natural Movement. Positioning the body at the centre of this investigation afforded new insights into the epistemological possibilities of the body when performing works of the past. We can consider the body as a gateway to knowledge of the past. However, through this investigation it became clear that the information gathered through embodied experience, through the tacit dimension, should not be considered evidentiary. Instead, it should be closely examined in order to determine the extent to which our body's experience is signalling the differences between our modes of being-in-the-world and past performances (i.e. the music example mentioned in this chapter) or it is gaining access to the past (i.e. the experience of the use of the torso). Thus, the tacit dimension of the body can show us the areas that require further investigation and instigate the starting point of the quest. Whilst Ferguson's support and knowledge during the process proved invaluable, the impossibility of immersing oneself in the communities of practice of the past is a limitation to the embodiment of the technique supporting the performance of this solo. The idea of integrating the findings of the repertoire and the archive in a network of systems of transfer proves useful as it puts into dialogue the embodied and archival data in a way that allows us to discover new relationships and findings. These findings shifted the idea of envisioning *Wind Tossed* as a unique work of art to introduce us to a shifting practice, making us aware of the multiple incarnations and corporealities that coexisted in the transmission of *Wind Tossed* throughout time as well as the different approaches to Atkinson's choreography by Natural Movement practitioners. As Polanyi argues, knowledge is embedded in living processes and in history, thus incarnations of this solo will keep bringing light to our understanding of Natural Movement, Atkinson's choreographic practice and the bodies of the past.

NOTES

1. My intention is to move away from the influence of the affective turn in the theorization of reenactment practices. This decision responds to the existing concern in the field regarding how the epistemological

possibilities and the value of personal experiences can construct or help the acquisition of knowledge about the past. Agnew argues that for practices to gain legitimacy and become new forms of historical representation they must foreground their interests, disambiguate experience and understand the extent to which affect can be considered evidentiary (Agnew 2007). Most importantly in Agnew's assertions is her acknowledgement that any identification with the past needs to "be accompanied by a hard-eyed investigation of historical processes and rigorous coming to terms with the past" (Agnew 2007, 307).

2. Looking at the materials in the archive it seems that the solo was performed for the first time on December 17, 1936. It was performed at Madge Atkinson's studios (Kensington, London). The program was titled 'Studio evening' and *Wind Tossed* was performed by Jean Rogerson (NM/H/1/3/54). Jean Rogerson performed the solo again at the July 1937 ISTD Technical school (NM/H/1/3/53), and on the 8th and 9th of July 1938 at the Rudolf Steiner Hall (London) in a program titled 'Dance, Mime and Music' performed by Jean Rogerson (NM/H/1/3/55).

3. Nancy Watson Morris traveled to London, studied Natural Movement with Madge Atkinson and took the Member examination of the Imperial Society of Teachers of Dancing (NRCD, NM/M/4).

4. One could argue that that the paintings the critic is referring to in this instance are those of Constable. The intricate designs and use of color in Madge Atkinson's costumes and her collaborations with costume designers in Manchester can be accessed in Fensham's (2015) article "Designing for Movement: Dance Costumes, Art Schools and Natural Movement in the Early Twentieth Century."

5. Dance practices that emerged during the first part of the twentieth century, such as Ruby Ginner's revived Greek dance, Atkinson's Natural Movement, Margaret Morris' technique and the proponents of natural and Greek dancing, vacillated "between dance as a theatrical art and dance as a means of developing a student's physical and spiritual well being" (Anderson 1990, 255).

6. Note that the term 'score' is used here in a broad sense. Madge Atkinson created her own notation system that combined movement descriptions with a set of symbols (some created by her and others inspired and adapted from Feuillet's notation system).

7. The score of *Wind Tossed* appeared in 1937 in *Dance Journal*. The solo was taught to ISTD teachers at congress, they could use the solo for performances or as part of the advanced examinations of the Natural Movement Branch. Natural Movement students had to do this solo variation for dance exams, but the solo could be slightly adapted to suit individual students (Ferguson 2015, interview).

8. The notion of cultural memory elicited here is the one delineated by Assmann (2008) in his writings on communicative and cultural memory.
9. Traces or remains of this solo can also be found outside the archive, embedded in dance journals of the period. For example, *Dancing Times* also hosts a photograph of Rogerson leaping in the air (*Dancing Times* 1938, 297).
10. The archive has its own logic, it organizes and groups artifacts in particular ways. To find the scores of *Wind Tossed* in the archive, one has to look into a folder or section called 'examinations'. Thus, in the archive, this solo is classified in relation to its educational realm, as part of the Natural Movement examinations conducted by the Imperial Society of Teachers of Dancing. The traces of *Wind Tossed* (1936) as part of Madge Atkinson's performance group are obscured by the classification of the archive. They remain hidden, inside performance programs, photographs, newspaper cuttings and a music score.
11. Jacqueline Ferguson studied at London College of Dance from 1956 to 1959. She returned in 1967 to be part of the faculty. Note that in 1955, the college had relocated from Maidenhead to central London (8 Addison Road, W.14).
12. Archival research showed the existence of different scores for this solo. The main difference was in the movement material choreographed for bars 25 to 28.
13. I completed my MA dissertation on this topic at the University of Surrey (2007) and I am currently completing a practice-based PhD in the practice of Natural Movement.
14. The importance here is placed in the technique of the body as the key and gateway to engage in the epistemological potentialities of practice. The focus moves beyond the artistic artifact to the technique embedded in the artifact itself. This approach resonates with Spatz's (2015) ideas regarding technique, the body and epistemology.
15. The music score seems to be organized in two-bar phrases that repeat or reoccur. Thus we can see a repetition of the music motif. For example, a musical motif will be introduced in bars 1 to 4, and recalled/repeated in bars 9 to 12. The same takes place in bars 17 and 18 (repeated in bars 37 and 38); bars 19 and 20 (repeats in bars 39 and 40); and 29 and 30 (repeated in 31 and 32). This raises issues in relation to authenticity and the idea of different scores, versions being slightly modified to suit performers and the different approaches.
16. The score used by Ferguson and published by the Imperial Society of Teachers of Dancing introduces in bar 28 a different sequence, one that includes an upright position of the foot facing upstage. This movement, unlike the other movements in the solo, does not reoccur. in Atkinson's

notes we can see a mirroring of the actions of bar 27 in bar 28, this follows the way in which she had crafted the piece. Thus the repetition of the musical motif of bar 27 in bar 28 would result in the repetition of the movement material in a different spatial orientation.

BIBLIOGRAPHY

Agnew, Vanessa. 2007. History's Affective Turn: Historical Reenactment and Its Work in the Present. *Rethinking History* 11 (3): 299–312.

Anderson, Jack. 1990. London Contemporary [Review]. *Dance Chronicle*, 13 (2), No. 2: 254–257.

Assmann, Jan. 2008. Communicative and Cultural Memory. In *Cultural Memory Studies: An International and Interdisciplinary Handbook*, vol. 8, ed. Astrid Erll, Ansgar Nünning, and Sara B. Young. Berlin: De Gruyter.

Atkinson, Madge. 1926a. The Dance Based on Natural Movement: An Introduction to my System of Teaching. *Dancing Times*, December 195: 290–299.

Atkinson, Madge. 1926b. Blending Nature and Art in 'Natural Dancing'. *The Ballroom* 7/12: 27–28.

Connerton, Paul, and Jack Goody. 1989. *How Societies Remember*. Cambridge: Cambridge University Press.

de Certeau, Michel. 1992. *The Writing of History*, trans. Tom Conley. New York: Columbia University Press.

Dean, D., Yana Meerzon, and Kathryn Prince (eds.). 2014. *History, Memory, Performance*. Basingstoke: Palgrave Macmillan.

Fensham, Rachel. 2015. Designing for Movement: Dance Costumes, Art Schools and Natural Movement in the Early Twentieth Century. *Journal of Design History* 28 (4): 348–367.

Foucault, Michael. 1991. *Discipline and Punish: The Birth of the Prison*, trans. Alan Sheridan. London: Penguin.

Johnson, Katherine M. 2015. Rethinking (Re)doing: Historical Re-enactment and/as Historiography. *Rethinking History* 19 (2): 193–206.

Johnstone, Mary Anderson. 1924. *The Physical Training of Girls*. London: Sidgwick & Jackson.

Kirshenblatt-Gimblett, Barbara. 1998. *Destination Culture: Tourism, Museums and Heritage*. Oakland, CA: University of California Press.

Ness, Sally Ann. 2008. The Inscription of Gesture: Inward Migrations in Dance. In *Migrations of Gesture*, ed. Noland and Ness. Minneapolis: University of Minnesota Press.

Parviainen, Jaana. 1998. *Bodies Moving and Moved: A Phenomenological Analysis of the Dancing Subject and the Cognitive and Ethical Values of Dance Art*. Tampere: Tampere University Press.

Parviainen, Jaana. 2002. Bodily Knowledge: Epistemological Reflections on Dance. *Dance Research Journal* 34 (1): 11–26.

Polanyi, Michael. 1966. *The Tacit Dimension.* Garden City, NY: Doubleday.

Polanyi, Michael. 1969. *Knowing and Being: Essay by Michael Polanyi*, ed. Marjorie Grene. London: Routledge & Kegan Paul.

Rokem, Freddie. 2000. *Performing History: Theatrical Representations of the Past in Contemporary Theatre.* Iowa City: University of Iowa Press.

Schneider, Rebecca. 2011. *Performing Remains: Art and War in Times of Theatrical Reenactment.* New York: Taylor & Francis.

Sheets-Johnstone, Maxine. 1999. *The Primacy of Movement.* Amsterdam and Philadelphia: John Benjamin's Publishing Company.

Spatz, Ben. 2015. *What a Body Can Do.* London: Routledge.

Taylor, Diana. 2003. *The Archive and the Repertoire: Performing Cultural Memory in the Americas*, 2nd ed. Durham, NC: Duke University Press.

Archival Sources

National Resource Centre for Dance:

NM/H/1/3/55: Natural Movement Programmes (1931–1939): Madge Atkinson Presents Dance, Mime and Music at the Rudolf Steiner Hall.

NM/H/1/3/54: Natural Movement Programmes (1931–1939): Studio Evening.

NM/H/1/3/53: Natural Movement Programmes (1931–1939): Natural Movement at the Technical School.

NM/M/4: Newspaper Cuttings: Madge Atkinson's Work in Cape Town Under the Direction of Nancy Watson-Morris.

NM/T/1/25/7: Notation Scores/Music Scores: Russian Music for Piano, Russian Album Book II.

NM/T/2/4/3/2 and NM/T/2/4/3/2d: Notation Scores/Notation: Exam work, Advanced Dances, "Wind Tossed."

V&A Theatre and Performance collection:

Natural Movement Collection, Ref: 003: Images: Jean Rogerson.

Interview

Jacqueline Ferguson, London. April 24, 2015.

CHAPTER 5

The Transmission–Translation–Transformation of Doris Humphrey's *Two Ecstatic Themes* (1931)

Lesley Main

INTRODUCTION

Doris Humphrey choreographed the solo, *Two Ecstatic Themes*, following significant artistic and personal encounters in 1931. Humphrey had been searching for a philosophical parallel that closely reflected her own movement explorations since leaving Denishawn in 1928. The discovery of Nietzsche's Apollonian–Dionysian concept in *The Birth of Tragedy* was a revelatory moment and she was subsequently to define her movement philosophy as 'Fall and Recovery'.[1] The second encounter was with her husband-to-be, Charles Francis Woodford, later known as 'Leo'.[2] The combination of these two happenings resulted in a work that came to be regarded as her signature solo.

Two Ecstatic Themes is formed in two parts: *Circular Descent*, set to Nicholas Medtner's *Tragedie-Fragment in A Minor*, Opus 7.2 (1904), and *Pointed Ascent*, to *Maschere Che Passano 1* (1918) by G. Francesco Malipiero. The dance premiered on October 31, 1931 in

L. Main (✉)
Middlesex University, London, UK
e-mail: l.main@mdx.ac.uk

© The Author(s) 2017
L. Main (ed.), *Transmissions in Dance*,
https://doi.org/10.1007/978-3-319-64873-6_5

a Humphrey-Weidman concert at Washington Irving High School in New York City. Writing not long after the premiere, dance critic John Martin described the dance as "a study of motion applied to the simplest of ideas" (*New York Times* November 25, 1931). In a subsequent review, he wrote "there is no other dancer in the field who could have conceived it in just this form or who could dance it with such a complete sense of fulfilment. Miss Humphrey's style is seen perhaps here at its best" (King 1978, 113). A program note came later: "*Two Ecstatic Themes* is the keynote to Miss Humphrey's mature work. The first part is in circular and spiral movements, soft and sinking, to convey a feeling of acquiescence. The second part, in contrast to the first, moves in pointed design to a strident climax suggestive of aggressive achievement. The whole is a counterpoint of circular and angular movement, representing the two inseparable elements of life as well as design" (Program note 1935). The fact that the program note came some years after the premiere was not unusual. Dance writer Margaret Lloyd, commenting on a Humphrey-Weidman program that included *Two Ecstatic Themes*, observed: "A modern dance does not spring full-panoplied into life, but undergoes many changes before it begins to arrive and sometimes after it has arrived. Doris and Charles were no exception to the fact that good work is usually good because it has been worked over" (Lloyd 1987, 117).

In 1975, Muriel Topaz, then director of the Dance Notation Bureau, invited former Humphrey-Weidman dancer, Ernestine Stodelle, to recreate *Two Ecstatic Themes* and *Air for the G String* (1928) for the Limón Dance Company. The solo was to be performed alternately by Carla Maxwell, the artistic director, and Nina Watt, principal dancer. According to Stodelle, *Circular Descent* and *Pointed Ascent* were solo declarations of Humphrey's newly emerging theory of Fall and Recovery:

> Each dance acted as a metaphor in itself: the curving, falling forms of the first suggested the intoxicating experience of Dionysian release; the aggressive thrust of the second suggested a frantic attempt to regain the security of Apollonian stability. *Two Ecstatic Themes* made a concise, eloquent avowal of the dual philosophical theme that Humphrey had converted into a movement language of her own. (Stodelle 1995a, 267)

Stodelle recreation has remained in the Limón Company's repertoire ever since, eliciting reviews from contemporary dance critics who share similar standing to that enjoyed by Martin and Lloyd in the 1930s and

1940s. Marcia Siegel, writing about the dance in 1980, states that "we see a clear movement idea, detailed with fine craftsmanship and deliberate emphasis... The dance is a perfectly fused meeting of passion and will" (Siegel 1993, 103). Jennifer Dunning describes *Two Ecstatic Themes* as a transcendent signature work (Dunning 1989), and in the same review notes: "It is good to see those lyrical descents and rises—Miss Humphrey's inspired and inspiring contribution to modern dance's rendering of human existence." In 1994, Dunning wrote in greater detail about the solo, performed by Watt in a program of Humphrey-Weidman dances titled "The Legacy of Doris Humphrey," introduced by Stodelle at the 92nd Street Y:

> Ms. Watt made every moment clear and meaningful in the more familiar *"Two Ecstatic Themes,"*... The solo is one of the most fascinating works of the period, a piece that manages to be analytical and deeply emotional at the same time. In the first part, "Circular Descent," a woman lowers gradually to the floor, her body spiralling slowly. In "Pointed Ascent," the woman rises, almost thrusting up into the air.

> As Ms. Stodelle commented, *"Two Ecstatic Themes"* could portray Everywoman in the 20th century. It illustrates in deceptively simple detail Humphrey's concept of falling and recovering from falls as a central principle of movement. Most of all, the solo is choreography that never looks dated and that, despite its spare and chiseled look, is rich with psychological detail. (Dunning 1994)

These critics' viewpoints concur with Stodelle's assessment that this dance did not have an overtly literal narrative but that the underlying emphasis on falling in love was fundamental to its success. Humphrey would seem to agree. In the summer of 1934 she wrote to her husband from Bennington, *"our* love dance—The *Two Ecstatic Themes* made a big impression. Some of the ecstasy that was and is ours must be in it" (Cohen 1995, 128; DH's emphasis).

The occasion of 'Transmission—A Performance Symposium'[3] in London in 2014 offered an opportunity to evaluate my staging process for *Two Ecstatic Themes* and to consider how the notion of 'transmission' was exemplified in that process. To foreground the discussion, I would offer a definition of transmission within the context of staging dances as 'the means through which the conceptual framework and choreographic intention of a work is conveyed'. The variant forms of staging practice currently employed in dance include reconstruction, recreation, reinvention, reenactment, reimagining. All are important and valid modes of practice, not least because a director makes a conscious choice to operate from a particular contextual perspective. Further, whichever mode has been employed signifies to the audience that the dance has been staged from that particular perspective. That said, an approach that has 'transmission' at its core is especially useful for the director who wants to locate the exploration of a work from the present, because it allows for a staging perspective that resides *in* the present, without the habitual presence of the 're' prefix and its connotations of 'past'.

Having danced and directed Humphrey's solo and ensemble works many times, I have an experiential and informed understanding of what is required of the performer on corporeal and intuitive levels. From a directorial perspective, therefore, the essential task is to transmit knowledge from a range of sources that are drawn together to form a coherent whole for the performer's artistry to inhabit. The performer, likewise, goes through a process of transmission, by making sense of the received knowledge intrinsically and being able to convey that knowledge outwardly, to the audience. How the aforementioned 'coherent whole' is manifest will be examined through the course of this essay.

Performing *Two Ecstatic Themes* and the earlier solo from 1929/1930, *The Call/Breath of Fire*, are different encounters when compared to the large ensemble dances that constitute much of Humphrey's canon. The solos, arguably, are not suitable for young, inexperienced dancers in the way that works such as *Water Study* (1928), *The Shakers* (1931) and *Passacaglia* (1938) can be. Humphrey was in her early 30s when she made both dances and choreographed them for herself. There is also something about the idiom of the solo work that sets these dances apart from the soloist roles Humphrey danced in her ensemble works, including 'The Eldress' in *The Shakers*, 'The Matriarch' in *With My Red Fires* (1936) and the leading role in *Passacaglia*. These solo works are for the experienced performer who can bring a mature level of artistry to the staging process. Such experience is important because of the conceptual and dynamic subtleties and connections that have to be located and embodied in order to make sense of the choreography. An example is the opening series of falls, which Stodelle and past performers of the work acknowledge as the most significant part of the dance.[4] Humphrey establishes the essential theme of the work in this opening statement. Here, through a series of progressively deepening back falls, Apollonian equilibrium gives way to Dionysian abandon, to be followed by a reassertion of will before swiftly tumbling again into recklessness, and so the pattern continues for the rest of the dance. Once the performer locates the duality inherent in this dynamic experience, the rest of the work is unlocked.

To examine how a transmission process can unfold to the point of performance, this essay is presented in two parts. The first part focuses on the interconnecting ideas of transmission, translation and transformation as they relate to the evidence base for a dance work; the second, 'Performing *Two Ecstatic Themes*', comprises reflections from dancers with a long performance history of the work, the impact of the music, and the significance of the spiral curve as a movement concept (Fig. 5.1).

Interconnecting Transmission, Translation and Transformation

The introduction to this essay suggested that the essential task for a director is the transmission of knowledge from a range of sources in order to form a coherent whole for the performer to explore further. A performer undergoes a similar set of processes but I would argue that the director has greater latitude to make choices in terms of what to include from evidentiary sources. I have written previously in some detail on the subject of the selection of evidence in relation to the staging process for dance works.[5] By way of a brief summary, and in specific relation to a choreographic work, a body of evidence exists that comprises a variety of sources. Primary sources include any visual and literary accounts of the dance that can be directly attributed to the choreographer and her/his close associates. Other traces of the work can be found in reviews, photographs, a Labanotation score if one exists, and secondary written accounts. In relation to Humphrey's work, for example, commentary from the dance writers and critics of her time, including John Martin, Margaret Lloyd and Selma Jeanne Cohen, is widely regarded as being authoritative from the spectator perspective because they witnessed these dances on numerous occasions during the 1930s and 1940s and, importantly, could write knowledgeably about what they saw.

The evidence base that I chose for staging *Two Ecstatic Themes* in 2014 comprised Humphrey's writing about the work; firsthand accounts from close associates of Humphrey who saw her performing the work on multiple occasions, namely Stodelle, Martin and former

Fig. 5.1   Gail Corbin in *Two Ecstatic Themes*, Circular Descent. Photograph by Jennifer W. Lester

Humphrey-Weidman dancer, Eleanor King; Stodelle's subsequent recreation and coaching of the work; and my own embodied knowledge of the work. Two further significant aspects were the musical recording by pianist Vivian Fine, who accompanied Humphrey's performances of the dance on numerous occasions, and the notion of the 'spiral curve' as a movement concept within this particular choreographic context. Other evidence exists, including a Labanotation score and secondary written accounts that could form part of a body of evidence but did not on this occasion. From the performer perspective, written testimony by past performers of the dance proved to be a useful additional source for dancer Louise Kelsey, who performed the work in 2014.

Before looking in more detail at the 2014 staging process, I would like to first consider the transmission of evidence in a broader context. In his essay, "The Body as Archive: Will to Re-Enact and the Afterlives of Dances" (2010), André Lepecki offers the term 'archive' to describe what I refer to as the selection of evidence. Here, he is referring to the trend for reenactments exemplified by the work of dance artists such as Richard Move and Fabián Barba in their respective performances of the work of Martha Graham and Mary Wigman. Lepecki argues:

> I am suggesting that the current will to archive in dance, as performed by reenactments, derives neither exclusively from 'a failure in cultural memory' nor from 'a nostalgic lens'. I am proposing 'will to archive' as referring to a capacity to identify in a past work still non-exhausted creative fields of 'impalpable possibilities'. (Lepecki 2010, 31)

Lepecki goes on to talk about this form of approach—not 'fixing' a work in its original form, but unlocking and releasing new possibilities—which is similar to the approach I have developed for staging Humphrey's dances.[6] The parallel with Lepecki's position occurs in two ways: the notion of releasing new possibilities and, prefacing that, the selection of evidence by the director to form an interpretive base. Consequently, directorial choice will frame the outcome—the performance—each time and, inevitably, each of these instances of performance will be ever so slightly altered by the choice of evidence, the passage of time, changes in emphases and changes in performer, as but some examples.

In an apt analogy for dance, the notion of being 'ever so slightly altered' is drawn from T.S. Eliot's essay, "Tradition and the Individual Talent." Eliot observed that "the arrival of a new work affects existing work...[thus] the whole existing order must be, if ever so slightly altered" (Eliot 1917, 38). One interpretation of his idea is that knowledge and understanding can increase without deliberate intervention. The 'new' arrival, be it a planned or random occurrence, changes the existing context simply by its presence. This idea suggests a simultaneous shift and expansion. The fluidity inherent in this position is attractive because of the implication that knowledge, a work, a fact, whatever is being considered, is never entirely fixed.

In a later passage in the same essay, Lepecki makes a broader point in relation to dancing the work of another when he says, "to understand dance as a dynamic, transhistorical, and intersubjective system of incorporations and excorporations is to understand dance not only as that which passes away (in time and across space) but also as that which passes around (between and across bodies of dancers, viewers, choreographers) and as that which also, always, comes back around" (2010, 39). Here, Lepecki seems to be suggesting an ongoing continuum of activity within the realm of a work and its performance manifestations. He continues: "Dance is the passing around and the coming around of corporeal formations and transformations... Thanks to transformative exchanges of steps and sweat, thanks to on-going transmissions of images and resonances, choreography allows dancers to turn and return on their tracks in order to dance via ex- and incorporations" (ibid.). One reading of his terms 'incorporation' and 'excorporation' could be what one decides to leave in and leave out of the evidence base of a work. This is a useful approach for dance because it places the work as a vital, 'living' entity that has transformative capacities and avoids the 'fixed' empirical state that can suffocate performance-based art works.

Lepecki refers to 'transmission' and 'transformation', both of which are relevant to a staging process. I would add a third idea, that of 'translation' as identified by Walter Benjamin in his essay, "The Task of the Translator" (1921/1996). Walter Benjamin suggests that "translatability is an essential quality of certain works, which is not to say that it is essential for the works themselves that they be translated; it means, rather, that a specific significance inherent in the original manifests itself in its translatability" (Benjamin 1996, 254). The idea of 'a specific significance inherent in the original' indicates there is something important to be found and I equate this idea with capturing the essence of a choreographer's intention. Without that person in the studio, a director is always going to be in a position of making their best judgment and that judgment has to be based on evidence that is substantively linked to the choreographer to capture the 'inherent significance'. Further, Walter Benjamin goes on to say, "the life of the original attains its latest, continually renewed and most complete unfolding" (Benjamin 1996, 255), which ties in with Eliot's 'ever so slightly altered' notion.

Jacques Derrida offers a post-structuralist response to "The Task of the Translator" that questions Walter Benjamin's stance in his own essay, "Des Tours de Babel" that has garnered some favor within the field of dance studies and beyond. It would be remiss of me, therefore, not to make reference to the diverse positions taken by the two writers on notions of meaning, of language and the position of translation in comparison to 'the original' (see Derrida 1985, 181). I am not going to attempt to reconcile these positions here because the writing in question is too substantive to do it justice within the confines of this essay. My objective, rather, is to draw together ideas that resonate with the form of staging practice in which I choose to engage. Lepecki, Walter Benjamin and Eliot offer ideas that mesh with the notion of a work's capacity to grow in the present but with a continuing connection to and with the source, the choreographer and/or dance work in this context.

As examples, the performance work of Richard Move and Barba provide apt reference points for the idiom of the solo work. Move's performances of Martha Graham's repertory progressed far beyond the cabaret style of his first rendering of Graham's solos in his *Martha@...* series, which began in 1996 at Mothers in Manhattan. By 2006, he was performing with the Martha Graham Company *as* Graham, on one occasion partnering Desmond Richardson in a reconstructed duet from Graham's *Part Real–Part Dream* from 1965. Move describes his approach as "deconstructions or synoptic re-inventions" (Lepecki 2010, 43). Lepecki describes Move as a 'corporeal archive' (ibid.). For those who have seen him perform, the novelty aspect and perceived parody fade swiftly, not simply because he has captured Graham's persona convincingly but because he can dance the movement convincingly, and it is the latter aspect that seals the deal, as it were, and allows his work to transcend parody into mainstream theatre.

Barba's reenactment project focused on Mary Wigman and, specifically, a program of nine solo dances including the dance cycle, *Schwingende Landshaf* from 1929 that he performed in Belgium in 2009. Barba's approach was to capture not simply the dances but the environment in which the dances were viewed, including audience conventions of the time (see Barba 2011; Stalpaert 2011). The reenactment process, therefore, reached some way beyond the choreography. In relation to the dancing aspect, Barba's training and performance experience was largely in contemporary release-based techniques. Whilst his initial response to seeing the solos on film was of witnessing something that was profoundly 'familiar', he acknowledged the necessity of seeking stylistic, technical underpinning before attempting to learn the solos, which he subsequently did with Susanne Linke, one of Wigman's last students (Barba 2011, 83). He observed:

These tools included exercises to relate the movement of the limbs to strong centric abdominal muscles; control of breathing, stressing the relation of inhalation and exhalation to different movement qualities; the suspension of an impulse in time to increase its dramatic tension; and the creation of movement phrases that foreground the dynamic tension between gravity and muscular resistance in clear geometrical shapes. (ibid.)

Aside from the reference to geometrical shapes, there are parallels here with Humphrey's 'Fall and Recovery' philosophy, perhaps not unsurprising given the emphases on natural movement that Humphrey and Wigman explored during that period. Move and Barba provide pertinent examples for this discussion because of the emphasis both artists place on capturing the requisite style of dancing in order that the choreography can be fully read and, thus, appreciated.

PERFORMING *TWO ECSTATIC THEMES*

In comparison with Barba and Move, the stylistic issue for Humphrey-trained dancers is a different one because they already embody 'Fall and Recovery' implicitly. It is more a question of inhabiting movement vocabulary from 1931 and making sense of that within a twenty-first-century dancing body. Furthermore, securing the requisite physicalized state for the choreography is but the starting point. Muriel Topaz observed: "What distinguishes the performing technician from the performing artist is his or her ability to absorb all the information provided by the director, the score and/or individual investigation, and to conceive and project a viable interpretation of a role based on everything he or she has discovered" (Topaz 1995, 71). Topaz highlights the importance of the performer engaging in a process of exploration in order to create the 'coherent whole' referred to earlier. Stodelle recalls Humphrey's methods of transmitting ideas to her dancers, in words, gestures or movement dynamic, because she realized the necessity of establishing the timing of the movements and, as importantly, the 'why' behind the dance as a creative conception. "Every motion has meaning—Humphrey's working methods were to devise only those movements which logically issued from the dance's conceptual theme" (Stodelle 1995b, 5). With regard to *Two Ecstatic Themes*, making sense of it in performative terms is only possible once the dancer has a secure grasp of the conception. Learning the movements in a few days of rehearsal is not the same as 'knowing' the dance and being equipped to perform it. More specifically, Stodelle commented, "To dance *Two Ecstatic Themes* requires technical abilities of a special kind: fluent body movement, perfect balance, skill in falling at all levels and in all directions, and floor work of a highly dexterous kind. Most essential is an innate gift for both lyrical and dramatic projection, a projection that is muted with an awareness of the composition's underlying significance. When that final moment of "truth" arrives, and the choreographer's idea is fully translated into the visceral world of movement, then something extraordinary happens: the choreographer's impulses and the dancer's instinctive responses become one" (Stodelle 1995b, 12). Here, Stodelle signifies the importance of the performer's role in conveying meaning, as in the choreographic intention (Fig. 5.2).

Fig. 5.2 Gail Corbin in *Two Ecstatic Themes*, Circular Descent. Photograph by Jennifer W. Lester

Successional movement is a primary marker of the Humphrey style. When initiated by the breath, energy travels successively through pathways of the body, as determined by the choreography. The dynamics of successional movement are all-inclusive, propelled by feeling or by gravity (Stodelle 1995b, 9). From its initial gesture until its last slow fall, the movement in *Circular Descent* is lyrically expressive, captured in the language of successional flow. *Pointed Ascent*, conversely, could be described as a forerunner of the feminist point of view, the first dance that epitomized the needs of women to live independent, creative lives (Stodelle 1995b, 12). Together, performing these dances is like reliving an experience that had made deep inroads into one's consciousness. As Stodelle observed: "Never before had our choreographer created a dance that revealed such deeply experienced feelings" (1995b, 7). Her inference is that there is a weight of responsibility on subsequent performers, which is a view shared by dancers Gail Corbin, Jeanne Yasko and Sandra Kaufmann. All three learnt *Two Ecstatic Themes* from Stodelle, and agree that the work is the epitome of Humphrey's philosophy of the 'Arc between Two Deaths'. There is also consensus that the essence of the dance is captured in the first series of falls and that this initial sequence of movement is hardest to grasp, which is the reason why Stodelle would spend so much time on this section.

Corbin, Humphrey-Weidman dancer and director, holds a distinctive place in the history of Stodelle's recreation. She was one of two dancers on whom Stodelle set the work initially as she worked through the recreation process in 1975 and before she staged the dance for the Limón Company. Corbin began studying and performing with Stodelle from the age of 18 and the second dancer, Penelope Hill, had also danced with Stodelle for many years. Both dancers, therefore, brought a deep-rooted knowledge of the Humphrey style and the core principles of Fall and Recovery into the recreation process. Corbin observed: "As the body who Ernestine reconstructed on I saw the logic and intent first hand. The difficulty for any dancer is to make it *real*—not to superimpose shape on *movement*. The body is the source of the curve, the arms follow what the body initiates" (Corbin 2014, interview). Corbin went on to perform and stage the dance countless times over the years in the USA and Europe, and can be regarded as the authority on the dance, notably so since Stodelle's passing in 2008.

Corbin's assessment of *Two Ecstatic Themes* adds to Stodelle's viewpoint and is important because her experience encompasses both performing the work, probably more than any other dancer, and directing it:

Understanding the Idea is difficult for some dancers. The idea of resisting yet giving into the fall is hard to wrap your head around! And then put it in your body but you must. We always talked about falling in love with Ernestine. That scary uncertainty that made you ecstatic and stiff at the same time! Then of course the music must speak to you and guide your timing through all the falls and pulls. They are graded and uneven. Being off balance is what you are and you have to "go" there. Contrarily *Pointed Ascent* has just the opposite impulse. Staccato and angles but again the idea must be in every gesture. That strength to say no and combat that thing that made you fall in the first place. This dance made me an actress. I feel this dance very much in my soul. (Corbin November 2014, interview)

Yasko's route into the dance was through extensive experience in Limón's style and taking Stodelle's Humphrey class when the latter taught the Limón Company. She first learnt *Two Ecstatic Themes* from Corbin in Ireland. They set the work in a week and when Yasko returned to the USA, she then worked with Stodelle in some detail. Yasko performed this dance in a solo program in Europe that also included *Waltzer*, a work made especially for her by renowned Limón exponent, Clay Taliaferro, and Humphrey's earlier solo, *The Call/Breath of Fire*. Yasko would return to work with Stodelle whenever she was in the USA, noting the subtleties Stodelle added on each occasion that, in turn, deepened her own performative sense of the dance (Yasko 2014, interview). Corbin, likewise, would work with Stodelle before each performance, noting: "As time went on she would change minor things—not even worth pointing out…so that the clarity of the idea was purified" (Corbin 2014, interview). This comment resonates with the emphasis Stodelle placed on the conception of the dance, referred to earlier, and how important it was for the dancer(s) to understand the idea in tandem with the choreography. Yasko's recollections of performing the work include it being fulfilling, a 'complete' piece in which she felt artistically at home. "*Two Ecstatic Themes* was an absolute statement of why Doris was on earth. Everything for her was crystallized in this one work. You could sense her heart soaring to the heavens" (Yasko 2014, interview). Corbin noted: "I always felt as performer I was moving through a pattern that was in the space already" (Corbin 2014, interview), which is a most evocative image that conjures up the idea of past spirals in space, first traced and inhabited by Humphrey in the 1930s and then found again in 1975 by Corbin, and Hill and the dancers that followed (Fig. 5.3).

Fig. 5.3 Gail Corbin in *Two Ecstatic Themes*, Circular Descent. Photograph by Jennifer W. Lester

By way of contrast, Graham dancer Sandra Kaufmann came to the solo via *The Call/Breath of Fire*. Kaufmann performed with the Martha Graham Company for more than ten years and thus has a body ingrained with the dynamic principles of 'Contract and Release'. She first saw *Two Ecstatic Themes* in 1989, performed at the Academy of Music and Movement in Oak Park by Miroslava Pospisil, another of Stodelle's principal dancers, who performed the dance many times. Having not previously encountered Humphrey's work, Kaufmann recalls not knowing what she was seeing but she knew the work was important. Something in the work resonated and captivated her. Before learning either solo, Kaufmann witnessed Stodelle setting *Two Ecstatic Themes* on Sarita Smith Childs, a process that was filmed at the Academy in Oak Park for the series of videos of Stodelle coaching Humphrey works, produced by the publishing house, Dance Horizons. After some years of coming to understand Humphrey's style and philosophy, and working on *The Call/ Breath of Fire* with Stodelle, Kaufmann travelled to Stodelle's studio in Connecticut to learn *Two Ecstatic Themes* in 1998. She noted the similarities to the rehearsal process observed in Oak Park, with Stodelle spending a substantial amount of the rehearsal time on the first falls, the 'yielding' to gravity. *Circular Descent* took much longer to set than *Pointed Ascent*, the latter coming more naturally to her Graham-trained body. For Kaufmann, predominant memories are the emphasis on the opening successional falls, circularity and yielding. Alongside, she recalls the contrast within *Circular Descent*—the moments of doubt before giving in and falling again (Kaufman 2014, interview). In a neat connection, Kaufmann performed *Two Ecstatic Themes* and other solo works in Richard Move's *Martha@...* series at Mothers in New York City in the early 2000s. Deborah Jowitt, reviewing the event for *Village Voice*, called her performance of the Humphrey work 'dramatically compelling', which Kaufmann particularly appreciated because the drama inherent in the work had been a strong focus for Stodelle in rehearsal.

Naomi Mindlin, former Limón dancer, learnt *The Call/Breath of Fire* solo with Stodelle in 1994. The experience she describes is worth documenting here because it closely mirrors the rehearsal process for *Two Ecstatic Themes*. "The motivation of the movement was paramount. The movement is presented as material to be mined for all the nuances it contains. The movement is worked and re-worked until it evokes a deeper meaning than first or superficial contact could afford. Images are used throughout the coaching process that urge the dancer to engage her imagination and to find meaning from her own life in the movement" (Mindlin 1995, 131). Mindlin recalls important coaching notes Stodelle gave her as the rehearsal process progressed: "You have to uncover it for yourself. What actually happens is that it emerges. You get to the core of it. It emerges in you and out of you, so that you're really in the centre of it"; "You are the gesture, don't just do it"; "Your body is your face"; "Any repeat of something is because it is being resolved" (Mindlin 1995, 131). These ideas have a wide reach in terms of being available and understandable for a performer, no matter what the individual stylistic history may be. Kaufmann observed that the process of learning and rehearsing was both exhausting and mysterious (Kaufmann 2014, interview). Arguably, she had to work harder to capture this dance because her intuitive kinesthetic responses were further removed than Humphrey/Limón-trained dancers such as Corbin and Yasko. These accounts provide important insights into the performer's experience of *Two Ecstatic Themes* and, collectively, allow glimpses of both the thought and movement processes that are worked through by the individual in rehearsal and how these processes then come together in the moment of performance.

As a director, I am drawn to a staging approach fuelled by the interconnecting notions of 'translation–transmission–transformation' because these concepts have the propensity to be applied in more than one context and, thus, provide a fluid but connected base from which to operate in the present. The act of *translation* for the director is selecting and making sense of the evidence. The act of *transmission* is the transference of this knowledge and understanding to the performer who will, in turn, go through a related but distinct process of transmission to inhabit the work for performance. Inevitably, there will be a degree of *transformation* of the work in the resulting performance because it is the latest manifestation of that work.

The staging process in 2014 began by first considering Humphrey's writing around the time she choreographed the dance. An example comes from a letter to her husband-to-be, dated July 21, 1931, in which Humphrey speaks of her love for him as an "impalpable white center from which I draw new strength for work, new love for people, increased sensitivity to all things in my world" (Cohen 1995, 102). She also refers to 'a spiral curve' later in that same letter. The costume for *Two Ecstatic Themes* is a pristine white dress, long sleeved, ankle length with close fitting bodice and full circular skirt. The suggestion of an 'impalpable white center' engenders a sense of presence both within and around the solo dancer. Stodelle's description of the opening of the dance provides an indication of the starting point for this presence: "The interplay between the physical act of falling/recovering and its implications as an expression of deep feeling comes to light as the curtain rises on *Circular Descent*, and the dancer is discovered standing stage centre, her legs planted firmly apart, her arms stretched sideways in taut, straight lines. Linearly, here is perfect symmetry; kinetically, the dancer's stance suggests absolute control; the emotional tone is one of security, of complete rationality" (Stodelle 1992, 2). These pieces of primary evidence—writing from the choreographer, the costume design, and Stodelle's firsthand observation of Humphrey dancing—when considered together, enable the creation of a landscape from which the transmission of the dance can unfold. The opening of the dance evokes stillness, silence and presence, albeit momentary. The advent of the musical accompaniment changes everything.

Humphrey came to choose the music for the dance after she had begun work on the choreography. She conferred with Louis Horst, a former colleague at Denishawn and the musical director of her early concerts, with the hope of his recommending suitable music (Stodelle 1992, 3). Horst's suggestion of Medtner's resonant *Tragedie-Fragment in A Minor, Opus 7.2* for the first theme, *Circular Descent*, provided Humphrey with an ideal accompaniment for movement phrases described later in the program note as "soft and sinking, to convey an emotional feeling of acquiescence." Against this quasi-abstract interpretation, Humphrey set her second theme, analyzed in the same program note as moving "in pointed design to a strident climax suggestive of aggressive achievement." The similarly energetic *Maschere Che Passano 1* (1918) by Malipiero reflects the vigorous spirit of the contrasting *Pointed Ascent*. Humphrey's contemporary, composer/pianist Vivian Fine, accompanied her performances live on many occasions and it is her recording of both musical pieces that continues to be used today. The musical recording, therefore, is a significant piece of evidence for the director and performer to acknowledge in the transmission process because of the insights it offers into timing, phrasing and dynamic nuance.[7]

The knowledge that Fine's interpretation of these musical pieces was built through watching Humphrey perform the dance over an extended period allowed us to use the music as a source beyond that of accompaniment in 2014. One example, evident in both pieces, comprises the suspended silences and pauses that create space for the drama of the work to unfold and heighten. Another example is the use of accelerando and decelerando throughout. Such musical inflections occur within and at the end of phrases and provide director and performer with an insight into how Humphrey paced particular movement phrases and an opportunity for further exploration in relation to meaning and to dynamic.

The dancer I worked with in 2014, Louise Kelsey, had danced in the Humphrey style for more than a decade and had previously performed *Water Study* (1928), *With My Red Fires* (1936) and *Passacaglia* (1938). Readers familiar with those dances will appreciate the array of dynamic nuance and challenge demanded of the performer. Kelsey, therefore, came to *Two Ecstatic Themes* with an innate sense of stylistic underpinning. This initial transmission of ideas from director to performer allowed Kelsey to unlock the key to the choreographic intention and, in doing so, find her own way into the dance. The work we did in the studio focused on the dual ideas of 'yielding' and 'striving'. Reflecting back on the process, these two ideas were present in every rehearsal in some form, in relation to execution, dynamics, expression or musicality. The idea of 'yielding' is most at play in *Circular Descent*. A second, connecting idea is that of 'inhabiting the spiral curve'. Together, these aspects are central to capturing the conceptual idea of this first part. In order to yield, one must inhabit the spiral; in order to inhabit the spiral, one has to yield.

From the opening moments of the dance, in the stillness and silence, the 'impalpable white center' begins to move from within, taking the dancer imperceptibly outward toward the edge of the spiral on the first notes of the music. Hovering momentarily at a point of suspension, the breath then releases and the body falls around and downward, through a backward arcing hinge, before climbing upward into the high point of the spiral curve. This first section sees the dancer navigate her way around a series of five falls, each distinctive from the last, the form of the spiral curve nuanced from one to the next, 'ever so slightly altered' from the one that has gone before. The volume of each spiral grows with a quiet intensity, progressively building to a point where the body is pulled so far off-balance that the dancer has no option but to follow the pull as it travels across space.

The pattern of *Circular Descent* is established in this first series. The dominant theme of the spiral curve is punctuated, first by a downward lunging thrust that offers a glimmer of what is to come in *Pointed Ascent*. The lunging action yields into a sequence of subtle spirals, falling and climbing through the shoulders and feeling propelled from the inside of one's chest. A fleeting return to the opening, Apollonian stance follows, but this time the force of the spiral pulls the dancer upstage, then downstage and then around the stage in spiral turns, back and forth, on a spiral pathway that leads upstage to the furthermost point the dance will reach. Here, the dancer falls precariously from one leg, the upper body and arms tracing an 'hour glass' figure, as described by Stodelle earlier. These falls give way to a descent to the floor, beginning from a high, suspended rise facing out to the side, and falling downward through backward steps to the floor. The movement of the torso is at its most expansive and 'striving' here, reaching and pulling from the one side to the other then around to the back before the body is seemingly dragged back round to the front again. A reassertion of will sees a return of the opening stance, this time with the body placed up on the knees. A reprise of the opening series of spiral curves from this kneeling position follows, with the lower plane making the movements feel correspondingly more restrained and adding to the sense of downward pull. A final flurry of turning, accelerating spirals on the spot is halted by a piercing strike down to the left, swiftly followed by a swing up to the rise with the right arm high. The final moments of *Circular Descent* comprise a slow hinging back fall to the floor, a seeming relinquishing of power and self but with a twist—the left knee is deliberately left pointing upwards as a hint that all may not yet be over (Fig. 5.4).

Throughout *Pointed Ascent*, the dancer strives relentlessly upward, ever climbing from the opening position, lying prone on the ground, physically and emotionally spent after the travails of *Circular Descent*. The angularity and thrusting nature of the movement act both as a spur to overcome recent acquiescence and as a counterpoint in design. The edges of both movement and spatial design are pierced directly, as opposed to the circumnavigation of what came before. *Pointed Ascent* takes place entirely on the spot, centre stage. Criss-crossing gestures and reaches repeatedly break the vertical plane. *Circular Descent* comprises a series of spiral curves that descend progressively. The pattern reversed, *Pointed Ascent* drives and jars its way back up, with occasional moments of lateral regrouping before charging on again. The concluding moments see the dancer rise up from a low, crouched-over position, as if gathering renewed strength and power. As she rises, the hands are drawn up in front of the body in a taut, trembling action, until she takes one final step out, back to the opening stance, and the arms simultaneously shoot upward in a sudden tight clasp. This final assertion, over will, over gravity, is triumphal.

It is widely acknowledged that through this dance and her subsequent movement explorations in the early 1930s, Humphrey both harnessed

Fig. 5.4 Gail Corbin in *Two Ecstatic Themes*, Pointed Ascent. Photograph by Jennifer W. Lester

and defined her artistic credo as 'Fall and Recovery' with successional movement at its core. It is fitting, therefore, that she has a final word that is applicable equally to *Two Ecstatic Themes* and to her broader movement philosophy: "All life fluctuates between the resistance to and the yielding to gravity... There are two still points in the physical life: the motionless body, in which the thousand adjustments for keeping it erect are invisible, and the horizontal, the last stillness. Life and dance exist between these two points and therefore form the arc between two deaths" (Humphrey 1959, 106). The task for us as translators and transmitters of her work, and the choreographic work of others, is to pursue the artist's intent through the evidence, crafting the strands we can uncover into 'coherent wholes' for performers and audiences. The notion that subsequent performances of a work can be 'ever so slightly altered', whether by design or simply the passage of time, supports the work as a vital, 'living' entity that has transformative capacities. At the heart of this argument is a work's capacity to grow in the present whilst acknowledging a continuing connection to and with the source, the choreographer.

NOTES

1. Friedrich Nietzsche's analysis of Greek culture in *The Birth of Tragedy* (1872) suggests that there exist within human nature two conflicting yet intertwining impulses—the desire to achieve perfection and stability, and the equally compelling urge to experience the danger of abandon. Nietzsche referred to this as his 'Apollonian–Dionysian' theory. This notion provided Humphrey with a philosophical framework in which to place the movement explorations she had been pursuing since leaving Denishawn in 1928. "Translating Nietzsche's observations into movement analyses of her own, Humphrey found the same quest for ecstasy in the pursuit of Apollonian idealism as in Dionysian abandon. To her, the static perfection of symmetry was as congealing as the trap of total self-forgetfulness. Between these two extremes lay 'the arc between Two Deaths', the movement realm of gravitational ebb and flow" (Stodelle 1992, 3).
2. On a restorative cruise in 1931, Humphrey met and, after some persuasion and gentle pursuit on his part, fell in love with the ship's captain, Charles Francis Woodford, whom she came to refer to as 'Leo' to distinguish him from her artistic partner, Charles Weidman.
3. 'Transmission—A Performance Symposium' took place at Middlesex University, London on Saturday, December 13, 2014. The program included performances of *Two Ecstatic Themes* and Martha Graham's 'lost' solo, *Imperial Gesture* (1935) alongside work by Robert Cohan—see full details on http://www.transmissionperformancesymposium.wordpress.com.
4. Accounts from former dancers Gail Corbin, Jeanne Yasko and Sandra Kaufmann are discussed in the section titled 'Performing *Two Ecstatic Themes*'.

5. See Main (2012), Chap. 1 for a full discussion.
6. As documented in Main (2012), Part 2.
7. See Stodelle (1983) for detailed exposition of Fine's work with Humphrey and Weidman in the 1930s.

BIBLIOGRAPHY

Barba, Fabián. 2011. A Dancer Writes: Fabián Barba on Mary Wigman's Solos. *Dance Research Journal* 43 (1): 81–89.
Benjamin, Walter. 1996. The Task of the Translator. In *Walter Benjamin: Selected Writings*, vol. 1, 1927–1934, ed. M. Bullock and M. W. Jennings. Cambridge, MA: Belknapp Press of Harvard University Press.
Cohen, Selma Jeanne. 1995. *Doris Humphrey—An Artist First*. Princeton, NJ: Dance Horizons.
Derrida, Jacques. 1985. Des Tours de Babel. In *Difference in Translation*, trans. and ed. Joseph E. Graham, 169–207. Ithaca, NY: Cornell University Press.
Dunning, Jennifer. 1989. Recalling the Spirit of Doris Humphrey. *New York Times*, March 11.
———. 1994. A Pioneer's Essence Distilled by Her Heirs. *New York Times*, December 24.
Eliot, Thomas S. 1975 [1st edn 1917]. Tradition and the Individual Talent. In *Selected Prose of T.S. Eliot*, ed. Frank Kermode. London: Faber.
Humphrey, Doris. 1959. *The Art of Making Dances*. New York: Rhinehart.
King, Eleanor. 1978. *Transformations*. New York: Dance Horizons.
Lepecki, André. 2010. The Body as Archive: Will to Re-Enact and the Afterlives of Dances. *Dance Research Journal* 42 (2): 29–48.
Lloyd, Margaret. 1987 [1st edn 1949]. *The Borzoi Book of Modern Dance*. Princeton, NJ: Dance Horizons.
Main, Lesley. 2012. *Directing the Dance Tradition of Doris Humphrey. The Creative Impulse of Reconstruction*. Madison, WI: University of Wisconsin Press.
Mindlin, Naomi. 1995. A Humphrey Tutorial. *Choreography and Dance: Doris Humphrey—A Centennial Issue* 4 (4): 123–134.
Siegel, Marica. 1993. *Days on Earth. The Dance of Doris Humphrey*. USA: Duke University Press.
Stalpaert, Christel. 2011. Re-enacting Modernity: Barba's 'A Mary Wigman Dance Evening' (2009). *Dance Research Journal* 43: 91–95.
Stodelle, Ernestine. 1983. Sensing the Dancer's Impulse. *Art Times*, November.
———. 1992. *The Collected Works*, vol. 2. New York: Dance Notation Bureau.
———. 1995a [1st edn 1976]. *The Dance Technique of Doris Humphrey and its Creative Potential*. Princeton, NJ: Dance Horizons.

————. 1995b. A Life Well Lived in Dance. *Choreography and Dance: Doris Humphrey—A Centennial Issue* 4 (4): 3–16.

Topaz, Muriel. 1995. Reflections on Style and Performance. *Choreography and Dance: Doris Humphrey—A Centennial Issue* 4 (4): 61–74.

Interviews

Gail Corbin—email correspondence, November 19, 2014.

Jeanne Yasko—in conversation, November 14, 2014.

Sandra Kaufmann—email correspondence, November 12, 2014.

CHAPTER 6

Transmission as Process and Power in Graham's *Chronicle* (1936)

Kim Jones

Martha Graham's *Chronicle*, a dance about the aftermath of war, was created in 1936 and performed until 1938. Originally consisting of five dances presented in three sections, *Chronicle* was one of a group of overtly political dances that Graham created during the 1930s. In this chapter, I investigate the history of production and reproduction of this work and discuss my own learning of *Chronicle* in 2002, as well as my subsequent restaging and teaching of sections of the work. Throughout my discussion of *Chronicle*, I return to the idea of 'transmission' as a theoretical touchstone and as an aspect of the reproduction process. Humphrey exponent Lesley Main suggests that transmission is the conveyance of the "conceptual framework and choreographic intention of a work" (Main 2017, this volume). I also find it useful to think about transmission in dance reconstruction like the transmission of a car, as governing power in the work. I mean this in three ways.

First, and especially in a work like *Chronicle*, which has been in constant flux since its first performance, 'transmission' reminds us to consider the creation and reconstruction of dances as a process, not a

K. Jones (✉)
University of North Carolina, Charlotte, USA
e-mail: kjonesdance@hotmail.com

© The Author(s) 2017
L. Main (ed.), *Transmissions in Dance*,
https://doi.org/10.1007/978-3-319-64873-6_6

product. It is important to remember that Graham, like other creative artists, altered, edited, reshaped, and discarded ideas as she created dances, and she also collaborated with others. With Graham's works, I find it as productive to think about the impact of her collaborators and critics—to carry on the analogy, of the combined impact of engine, transmission and wheels in driving a car forward—as it is to think about what the 'original' dance must have been like.

Second, I find that performance practices are especially significant in regulating the power in a dance. Understanding Graham's use of breath is all-important to reimagining her choreographic choices, and in shaping a work that is true to the emotional and physical nuances that drive Graham's dances. I am especially interested in considering how best to involve contemporary dancers in the performance of movement that comes from a different era, and how to convey the meanings of the historical works to the performers and to others. I understand much of Graham's technique and choreography as being as salient today as it was in her own time. An important consideration, therefore, is how does a Graham dancer in the present embody Graham technique and style of the past?

Third, transmission as the governance of power calls us to consider the privileges and responsibilities of those who guard and investigate Graham's legacy, among them the Martha Graham Center of Contemporary Dance, scholars, régisseurs, and performers. Those who reconstruct dances rely differently on resources and have different methodologies and goals. In addition, subsequent changes to costumes, body types, and training methods impact dance works. What exactly is 'the dance'? For whom and for what reason?

This chapter is informed by my long association with Graham's work, with the Martha Graham Dance Company, and a commitment to researching and reimagining historic dances. I danced with the Graham Company from 2002 to 2006 and performed in major works such as *Primitive Mysteries* (1931), *Chronicle* (1936), and *Deep Song* (1937). When I began teaching at the University of North Carolina at Charlotte (UNCC) in 2008, I used my experience to restage some of Graham's early dances: *Lamentation* (1930), *Primitive Mysteries* (1931), *Panorama* (1935), and "Steps in the Street" (1936), a section of *Chronicle*. These projects were supported by grants from the National Endowment of the Arts (NEA) and a UNC Charlotte Academic Program Improvement Grant (API). My reconstruction and restaging were evaluated by the Martha Graham resources in New York and, in 2004, I became a régisseur for the Martha Graham Center of Contemporary Dance—a specialist who is permitted and encouraged to restage Graham masterworks and to utilize the Center's resources for that purpose.[1]

In addition to my work as a régisseur, I reimagine 'lost' dances that have few historical artifacts and little archival support and/or experiential detail in the historical record. From 2011 to 2013, my research centered on reimagining Martha Graham's solo, *Imperial Gesture* (1935), which is from the same time period as *Chronicle*.[2] Last performed in 1938, *Imperial Gesture* presents images of monarchs and dictators using expansive gestures that reach across continents.[3] From 2015 to 2016, I reconstructed American choreographer Paul Taylor's *Tracer* (1962) for the Taylor 2 company.[4] In working with Paul Taylor, this project moves my research out of the purview of Graham and her legacy and into the generation of dancers who came after her (Fig. 6.1).

Fig. 6.1 Author Kim Jones coaching the final dress rehearsal for the premiere of her reconstruction of *Tracer* with the Taylor 2 Company, September 30, 2016. Photograph by Jeff Cravotta

These experiences impact my understanding of my earlier work with *Chronicle*. At this point in my academic and artistic career—and in my research in general—I am strongly committed to engaging a new generation of dancers and audience members in projects that bring dance history to life. I hope to animate past dances and to provide theatrical experiences, but moreover to engage current students and audiences in the processes and questions of reconstruction and/or reimagining. This transmission of ideas, artistic priorities, methods of working, and social and political concerns helps these works remain vitally relevant in today's world.

DANCE AS PROCESS: TRANSMITTING *CHRONICLE*'S HISTORICAL AND POLITICAL CONTEXTS

In a 1936 program (for Martha Graham and Dance Group), *Chronicle* consisted of five dances presented in three sections: "Dances Before Catastrophe" (including "Spectre-1914" and "Masque"), "Dances After Catastrophe" (including "Steps in the Street" and "Tragic Holiday–in Memoriam"), and "Prelude to Action." The look and impact of this version of *Chronicle*, as performed by Martha Graham's then all-female troupe (1926–1937), and critics' early singling out of "Steps in the Street" as a successful aspect of the dance, can be glimpsed from period writings. Owen Burke, as one example, observed

> *Prelude to Action* is restrained, taut dance of gathering energies, gathering forces. There is no goal marked, but following the *Catastrophe* the direction is plain. Right now there is a massing of strength; there must be no repetition of [death, despair, mourning] "Steps in the Street!"...for sheer artistry of movement, for brilliance of choreography, for the rush and force of energy there is little on the concert stage to equal..."Steps in the Street"...or "Prelude to Action." ...*Chronicle* undoubtedly is the most important work of the current season. (Burke 1937)

More important, perhaps, than the work's positive reception or success is that *Chronicle* was part of Graham's search for a way to wield choreography and movement as political statement. Critics, who discussed the success of Graham's efforts throughout this time, helped this process along by making clear the associations between current events and Graham's choreography. For example, Graham's solo *Deep Song* (1937)

GUILD   THEATRE

FIRE NOTICE: The exit, indicated by a red light and sign, nearest to the seat
you occupy, is the shortest route to the street.
In the event of fire or other emergency please do not run—WALK TO THAT EXIT.
JOHN J. McELLIGOTT, Fire Chief and Commissioner

SUNDAY EVENING, DECEMBER 20, 1936, AT 8:45 P. M.

MARTHA   GRAHAM
and DANCE GROUP
LOUIS HORST, Musical Director

Celebration . . . . *Louis Horst*
Dance Group

Frontier . . . . *Louis Horst*
Martha Graham

Primitive Canticles . . . . *Villa-Lobos*
 a. Ave
 b. Salve
Martha Graham

Primitive Mysteries . . . . *Louis Horst*
 a. Hymn to the Virgin
 b. Crucifixus
 c. Hosannah!
Martha Graham and Dance Group

INTERMISSION

Chronicle . . . . *Wallingford Riegger*
 Dances Before Catastrophe
  a. Spectre—1914
  b. Masque

 Dances After Catastrophe
  a. Steps in the Street
  b. Tragic Holiday—In Memoriam.
 Prelude to Action
Martha Graham and Dance Group

Dance Group: Anita Alvarez, Thelma Babbitz, Bonnie Bird, Dorothy Bird,
 Ethel Butler, Aza Ceskin, Jane Dudley, Frieda Flier, Marie Marchowsky,
 Sophie Maslow, Marjorie Mazia, May O'Donnell, Kathleen Slagle,
 Gertrude Shurr, Anna Sokolow, Mildred Wile.

Fig. 6.2 Program for the Martha Graham and Dance Group premiere of
Chronicle at the Guild Theatre, NYC, December 20, 1936. Program materials
provided by Martha Graham Resources, a division of the Martha Graham Center
for Contemporary Dance, Inc

demonstrates her response to the current events of 1937 in Spain (Fig. 6.2). The dance expresses the hardships of a woman, mother, sister, wife who feels anguish, repression, and loss in a war. Burke (1938) responded that the piece "poignantly express[es] Americans' knowledge of the profound sufferings of the Spanish people fighting for their liberties against the fascist invasion." This was an era of searching and experimentation across art-making genres, not of controlled, definitive statements.

During this period, Graham's work focused on the human condition, and her expression was both literal and abstract. A list of selected dances that Graham created leading up to and just following the premiere of *Chronicle* illustrates her focus on the human condition as it relates to what is happening in society. For each, I have included the title, the theme, and a quotation about the dance from a contemporary critic for context:

- *Strike* from *Immigrant* (1928), about revolution: "all the revolutions of the world in that slender body" ("Martha Graham Dance Program Wins Applause" 1928);
- *Heretic* (1929), about forces of societal intolerance: "stiff-necked recrimination, cruelty and oppression" (Watkins 1929);
- *Lamentation* (1930), about loss/grief: "unbearable desolation... the consummate grief of all ages" ("A Dancer and an Educator on Fascism" 1937);
- *Primitive Mysteries* (1931), an abstract work in response to indigenous culture: "Its blending of austerity and tenderness, its deep sincerity and simplicity, its clarity and richness of design, combine to make of it one of the few unquestionable masterpieces of the modern repertoire" (Martin 1935);
- *Frontier* (1935), about American identity: "built on serenity...a recreation in American backgrounds" (Burnshaw 1935);
- *Panorama* (1935), a cry for social action: "We may speak of *Panorama* as new and revolutionary. It is not a propaganda or proletarian work of art. It is to supply energy to mobilize the beholder as well as the dancer" (McCausland 1935);
- *Imperial Gesture* (1935), about power and avarice: "stunning picture of imperialist greed" (Burnshaw 1935);
- *Chronicle* (1936): "devoted to a consideration of the 'advent and consequences of war'" (Martin 1936a).

Program notes from performances of *Sketches from Chronicle* in 1994[5] make clear that the work is not about an 'incident' or real life, but rather about the emotional states that result from living fully as a human being.[6] Created between the World Wars, when memories of the first were still fresh and anxiety for the second was brewing in the human consciousness, Graham dancer and scholar Ellen Graff says, "Graham's dances began to reflect her fears for the world" (Graff 1997, 64). The sections of *Chronicle* expressed desperation, hunger, anxiety, fear of war, and the loneliness one feels to a rise of protest, and unity among the masses. "Full of symbolism...*Chronicle* was a theater piece" (Graff 1997, 117). By this, Graff is pointing to the fact that some of Graham's work had been criticized as being "too abstract and too formal (modernist)," but *Chronicle* called to a wider (Leftist) audience and had more mass appeal (Graff 2017, interview). Burke (1937) gives us a clearer picture of what the original audiences saw and felt: "The patterns are abstract; there is no miming. Program notes might clarify and save the audience the need to puzzle over subtleties in meaning, of intention. But although the ideas of the dancer are obscured in the over-abundance of choreographic movement, the emotional overtones carry through, and with them the meaning of the composition and its significance."

Graham was actively involved in political causes during this period, most famously through her refusal of Hitler's invitation to perform at the dance festival for the 1936 Summer Olympic Games in Berlin. Writing in the *New Masses*, Owen Burke (1938) contextualizes this incident:

> For twelve years Martha Graham has pointed the direction of the modern dance, and the best of our younger revolutionary dancers carry on through the technique she has taught them. Nor does her work end with her dancing. She set the pace for the dance world by refusing to participate in the Nazi Olympics and dance festival; she is a member of the anti-Nazi literature organ; she participates actively for the passage of the Fine Arts Bill.[7]

As a member and speaker for the Committee for Anti-Nazi Literature symposium, Graham "spoke on the manner in which art and education in Nazi Germany have been turned to imperialistic uses, not through changing the structure of the education system, or changing, say, the movement in dancing, but by changing the entire basic philosophy from which these things are taught and applied" ("A Dancer and an Educator on Fascism" 1937). In response to the Nazi philosophy of teaching and using art for the party's purposes, Graham felt that dancers had a responsibility to react in kind:

> Miss Graham's plea that dancers be watchful of their world and sincere in their art, carried over the emphasis that the very real and terrible developments taking place in the world leave no one unaffected. Spain is at present the scene of tragedy and horror; all Western Europe is looking on, vulture-like; America has its own enemies within. Such hysteria can be curbed only by united resistance against it, and dancers and other artists must know and play their part with others in that resistance. ("A Dancer and an Educator on Fascism" 1937)

We understand Graham as both an activist and artist, and her works from this period serve to demonstrate a communion of her political and artistic expression grounded in the human condition and performed through human movement. Graham responded, not only in her refusal to perform at the Berlin Olympics, but through her art as well. Graff (1997, 113) notes that in December 1935, Graham performed *Celebration* and *Imperial Gesture* on a benefit program for the International Labor Defense (ILD) at Carnegie Hall, appearing with groups headed by Humphrey, Weidman, Tamiris, and Sokolow. Graham became an active presenter with the American Artists Congress from 1935 to 1937. She was also a signing member of the Congress' declaration that strove to not only oppose fascism in Europe, but to champion civil liberties in the struggle for workers' rights at home in the United States.

Interestingly, Graham's aesthetic development was the topic of an article in the (1935) publication *New Theatre*, in which Irving Ignatin takes issue with critics Paul Douglas (1935) and Edna Ocko regarding their reviews of Graham's "revolutionary" work (Ignatin 1935). Central to their reviews was an analysis of the relationship between form and content in Graham's work. Graff observes that in reference to the International Labor Defense benefit at Carnegie Hall, Edna Ocko found that "[a]mong the Graham contributions were compositions...singled out as socially conscious; despite their formal values, they had earned the tentative approval of left-wing ideologues" (Graff 1997, 113). Douglas questioned whether form and content were inseparable in art, and commented that Graham's exact attention to form did not always demonstrate a relationship to the content of her work (Ignatin 1935). Ocko is quoted as praising Graham's exquisite *"system* of dance technic[sic]" in which "she has developed a science of modern dance movement which seems remarkably suited to make the body a fit instrument for expression" (Ignatin 1935). Referring to the body of movements that Graham created for her company, Ocko says "It would be almost impossible to do meaningless dances with this equipment" (Ignatin 1935). It is well known, however, that Ocko sometimes criticized Graham's choreography for not matching its revolutionary content. Ignatin's analysis of Graham settles in between Douglas and Ocko. He states, "the dance with proletarian content will in time create its distinctive formal structure" (Ignatin 1935). The dance works from this era, led mostly by Graham, speak to the working-class people. Most of the dancers from her company by the mid-1930s established the New Dance Group, which was made up of artists and dance makers dedicated to social change. The fact that Graham's work generated such lively and impassioned debate says much about her impact on both the contemporary and artistic communities. For our purposes, we must evaluate these reviews for what they can teach us regarding representing this work for current generations.

When we attempt to restage, reconstruct, or reimagine a work, going back to original sources is invaluable. Specific to *Chronicle*, dance critics of the time provide important insights of early performances of the dance. Writing in the *New York Sun*, critic I.K. (1936) describes the work as follows:

> The time chronicled is 1914 to the present [1936], and in motivation the impulse is not unlike that which prompted Kurt Jooss's "Green Table". However, there is no sly mockery or gentle sophistication in Miss Graham's interpretation.... Her approach is serious, intense, and bitter. In her five dances she not only draws the picture of war itself, but depicts the desolation of the post-war period, and issues a call to action for the future.

> As a general prelude, Miss Graham offers a solo dance titled "Spectre-1914," in which taut, inhuman gestures of response to the off-stage trumpet and drums might be interpreted as the unwilling but uncontrollable participation of humanity in war.... In the succeeding sections, a lengthy group dance, "Steps in the Street," conveys to the mind a world of the unwanted—the unemployed shuffling along the avenues, now and then bursting forth in rebellious movements, succumbing once more to a futile resignation.

This review illustrates for the present-day researcher a rather detailed picture of what audiences saw and what Graham intended them to feel: helplessness, fear, isolation, futility. For me, I find that images of historical or current events that evoke emotion, intellectual and artistic curiosity, and movement exploration give power to the thought, words, and movement.

Henry Gilfond, writing in *Dance Observer*, provides another insight into "Dances Before Catastrophe." It was performed in front of a red, white, and black background—"no accident," said Gilfond, "but rather conscious selection and condemnation" (quoted in Graff 1997, 65), referring to Graham's explicit display of the Nazi colors. From this, we know that Graham used her set, not just her choreography, to make known her anti-Nazi sentiment. Regarding the last section of *Chronicle*, a contemporary reviewer reported the following:

> "Prelude to Action" was the title of the last number on Martha Graham's opening program at the Guild Theater Sunday night as the third sequence in her latest dance creation "*Chronicle*" (Wallingford Riegger). Appropriately enough, this was the keynote of the evening, for the numbers never approached action nearer than a prelude. A capacity audience that included several standees, crowded the theater and the cult of Graham enthusiasts watched rapt and spellbound the numbers, bursting into loud applause at the close of each. (Rhodes 1936)

I remember this same feeling at Sadler's Wells in London, when we (the Graham Company) finished dancing *Chronicle* in 2003—there was a huge standing ovation and the longest curtain call.

Jerome D. Bohm, in his review of the same performance for the *NY Herald Tribune*, adds a different dimension to this particular performance:

> "*Chronicle*" is in many respects an advance over Miss Graham's previous attempt at an extended choreographic work with historical and sociological implications. To begin with, Miss Graham's dance contribution is here an integral part of the creation. In "Panorama," first revealed at Bennington two seasons ago, there was a want of unity of purpose which weakened its effectiveness. While "*Chronicle*" marks a step forward in Miss Graham's career as a choreographer, and points the way to brilliant future accomplishments, it does not yet succeed in providing a wholly satisfactory

composition. Many of the ideas are expressed at too great a length.... The most convincing movement is "Steps in the Street," but even here greater brevity would be advantageous. Whether such an ideology as is implied in the titles of the divisions of "*Chronicle*" lends itself to choreographic interpretation is a moot question. But if one is willing to set aside the programmatic basis and consider "*Chronicle*" purely from the aspects of design and motion, it must be admitted that Miss Graham and her group accomplish much that is remarkable. Merely considered as controlled, directed energy, their efforts were amazing. (Bohm 1936)

I agree with Bohm's assessment of the "controlled, directed energy." When dancing this work, there is a sense of rising, gathering, and focused energy from self to the group. The movement feels powerful and full. It is a physically demanding piece that is quite satisfying to dance.

John Martin, renowned dance critic for the *New York Times*, provides a more considered and detailed perspective:

Martha Graham...last night revealed her latest and by far her most ambitious composition for soloist and group under the title of "*Chronicle*." The work...is devoted to a consideration of the "advent and consequences of war." It bears a definite relation to the present world situation, but it is in no sense literal in its choice of materials. It is rather an attempt to see the present situation in terms of a kind of heroic perspective, a chronicle of historic proportions as its title clearly states.... That there is passion aplenty in the material itself is not to be denied, but it is equally manifest that the composer has not been entirely successful in bridging the gap between her deeply felt intention and its ultimate form. It is at present much too long, especially in its final section. It abounds in striking phrases and develops them with great ingenuity into a kind of neo-classical formality.... In the second section, in the final movement of several "Dances in the Street" [original title for "Steps in the Street"], occurs quite the finest piece of choreography of the whole work. (Martin 1936a)

Martin's review from the following week's performance illustrates the degree of change that can occur with new work:

At the Guild Theater yesterday afternoon, Martha Graham and her group gave their second performance of the season before another completely sold out house. The chief feature of the program was the new suite called "*Chronicle*."

It had been so largely transformed, however, since last week that it could scarcely be considered a repetition so much as a new version. In some cases, as in the opening solo of Miss Graham's, the choreography itself had been widely remade; elsewhere the difference lay in large part in the spirit of the performance, which breathed life and passion into a work which had lacked them in its first presentation. The final movement still remains over formal and a bit more cutting can be profitably done in earlier movements, but the general result is distinctly impressive and clearly invites further performances. (Martin 1936b)

Such insights from the time of creation are important in relation to reimagining/reconstructing a piece, since the creation of dance is fluid and it was not unusual for original performances to change.

Like critics, artists in different media, especially Graham's collaborators, hold insights about her work. Graham asserted that "[t]he only record of a dancer's art lies in the other arts" (Morgan 1980, 11), that is, a dance can be recorded by film or on paper by writing or drawing. She understood the value of collaborative relationships with visual artists, costumers, and musicians. Her collaborators included Isamu Noguchi, Jean Rosenthal, Alexander Calder, Louis Horst, Aaron Copland, Halston, and Calvin Klein. Indeed when reimagining *Imperial Gesture*, for example, I too relied on the products of other artists from the 1930s, such as painter/photographer Barbara Morgan, theater professor Arch Lauterer, and writers Stanley Burnshaw and John Malcolm Brinnin, to help unlock the lost work. I also relied on the contemporary artistic knowledges of multigenerational dancers, a composer, lighting designer, dramaturge, and costumer as they reflected on specific artifacts and gave new creative input (Jones 2015). Understanding Graham's collaborations in the past required a collaborative effort in the present.

This process of collaboration is also setting precedents for reconstructions and reimaginings to happen in the future. The process used for the three sections of *Sketches from Chronicle* (1994)—that of a researcher/director working with a dancer who was actively performing Graham's roles to lend a particular authenticity—is similar to the one I used in reimagining *Imperial Gesture* and for reconstructing Paul Taylor's *Tracer* in 2016. Just as Graham and Morgan collaborated to make the photographs in order to leave Graham's dance within other arts, our current collaboration moves through personal memory and experience. They modeled a path toward the uncovering of essence, distillation toward abstraction, creating a gesture at once of the individual as well as universal. These paths and possibilities were meant to present the human condition as a shared experience beyond the specific incident during a specific time period. This is why I use the term reimagining in addition to the term reconstructing. *Imperial Gesture* is about the intent and purpose Graham assigned to the dance in 1935, and it is also representative of contemporary artists and our current world. As I perform *Imperial Gesture* now, I perform it for myself and for my current audience. As Graham observed: "Throughout time dance has not changed in one essential function. The function of the dance is communication. The responsibility that dance fulfill its function belongs to us who are dancing today" (Armitage 1937, 83). This resonates within me as I move in and out of performing, teaching, making new dance works, reimagining and restaging dances from the past, and every time I am in the dance studio.

DANCE AS POWER: TRANSMITTING *CHRONICLE* THROUGH PERFORMANCE PRACTICES

When approaching Graham's past dances (from the 1930s and 1940s), using a political lens is, arguably, a necessity because her dances are inextricable from the time period in which they were created. However, dance scholar Mark Franko (2006) noted the difficulty of researching a past dance using a political lens, stating that such areas of inquiry are under-investigated in dance studies. Franko stated that "the methodological challenge we face is to articulate awareness of the traffic between bodies and ideologies acquired by virtue of all that has happened both in dance and in dance studies with the close analysis of how dancing itself actually works" (Franko 2006, 10). By close analysis, I understand Franko to mean that I approach my research as both artist and scholar. Like the repetition of a movement phrase in rehearsal that attempts to transcribe the mechanics of a prescribed movement onto a body in flux, the work of dancing itself insists that dance scholars remain aware of the inter-sectional nature of movement and time. The corporeal knowledge unique to a body in the present as it moves in choreography of the past is complex. My close analysis, in these instances, includes physical expertise—embodied knowledge of the forms and philosophies within a particular canon, Graham for example—to be necessary if not obligatory in my process of the reconstruction/reimagining. The following will offer insight into the reconstruction, restaging and performances of *Chronicle* between (1994) and (2015).

During my education at the Martha Graham School of Contemporary Dance in New York (1992–1995), three of the sections of *Chronicle* were reimagined and/or reconstructed, and were performed by the Martha Graham Dance Company during the 1994 New York season. These were "Spectre-1914" (Drums—Red Shroud—Lament), "Steps in the Street" (Devastation—Homelessness—Exile), and "Prelude to Action" (Unity—Pledge to the Future). The reconstructed and reimagined sections of *Chronicle* premiered on September 30, 1994, as *Sketches from Chronicle* for the Next Wave Festival at the Brooklyn Academy of Music (BAM), in a program entitled "Radical Graham" in honor of Graham's centennial celebration (Martha Graham Dance Company 1994). A number of Graham veterans brought these sections from *Chronicle* back to life. Pearl Lang, who began her career with Graham in the 1940s, was the Centennial Artistic Advisor, and also my primary Graham teacher. Three out of five centennial artistic advisors, Ethel Butler, Jane Dudley, and Sophie Maslow, were in the original cast of *Chronicle*, and Yuriko, a former Graham dancer also from the 1940s, reconstructed the "Steps in the Street" section. The Brooklyn Philharmonic Orchestra, led by Stanley Sussman, Graham's principal conductor, played live music for all of the dances.

As one example of the reconstruction process, former principal dancer Terese Capucilli and rehearsal director Carol Fried used film footage to reconstruct the solo "Spectre-1914" that Capucilli premiered at BAM. The reconstruction process utilized Barbara Morgan's photographic documentation and only 16 seconds of film footage from the end of the "Drums" section. The sections following, "Red Shroud" and "Lament," were reconstructed using Morgan's photographs and Capucilli's and Fried's embodied knowledge of the Graham aesthetic (Capucilli 2017, interview) (Fig. 6.3).

Capucilli outlines the history of *Chronicle*'s reconstruction in the following extract from recent correspondence:

> A vibrant commentary on war and its destruction, *Chronicle* fell out of the active repertory in 1938 and was thought to be lost.... In 1989, former Graham Company principal dancer, Yuriko...reconstructed another version of this section on the student group, the Martha Graham Ensemble, and it was later transferred onto the company. With this one section intact,

Fig. 6.3 Principal dancer Terese Capucilli (red dress) in *Chronicle*'s "Prelude to Action" with dancer Virginie Mécène at the Joyce Theater, NYC, 1999. Photograph by Julie Lemberger

in 1992, I conducted with then-Associate Artistic Director Carol Fried a research project to further uncover what possibilities there were in the reconstruction of Martha's early dances, particularly her solos. To our delight, we found a short film of Martha in "Spectre-1914" and close to 120 of Barbara Morgan's photographs as well as film sections and photographs of "Prelude to Action." "Prelude to Action" was also reconstructed in 1994 with the help of Sophie Maslow, who had been in the work in the 1930s. Both sections contained solo roles danced only by Martha, and the challenge was how to bring to the surface the images and the life of the characters while having never seen the work and having very little definitive movement phrases, and most importantly not having Martha with us. (Capucilli 2017, interview)

This information from Capucilli tells us much about reimagining and reconstructing Graham's work. We see that the process is often multifaceted, with a long and varied cast of characters playing roles. It is important to utilize all resources available: research, film, recollections from former dancers, and embodied knowledge are all integral to the process. In addition, Capucilli and Yuriko mentioned how integral Stanley Sussman, Music Director of the Martha Graham Company, was to the rehearsal process for the dance reconstruction. Capucilli remarked that "Sophie would not have been able to define sections [of the dance] if I had not worked with Stanley and notated all of the musical sections for "Prelude [to Action]"" (Capucilli 2017, interview). In her memorial for Sussman in (1996), Capucilli wrote that for reconstructing the "Spectre-1914" section, "Carol Fried, Stanley and myself spent hour upon hour working with the 1936 score, moving slowly and tediously through section upon section to bring the work alive making cuts... undoing cuts...inspiring photos to move."

In 1994, the 'reconstruction group' included original cast members, current Graham dancers, Morgan's photographs, and a short clip of film from the 1930s. The Martha Graham archive also provided reviews with detailed costume descriptions. One example from critic Owen Burke provides a picture of the costuming of "Spectre-1914" and how it impacted the meaning of the dance: "In 'Spectre-1914,' the first of the *Dances Before Catastrophe*, the simple dipping into the red cascade of the skirt that the dancer wears is enough to recall all the brutalizations of imperial conquest. It is a less satirical, more savage *Imperial Gesture* that moves slowly but ravishes well and gluttonously" (Burke 1937). Detailed and graphic descriptions from contemporary critics, though not always reliable due to personal biases, are invaluable in imparting impressions to us. The description of the movement that "ravishes well and gluttonously" is obviously open to interpretation, but conveys a spirit to us.

The success of the "Steps in the Street" reconstruction led the company to research and reconstruct other sections from *Chronicle*. In 1994, "Prelude to Action" was reconstructed by original cast member Sophie Maslow assisted by Capucilli, Fried, and Associate Artistic Director Diane Gray using film from Bryan and photographs by Morgan. Capucilli primarily reconstructed the Graham solo in this section, and Maslow led the group reconstruction. "Prelude to Action" was reconstructed on the Martha Graham Ensemble (MGE), the members of which then taught sections of the dance to the Martha Graham Dance Company. Dancer Deborah Goodman recalls her experience in rehearsal for "Prelude to Action":

> Speaking of how things change to reflect current situations/technique, I remember Sophie being adamant that unison accents happened at the top

of the movement rather than on the ground. This happened in a few places but I remember it most in the first entrance. The accent of the movement was to be the breaking of the chest *up* as the leg reached its zenith (count three). Carol and Diane felt the body's accent should be (and now is) when the leg touches the ground (on four). (Goodman 2016, interview)

Also during this period, Yuriko reconstructed "Steps in the Street" as part of her work with the Martha Graham Ensemble (now known as Graham 2). Yuriko founded the Martha Graham Ensemble in 1983 with a "mission to bring fresh energy, passion, and vision to Graham's tradition."[8] This group was a training ground for young modern dancers to enter the profession as dancers, educators, choreographers, and critics, and many dancers from the Ensemble were subsequently hired into the Martha Graham Dance Company. Just as importantly, and with Graham's permission, the MGE allowed Yuriko to work through reconstructions of past dances including *Heretic* (1929), *Celebration* (1934), *Panorama* (1935), "Steps in the Street" (1936), *Every Soul Is a Circus* (1939), *Canticle of Innocent Comedians* (1952), and *Secular Games* (1962) before they were set on the main company. Yuriko stated: "The Graham style is specific and it is my goal to help make accessible Martha's work not only for today's dancers but also for different audiences. It was my goal to bring dances to new places that never or seldom saw Graham works or modern dance" (Tokunaga 2008, 174).

Alessandra Prosperi, former principal dancer, had a long history in the company as a member between 1993 and 2006. She recalls of Yuriko's teaching process:

I remember spending many hours working on the "silent steps" entrance of "Steps in the Street." Yuriko made us listen to the sound of our steps and she would tell us, depending on the quality of the swoosh sound, if it was correct or not! There were no pretenses! It had to be real! Same thing with the breadlines walks. You really had to have your pelvis driving you and carry your weight forward. Heavy! A feeling of carrying all the sorrows of the world on your shoulders. In one of the first versions of the first breadline, our arms were closed in front of our head, which was looking down. Later on Yuriko changed it and everybody ended up unraveling and opening their arms in different positions, always depicting a state of hunger, struggle, desperation, homelessness.... Pretty soon I learned that just trying to do these steps correctly was not enough, you had to psychologically put yourself in that particular situation and portray it in your very own personal way. (Prosperi 2017, interview)

Aside from providing insight into Yuriko's teaching methods, Prosperi's comments help us begin to explore the changes that Yuriko made to the original as she worked, adding her own nuances to make the piece more meaningful. According to Miki Orihara, also a former principal dancer, Yuriko "watched [Bryan's] film and used some movement, quality, [and] formation but changed [the dance] with her own creativity. She modified movements from the film" (Orihara 2015, interview). Former company dancer and current régisseur, Lone Kjaer Larsen was in the Martha Graham Ensemble when Yuriko reimagined "Steps." She recalls: "I remember how difficult it was to do the jumps (from parallel to turn out)! I also remember some issues with the music. When Yuriko finished her reconstruction, we showed it to Martha, and Martha liked it and wanted the company to perform it. Soon...each of us taught our role to someone in the company" (2016, interview). Larsen[9] further commented:

> I have been looking at the 1991 (Yuriko's original) version of the piece, as well as the 2004 and 2015 versions. When we performed the piece in the early 1990s, the ballet stood "alone"—by itself. At the end, the Leader would continue her movement back and forth as the lights faded out. It was very powerful this way, and the piece was a complete "crowd pleaser" on tour. Later, when "Steps" became part of the larger piece [*Sketches from Chronicle*], the end of "Steps in the Street" was changed: The lights stayed on and the leader would continue on stage in silence...so as to make a connection into the next section of the larger piece. This changed the piece completely. (Larsen 2016, interview)

In addition to the changes Yuriko made, there are two arguably controversial elements to Yuriko's work. First, Graham was not part of the rehearsal and reimagining process of the dance by her own choice because she trusted Yuriko; however, she did see and approve the final version. Also, the original Wallingford Riegger score was not found; rather, another Riegger score, composed for Doris Humphrey's piece *New Dance* (1935), was utilized. Yuriko worked closely with Sussman on the reimagining of "Steps in the Street." Yuriko recalls the reasons for some of these challenges in recreating the piece and for some changes such as the score:

> "Steps in the Street," I believe, there was a complete film which was transferred to video. I cannot remember if there was sound on the film or if I

constructed it in silence. After looking for many hours in Martha's archives and storage, I could not find the original score by Wallingford Riegger, and so I asked Stanley Sussman to find suitable music by Riegger that would fit the dance. He found "New Music," which was commissioned by Doris Humphrey, which was unknown to me, and I was happy to have music that I could use. Later on after I left the company, they found the original music. However, the company did not use the original score, because everything would have to be restaged.... This was set on the MGE July–September 1989, and set on the MGDC in April 1990. (Tokunaga 2008, 179–180)

An interview I conducted with Yuriko (2016, interview) imparted invaluable information regarding her reimagining process. She relayed that she researched the 1930s and the Great Depression, capturing images of masses of hungry people waiting on the 'breadline' for food. She said she had to add choreography before the music began because "Steps in the Street" begins with the 'silent walks'—individuals moving backwards slowly, shifting their weight backwards as if catching oneself from falling. With the body in a contraction and the upper back in a twisted rotation, using the 'spiral', eyes are cast downward. There is a sense of despair, and hunger. One body begins from upstage, and other bodies move onto the stage, catching the shift of weight of the first dancer. Yuriko decided that this group of 'silent walkers' would open the dance, and a solo figure would repeat this movement, but alone at the end. She explained the importance of bringing the historical context to movement choices in the dance. She recalled: "After the silence [end of dance], I had to add the solo section as a person who is hungry as everyone else, but she does not want to belong to the group, there is some reason that she is there ... necessity." This figure serves as the leader of the group.[10]

Yuriko then continued to shape my imagination with other images that inspired her creative choices in reimagining the group work. She commented: "An image that I used...we used to have [in the 1930s] the 3rd Avenue El.[11] There was darkness at night underneath it, there were a lot of homeless people wandering around.... Everyone knew each other but were not friends." This inspired Yuriko to create the 'silent walks'. She described her process regarding making the work current for the dancers: "I use current life...those images in the newspaper and show [the dancers]."

So much goes into recreating a lost work, and so whoever is leading the work must make many choices throughout the process. Such choices, of course, impact the transmission and reception of the work, and have implications on several levels within Graham's legacy. For example, former dancers who are undertaking reconstructions recall different things about the dance and have different experiences while dancing it. Artistic directors may make stylistic changes, such as to choreography or costuming,[12] once the final draft of the work is done. The reconstruction, as for most dances with multiple performances, shifts to fit the moment and reflects the ideas, experiences, and desired outcomes of all those involved in the production. However, there are also issues of plain and simple practicality when a work has already been performed as part of the repertoire. Changes cost money, effort, and time with a season otherwise devoted to keeping the public interested with new work.

2002 Restaging of Chronicle

As stated earlier, I was part of the Graham Company when *Chronicle* was restaged in 2002. Rehearsing *Chronicle* with then-co-artistic director, Terese Capucilli, created indelible memories for me. Both "Steps in the Street" and "Prelude to Action" contain movement that expresses extreme devastation, unity, and strength within the masses: we responded to this outcry for justice with flexed feet, our fists in the air then slamming down onto our thighs, warrior-like. We burst onto the stage, jumping with our legs in scissor-like action, running through the space with our chests held up high. Our movements were assertive, and we could feel the tension of muscles as the tension between the masses (groups of dancers) versus the individual (soloist) (Fig. 6.4).

I found this movement vocabulary to be both potent and transformative from a personal as well as an artistic perspective. The emotional context of the work was especially vivid for me because of my proximity to the horrors of 9/11 in New York City. Burke (1937) notes of "Steps in the Street" specifically "the marching of men without cause, without direction, self-destroying—is a movement that is at once a dance of despair, death and mourning," and when I performed this after my experience on 9/11, I definitely felt a sense of mourning. I also understood that the depth of Graham's movement material was unique in the manner in which she organized her gestures and how these gestures require a particular control of breath. I do not think Graham meant to show us where we have been; she meant to change the world—to make us reflect, think, and transform, as she did in her choreography. She wanted us to

Fig. 6.4 Author Kim Jones (left) with Fang-Yi Sheu (center) in dress rehearsal for *Chronicle*'s "Prelude to Action," coached by Artistic Director Terese Capucilli, Joyce Theater, NYC, 2003. Photograph by Christophe Jeannot

breathe. This is the vein of Graham's philosophy that animated our process. *Doing* Graham technique, therefore, is a method for researching her past dances. It is well documented that Graham created the technique for the purpose of teaching people how to dance her work. As her work changed, so did her technique. For example, Yuriko often acknowledges that Graham's ideas about movement were continually changing. The purposes for the vocabulary changed with each new piece/era (Goodman 2016, interview).

During my time with the Graham Company, the women's rehearsals included "Steps in the Street" and "Prelude to Action" almost on a daily basis from my first day in the company to my last. I remember the first time I heard the music for "Prelude": we were matching our new learned movement phrases to the music. The music was so powerful, driving, and beautiful. We were coached not only by Terese, but also by dancers who were in the original reconstruction, such as Alessandra Prosperi, Elizabeth Auclair and Miki Orihara. I specifically remember

Alessandra working with the dancers in the 'pops' section, and she recalls: "I saw us dancers as a union of powerful, strong women, finally seeing the light and dancing in the hope of a better future!" (Prosperi 2017, interview) During my tenure, there were four dancers in this section including myself. The 'pops' section comes about half way into the dance and shows four women who are moving away from the rest of the group, and creating a wall of resistance and unity. The member of this new smaller group, the four 'pops,' move in unison but into individual spaces, expressing the anguish and hardships of the times. As any dancer understands, unison in a group is difficult to achieve. Hours of repetition deepen the attunement between dancers, tighten rhythm, coordinate breathing, and solidify spatial awareness so that four bodies move as one. It is Graham's technique—how we each exercised core muscles to create shapes that moved with the shift of weight in space—that allowed unison to not only evolve, but to instantiate a specific Graham sense of unity with each performance. This process of transmission as an embodied archive led to a successful revival of this dance on a universal and timeless theme (Figs. 6.5 and 6.6).

My memories of this time include experiences both on and off stage about rehearsals, performances, and personal reflections. It seems the past can only be experienced from the present, and for me what remains indelible is the precision of directional changes, floor patterns, the percussive action of the body in order to drop to the floor and then rise with an extended high leg, past the ear on the side of the body to a drop again in Graham's fourth position. I also remember my personal research and thinking about women's rights, racial injustice, the Great Depression, and life between two World Wars in 1936, all of which gave me a personal, historical context for the work. I found that my traumatic experience of living in New York during 9/11 provided a real, visceral experience with which I chose to link the dance to my mind and body for performance.

2006 AND 2015 RESTAGINGS OF "STEPS IN THE STREET"

Unlike other popular performance genres of the time—like vaudeville and romantic ballet—*Chronicle* focuses neither on scenarios nor ethereal characters; rather it focuses on the human condition and how real people relate to issues of social justice and human welfare. The challenge for a historical restaging such as "Steps in the Street" was to help current

Fig. 6.5 Blakeley White-McGuire in rehearsal for the "pops" section of *Chronicle*'s "Steps in the Street," 2005. Photograph by Christophe Jeannot

performers gain perspective into the worldview of Martha Graham in 1936 while also making the dance relevant to its 2006 Italian cast/audience and then again in 2015 for the cast/audience in Charlotte, NC.

In 2006, I was invited to restage "Steps in the Street" for the Arke Compagnia d'Arte, Turin, Italy. At that institution, the dancers study baroque, ballet, and modern dance (Graham, Horton, Humphrey) techniques and styles. From the outset, the enthusiasm, passion, and hard work of these dancers to engage in an intense rehearsal period was impressive. The focus of the rehearsals, therefore, was on the style, shape, and intention behind the movement. I shared with them the 'tool kit' from the Graham resources, which includes photos, videos, floor patterns for each dancer, and notation of counts. Because I was still performing this work as a Graham Company member, the dancers also had a 'living'

Fig. 6.6 Author Kim Jones (right) with dancers Yuko Suzuki Giannakis (center) and Erica Dankmeyer (left) in dress rehearsal for *Chronicle*'s "Prelude to Action," Joyce Theater, NYC, 2003. Photograph by Christophe Jeannot

reference point in terms of how the movement should be performed. Due to a language barrier, I was able to use sound—expressions of breath—to assist with my teaching. For example, when one fully exhales, the body collapses in the torso, and then the body rises again on a deep inhalation. This changes the body's position, shape, and level in space. I used sounds to demonstrate the speed of the feet during the jump section. I discovered that you cannot count one to eight in Italian without falling behind the beat in English (uno, due vs. one, two—that gives you 2 extra beats!). I recall that I asked the dancers to find either current events or dig into their historical past to link the percussive movements, 'silent walks', and movements in unison to connect to the choreography. These dancers thought of economic issues, because Italy was in the midst of a depression. When they were asked to walk backward, we tapped into feelings and fears of the unknown.

For the 2015 staging of "Steps in the Street," the cast members were my students from the University of North Carolina at Charlotte. In order to examine the social context of the original performances, we found invaluable books, reviews, and articles about the working and living conditions in America in 1936, when *Chronicle* was first created. The work's creation occurred between the two World Wars, among the rise of fascism, existing racial prejudices, labor strikes, and the Great Depression, which of course resulted in mass unemployment and great social hardships. We studied images and activities of labor and struggle of the working class and the poor. Also, we examined how the US government created the Public Works Administration that organized the Federal Theatre Project (1935–1939), which funded new, modern dance works. These actions changed the face of American dance and theater. We also looked at the events of the early 1990s when the reconstruction took place, and we looked at current and historical events over a span of 80 years. Cast members and I discussed how modern dancers and choreographers of the 1930s, other than Martha Graham, responded to cultural issues using their work, such as Helen Tamiris's "The Individual and the Masses" (1935) and Jane Dudley's "Time Is Money" (1934). These two works speak to the working middle class in New York City, and the hardships of the daily life of industrial workers.

The 2015 cast also connected current events such as the Black Lives Matter movement across the USA, the Arab Spring, the Syrian war, ISIS terrorism, and the refugee crisis to what they were experiencing in Graham's choreography from 1936. Just as in the 1930s, class struggles still abound, as demonstrated by the 'Occupy' movement in 2013, which included international protest movements against social and economic injustices, such as the government bailout for banks and fighting for tax equity. We also discussed the multiple power struggles in various nations during the Arab Spring, including antigovernment protests, uprisings, and armed rebellions that spread across the Middle East in early 2011. The dancers began to understand how the movement might have felt in the body in the 1930s compared to the way it does now. We weaved historical context with different movement phrases, movement shapes, pauses, focus of the body and head, and the use of the Graham technique to find the expression of devastation, solitude, exile, homelessness. We worked on finding the intention, quality, and texture behind the movement. As an ensemble of performers, we worked on finding a way to convey a message that is similar to the original one from the 1930s but also reflects current issues of solidarity and fighting against injustices.

THE POLITICS OF TRANSMISSION: WHOSE WORK?

The staging of past dances, in the context of the Martha Graham Dance Company, seeks to connect audiences with the scope of Graham's prolific artistic life. Additionally, the performance of such work serves to confirm the significance of the current company within an historical lineage of American modern dance. Martha Graham and, after her death, the Graham Company acknowledged her earlier works, such as *Heretic* (1929), *Celebration* (1934), Panorama and *Frontier* (1935), *Chronicle* (1936), and *Deep Song* (1937), as a body of legitimate, reconstructed, and reimagined Graham pieces for performance and these became a part of the official repertory within the Graham legacy. These reconstructed and reimagined works contain the embodied gestures of dances past, and also contribute to the canon of American modern dance. They are also fundamentally acts of respect for one of the most influential dance artists of the twentieth century.

At the same time, it is important to recognize that current dancers, régisseurs, and scholars/artists find their own professional identities and practices, and through interacting with Graham's movement vocabulary, performance practices, and a body of dances and attendant traces thereof. In my work dealing with Graham's dances, for example, I use different labels—reimagining, reconstruction, or restaging—to signal different relationships to dances. I call my scholarship for *Imperial Gesture* a *reimagining* since so little source material of the original work was available.[13] The process of reimagining, then, contains a great deal of my own artistic vision. To *reconstruct* a Graham piece is to reset her past work in the present with performance qualities that resemble the original choreography as closely as possible, but not exactly, because a complete record of the original work is likely not available. To *restage* a Graham work is to set past repertoires on contemporary dancers. A restaging is conducted by a régisseur who is either a current or former member of the Martha Graham Dance Company. A régisseur continuously seeks to connect current dancers and audiences with the scope of Graham's prolific artistic life. Both a reconstruction and a restaging of a Graham dance produce performances that have already become part of American dance history (Fig. 6.7).

My research for *Imperial Gesture*, for example, has been disseminated in a number of ways.[14] In some cases, especially in my work with professional dancers, I reimagine dances that may exist only in memories,

Fig. 6.7 Blakeley White-McGuire in Martha Graham's *Imperial Gesture*, reimagined by Kim Jones at the Knight Theater, Charlotte, North Carolina 2013. Photograph by Jeff Cravotta

images, reviews, costumes, or music. In the practice-based research work of reimagining and restaging dances, embodied knowledge and lived experience become the resources and scholarly/artistic lenses through which I understand information and ideas developed from archival research. Creative, collaborative, and pedagogical methods are employed to recreate the dances on living bodies and to make these experiences meaningful for dancers and collaborating artists and for audiences. For professional dancers, I also use these methods to create new dance works that rely on modern dance traditions. In work that I undertake with students, I stage choreography that I know well, and that also has thorough documentation and video records.

In all of this work, the questions I pursue include: What about the past am I trying to capture and convey? How can I present historical movement practices, images, and ideas in ways that can be understood as history but also as contemporary performance? What meanings, past and present, are available in this material? How can I employ my own knowledge to make these meanings clear for dancers and for audiences?

Aside from transmitting meaning and intention from the past to present-day audiences, there is a desire to preserve the past in some way. Preserving one's past is part of the nature of all humans, but artists especially so. For example, Burke (1937) noted that Wallingford Riegger, the composer for *Chronicle*, "wants American capital to do something about preserving 'such distillation of sheer beauty, such economy yet wealth of means, such mastery of technique, clarity of thinking' which he ascribes to Martha Graham's work. Otherwise, the appreciations, as is usual in such cases, fall into the category of the purely personal, ecstatic and useless." Riegger realized that the worst fate for an artist would be to fall into the realm of the forgotten and useless, and he wished for more permanence for Graham's work. It is Riegger's realization that motivates my practice-based research. I endeavor to bring Graham's experience of the past forward into our current world. The ephemeral delicacy of dance escapes us when the curtain comes down. If only I can capture a sense of Graham's experience of our humanity, the movement I reimagine may reveal a fragment of her expression once more.

CONCLUSION

The artists who work to restage/reconstruct/reimagine past choreographies are not acolytes; rather they are researchers/scholars, dancers/performers, choreographers, archivists, and collaborators. It is precisely the experience of dance making and performing that informs this kind of work and moves the régisseur, director, or researcher quite literally, toward a process rather than a product. Fundamentally, a process of this kind requires a back and forth between past and present in a process that conjoins what is embodied and what is/has been transmitted about the work, its creator, and its current recreator. Transmission, perspective, and interpretation in any dance creation and performance includes a constant reshaping of the work through embodied experiences of those who, collectively, endeavor to bring the possibilities of the past into the present. The processes of restaging/reconstructing/reimagining make visible the many layers of relating what is possible from a past with the multiple choices and resulting relationships that bring the work into the present as a 'new' dance. Transmission, and the power it directs, is a process that provides unique opportunities for honoring what should be guarded vs. creating within a tradition in flux. Martha Graham's creative life and legacy provide us with masterworks that can and do inspire dancers, artists, designers, researchers, and audiences through time. More importantly for me, as a Graham dancer, the Graham legacy also models how, through transmission and collaboration, masterworks remain exciting sites for knowledge of both the past and present.

NOTES

1. According to the Martha Graham Resource Director, Oliver Tobin, there are approximately fifteen to twenty Graham company dancers currently doing this work.
2. As noted by the contemporary critic Owen Burke (1937), "Martha Graham's *Chronicle* follows the tradition of *Imperial Gesture*. It is a brilliantly ambitious choreographic development that has for its subject matter the imperialist World War and a *Prelude to Action*."
3. The reconstruction was supported by a University of North Carolina at Charlotte Faculty Research Grant. The work received its premiere in January 2013 at the Knight Theater in Charlotte in a performance by former Martha Graham principal dancer Blakeley White-McGuire presented by the College of Arts + Architecture. *Imperial Gesture* had its New York City premiere at the Joyce Theater in February 2013 and is now part of the Martha Graham Dance Company repertoire.
4. It premiered at the University of North Carolina at Charlotte on September 30, 2016, followed by multiple performances at the 92nd Street Y in New York City in December of the same year [see the review by Macaulay (2016)]. (The Taylor organization confirmed that I am the

first person to reconstruct one of his 'lost' dances [Correspondence with Thomas Patrick, March 2017]).

5. In 1994, the three sections that were reconstructed and premiered at Brooklyn Academy of Music (BAM) in 1994 were called "Sketches from *Chronicle*" (Martha Graham Dance Company 1994).

6. The program notes from the 1994 reconstruction of *Sketches from Chronicle* read: "*Chronicle* does not attempt to show the actualities of war; rather, by evoking war's images, it sets forth the fateful prelude to war, portrays the devastation of spirit which it leaves in its wake, and suggests an answer" (Martha Graham Dance Company 1994).

7. The Fine Arts Bill, or the Federal Art Project (1935–1943), was part of a New Deal initiative to fund works of visual art. It was meant to employ artists, not necessarily to further the arts. See Kennedy and Larkin (2009).

8. Yuriko danced with the Martha Graham Dance Company (MGDC) between 1944 and 1967. Graham invited her back in1980 for workshops and reconstructions of works. Following conversations with Graham in 1982, Yuriko established and was director of the Martha Graham Ensemble (MGE) from 1983 to 1992. She was Rehearsal Director of MGDC from 1984 to 1991 and Associate Artistic director of MGDC from 1991 to 1992. Reconstructions/Recreations: For the MGE: Heretic, Celebration, Panorama, Steps in the Street (*Chronicle*), Primitive Mysteries. For MGDC: Primitive Mysteries, Every Soul is a Circus, El Penitente, Dark Meadow, Canticle for Innocent Comedians, Secular Games, Salem Shore, The Eyes of the Goddess.

9. Larsen was preparing to teach "Steps in the Street" in the workshop class at the Graham School.

10. In an interesting example of reconstructors' different interpretations of Graham's original intention, Larsen (2017, interview) recalled: "I always thought that the solo figure was there just to offer another perspective on the loneliness and alienation…. She is of course so clearly ignored by the other women as they walk by her on the diagonal crossing."

11. The Third Avenue elevated subway line was one of four elevated train routes that ran across 2nd, 3rd, 6th, and 9th Avenues in Manhattan. They were demolished between 1938 and 1942.

12. According to Graham Company principal dancer Miki Orihara (2016, interview), regarding changes to works: "As a work goes, over the years, movement and quality were changed by directors/dancers. As for 'Sketches…,' the ending was changed to fit into the transition. When the company perform it as a single work, not many people know about the ending timing, so I tried so many times to maintain what Yuriko did, but it is hard to fight so many times, so the curtain comes down at

the different timing." Regarding changes to costuming, Orihara (2016, interview) recalls, "in this section, the Center figure's costume keeps changing red to white back to red and white with black lines...then settle. We, as the chorus, had a bib—a white bib...that was not good. So we took it off pretty much on the second performance. Then it became just all same as 'Steps.'"

13. See Jones (2015) a full account of my process for reimagining *Imperial Gesture*, and how little was available to begin the process.

14. The reimagining of *Imperial Gesture* premiered in January 2013 at the Knight Theater in Charlotte in a performance by the Martha Graham Dance Company (MGDC) presented by University of North Carolina at Charlotte's College of Arts + Architecture. *Imperial Gesture* had its New York City premiere at the Joyce Theater in February 2013 and is now part of the repertoire for the MGDC. I performed the solo at the 92nd Street, YM-YWHA in New York City for the American Dance Guild and for the Fridays at Noon series Historic and Significant Female solos, at the 2014 Transmission Symposium in London and at the Framing Justice: Modernism and Social Advocacy in American Visual Arts and Dance 1920–1945 at Loyola University Chicago in October 2016. I have delivered papers and presentations at conferences and gallery events such as the South Eastern Colleges Arts Conference, the National Dance Education Organization (NDEO), and Art Fusion at the Mint Museum. Video and audio recordings of rehearsals and transcribed interviews were disseminated on social media sites and other digital platforms including http://imperial-gesture-2013.tumblr.com/.

BIBLIOGRAPHY

Armitage, Merle. 1937. *Martha Graham*. Los Angeles: Lynton R. Kistler.

A Dancer and an Educator on Fascism. 1937. *Dance Observer*, March. https://www.loc.gov/resource/ihas.200154357.0. Accessed 4 Aug 2017.

Bohm, Jerome D. 1936. Suite Features Martha Graham Dance Program. *New York Herald Tribune*, December 21. Library of Congress. https://www.loc.gov/item/ihas.200153992/. Accessed 4 Aug 2017.

Brinnin, John Malcolm. 1942. *The Garden is Political*. New York: Macmillan.

Burke, Owen. 1937. The Dance. *New Masses*, January 12. Library of Congress. https://www.loc.gov/resource/ihas.200153996.0. Accessed 4 Aug 2017.

———. 1938. Martha Graham: Revolutionary Dancer. *New Masses*. February 22.

Burnshaw, Stanley. 1935. The Dance: Five Dancers and Fourteen New Works. *The New Masses*, December 10, 27. http://www.unz.org/Pub/NewMasses-1935dec10-00027:27. Accessed 4 Aug 2017.

Capucilli, Terese. 1996. Piece written for Stanley Sussman's memorial. *MG Center for Contemporary Dance*, October 28.

Douglas, Paul. 1935. Modern Dance Forms. *New Theatre*, November.

Franko, Mark. 2006. Dance and the Political: States of Exception. *Dance Research Journal* 38 (1/2): 3–18.

Graff, Ellen. 1997. *Stepping Left: Dance and Politics in New York City, 1928–1942*. Durham, NC: Duke University Press.

I.K. 1936. Martha Graham Offers New Dance. *New York Sun*, December 21. https://www.loc.gov/resource/ihas.200153986.0. Accessed 4 Aug 2017.

Ignatin, Irving. 1935. 'Revolutionary' Dance Forms. *New Theatre*, December.

Jones, Kim. 2015. American Modernism: Reimagining Martha Graham's Lost *Imperial Gesture* (1935). *Dance Research Journal* 47 (3): 57–69.

Kennedy, Roger G., and David Larkin. 2009. *When Art Worked: The New Deal, Art, and Democracy*. New York: Rizzoli.

Macaulay, Alastair. 2016. Review: Paul Taylor's 'Tracer' Recalls a Dance and an Artist. *New York Times*, December 18. https://www.nytimes.com/2016/12/18/arts/dance/paul-taylor-robert-rauschenberg-review.html?_r=0. Accessed 4 Aug 2017.

Main, Lesley. 2017. The Transmission–Translation–Transformation of Doris Humphrey's *Two Ecstatic Themes* (1931). In *Transmissions in Dance: Contemporary Staging Practices*, ed. Lesley Main. London: Palgrave Macmillan.

Martha Graham and Dance Group. 1935. Carnegie Hall Program 1935–1936, New York, NY, December 15. Library of Congress. http://lcweb2.loc.gov/diglib/ihas/loc.natlib.ihas.200154332/default.html. Accessed 4 Aug 2017.

———. 1936. Guild Theatre Program, December 20. Library of Congress. https://www.loc.gov/resource/ihas.200153984.0/?sp=1. Accessed 4 Aug 2017.

Martha Graham Dance Company. 1930. *Martha Graham*. Metropolitan Theatre, Seattle WA, June 2. Library of Congress. http://www.loc.gov/item/ihas.200153697/#about-this-item. Accessed 4 Aug 2017.

———. 1994. *Radical Graham*. Directed by Ronald Protas and Diane Gray. Brooklyn Academy of Music, Brooklyn, NY, September 28–October 9.

———. 2012. Graham 2.

Martha Graham Dance Program Wins Applause. 1928. *NY Herald Tribune*, April 23. https://www.loc.gov/resource/ihas.200153316.0. Accessed 4 Aug 2017.

Martin, John. 1935. Martha Graham Wins an Ovation. *New York Times*, November 18. Library of Congress. https://www.loc.gov/resource/ihas.200153879.0. Accessed 4 Aug 2017.

———. 1936a. Martha Graham in Dance Recital. *New York Times*, December 21. Library of Congress. http://lcweb2.loc.gov/diglib/ihas/loc.natlib.ihas.200153985/pageturner.html. Accessed 4 Aug 2017.

———. 1936b. Martha Graham and Her Group Present Second Program of Season at the Guild Theatre. *New York Times,* December 28. Library of Congress. http://lcweb2.loc.gov/diglib/ihas/loc.natlib.ihas.200153993/default.html. Accessed 4 Aug 2017.

McCausland, Elizabeth. 1935. Modern Dance Takes Another Step Forward. *Union,* August 6.

Morgan, Barbara Brooks. 1980. *Martha Graham, Sixteen Dances in Photographs.* Dobbs Ferry: Morgan & Morgan.

Rhodes, Russell. 1936. Graham Dance Hailed at Guild. *New York Telegraph,* December 22. Library of Congress. https://www.loc.gov/resource/ihas.200153990.0.

Selections from the Martha Graham Collection. 2015. Library of Congress. http://lcweb2.loc.gov/diglib/ihas/html/marthagraham/marthagraham-home.html. Accessed 1 Aug 2015.

Tokunaga, Emiko. 2008. *Yuriko: An American Japanese Dancer: To Wash in the Rain and Polish with the Wind.* New York: Tokunaga Dance Ko.

Watkins, Mary F. 1929. [Review]. *Dance Magazine.* July. Library of Congress. https://www.loc.gov/resource/ihas.200153353.0/?sp=1. Accessed 4 Aug 2017.

Interviews/Communications

Terese Capucilli—personal communication/email. January 24, 2017.

Deborah Goodman—personal communication/email. November 22, 2016.

Ellen Graff—personal communication/email. February 10, 2017.

Lone Kjaer Larsen—personal communication/email. November 21, 2016.

———. personal communication/email. March 11, 2017.

Miki Orihara—personal communication/email. May 10, 2015.

———. personal communication/email. November 21, 2016.

Alessandra Prosperi—personal communication/email. March 14, 2017.

Yuriko—interview with the author. New York, December 2, 2016.

CHAPTER 7

Transmitting *Trio A* (1966): The Relations and Sociality of an Unspectacular Dance

Sara Wookey

INTRODUCTION

Trio A, a dance made in 1966 by Yvonne Rainer, is a dance that I somehow always felt I knew. Not that I knew the movements or how to execute them, but I understood the dance on a conceptual level. Texts such as Yvonne Rainer's "The Aesthetics of Denial" in *Terpsichore in Sneakers* (Banes 1987, 41–54) stuck to my memory in a way that other texts about other dances did not. The movements seen in Banes' 1978 film of the dance could also be felt in my body. Those weighted swinging arms, the tapping foot, the head turned to one corner or the other, the general lack of 'look at me' attitude that, for me, as a trained dancer of hybrid forms of Post-Modern dance and this thing called 'release-technique' seemed so tangible, so absolutely do-able. Then, in an unexpected turn, I began learning the dance from Rainer in an impactful stretch of time in my career. What I thought would be a somewhat speedy dance learning experience turned into sixty hours of dance labor over the course of three months in a studio in Los Angeles, California. I sweated my way

S. Wookey (✉)
8 Cliff Road, Flat D, NW1 9AN London, UK
e-mail: info@sarawookey.com

© The Author(s) 2017
L. Main (ed.), *Transmissions in Dance*,
https://doi.org/10.1007/978-3-319-64873-6_7

Fig. 7.1 Sara Wookey performing *Trio A* (1966) at VIVA! Art Action Festival, Montreal. 2011. Photograph by Guy L'Heureux

through the arduous task of learning a dance in which nothing except walking repeats, only right angles and curves are allowed as directional shifts, and juxtapositions of various body parts are expected to be executed with a kind of evenness and unfaltering quality (Fig. 7.1).

The dance focuses on the body. The body moving, dancing in silence, with no specific costume, no designed lights, objects nor narrative. The body moving in time and space. Rainer, now just over eighty, keeps moving and making new work while her dances of the past endure the test of time. More on that and my role in the dance remaining in existence later, but first some context on the dance and its maker.

Rainer emerged as a choreographer as part of the Judson Dance Theater, a collection of young artists, including dancers, composers and visual artists, among them Trisha Brown, Lucinda Childs, Douglas Dunn, Simone Forti, David Gordon, Steve Paxton, and others, who worked out of a church space in Greenwich Village in New York City (NYC) in the early part of the 1960s. The collective grew out of a composition class taught by Robert Dunn, a musician who had studied with John Cage. Many of the dancers, some having already studied with Anna

Halprin in San Francisco, also studied with Merce Cunningham and Martha Graham in NYC at that time. They experimented with everyday movements such as walking, standing and running in order to break free of the conventions of modern dance that demanded expression, narrative, virtuosity and spectacular gestures. They were highly influenced by the visual arts movements of that time and collaborated with artists such as Robert Rauschenberg and Robert Morris.

In an interview in 2016 for *WHO CARES? Dance in the Gallery & Museum*, Rainer describes a fluidity between the dance and visual arts community in New York City at that time:

> My generation were more integrated with the art world. Our ideas came out of art world ideas such as Minimalism and Pop Art. We were conscious of coming out of a more embraced and cohesive avant-garde. The visual artists were dancing and performing with the dancers. The artists who were a part of Judson, with the exception of [Robert] Rauschenberg, were not that well known or successful yet. All that seemed to change in the 80s and 90s. Now these worlds seem much more separate and autonomous than they were back then. (Wookey 2015, 59)

This was a time when Cunningham was collaborating with contemporary musician and personal partner John Cage, whose chance procedures and working with an unmodulated, atonal approach to making music was appealing to choreographers searching for something different in dance. Claiming that silence could be considered music, Cage set the stage for dance to also experiment with what else dance could be. This approach influenced Rainer's work and her making of *Trio A*, a dance approximately four-and–a-half minutes long, performed in silence and consisting of a series of ongoing movements. There are no recognizable rises and falls of movement, no climaxes where the movement gathers itself, hits a top edge and then resolves itself. It is a continuous phrase of movement that has been evened out and is unmodulated.

Trio A is not an easy dance, by any means, to learn and perform. The actual rigor of its choreography and labor involved in performing it can be confusing to those learning the dance as it looks easy-to-do. Within minutes of my transmitting *Trio A*, the person learning it (both dancers and non-dancers alike) often show surprise in regard to the dance's complexity that will demand much of that person's physical and mental energy in order to 'get it'. As unspectacular as it is, this is a dancer's dance. What I mean by that is the dance demands a committed focus and mental capacity that is attractive to the dancer trained to work in a way that demands presence of body/mind.

Although the dance was made at a time when dance artists, such as Rainer, were being influenced by Minimalism it is not, in my experience, a minimal or pedestrian dance. What may be considered minimal or pedestrian, however, is found in the dance's pacing or use of time. It is a dance built by a series of complex sequences done in an ongoing manner. There are no stops or pauses, only one long movement phrase that stops only when the last movement is executed: a quiet touch of the right foot, relaxed and balanced on the toes, behind the left foot while the body faces the back corner, eyes looking into the palms of the hands clasped on the left side of the body and standing in proximity to where the dance began.

The movements themselves feel anything but minimal or 'everyday'. There are usually 2–3 movements happening in the body at once and unrelated to each other. They sometimes reference or cite other dance forms including classical ballet, Cunningham or Graham technique. Every reference is altered in some way so as to render it recognizable yet slightly off. One example is the balletic 'coupe' where, traditionally, one foot is pointed behind the other, ankles touching lightly, Rainer turns the foot back and into a sickled position and pointed the other way around while it wraps itself around the other foot. In another example, where a fifth position might occur in ballet, she turns both feet inwards, almost mockingly. It is a dance commenting on dance, a critique, a question. *Trio A* is also a thinking dance. It comes from the mind of a choreographer intent on making the dancer and its audience think about what else dance can be by citing and disturbing dance techniques, questioning dance as it was then and prompting a consideration of what it might be and, eventually, become.

Trio A is an iconic work and 'paradigm shifter' in dance. It is arguable that many choreographers, such as Meg Stuart, Anne Teresa De Keersmaeker, Jérôme Bel, and Boris Charmatz have been highly influenced by the work of Rainer and her cohorts of Judson Dance Theater. *Trio A* played a part in heralding in a Post-Modern period in contemporary Western dance that no longer assumed the dancer had to be well trained, of a particular shape, size or weight. Nor did dance have to be visually pleasing to look at because many of the movement sequences in *Trio A* are absurd and to some extent unpleasant, such as collapses in the chest where the chin goes up and the mouth hangs open.

It took Rainer six months to create the dance. In her words, she "worked doggedly every day, accumulating tiny bits of movement" (Rainer 2006, 266). *Trio A* was first seen in a performance called *The Mind Is a Muscle, Part I* that was performed at Judson Church on January 10, 1966. On April 29, 1966 *Trio A* became the first section of a 40-minute version of *The Mind Is a Muscle* at the "Now Festival" in Washington D.C., and the evening-length version was performed at the Anderson Theater in New York City on April 11, 14, and 15. After that, when the larger work was no longer performed, *Trio A* was on its own. It was in a kind of hiatus when Rainer turned to film in 1972 until Sally Banes produced the film of Rainer dancing the work in 1978. Some time after that she taught it to the first of its transmitters, Pat Catterson. It would be, today, considered open source data, and primarily because Rainer insisted this be the case at the time. As the choreographer of the dance, she gave it away. Anyone could perform or teach it. I will speak later on in this chapter to Rainer's change of mind and her more current insistence that the dance be executed to a degree of correctness and be passed on only by one of five certified transmitters, including myself.

As part of the program of *The Mind is A Muscle, Part 1* at the Anderson Theater in 1968 Rainer wrote a one-page statement clarifying her love of the body, despite the rather non-communicative approach in *Trio A*. In her statement she says: "The choices in my work are predicated on my own peculiar resources—obsessions of imagination, you might say—and also on an ongoing argument with, love of, and contempt for dancing. If my rage at the impoverishment of ideas, narcissism, and disguised sexual exhibitionism of most dancing can be considered puritan moralizing, it is also true that I love the body—its actual weight, mass and unenhanced physicality" (Wood 2007, 4).

Trio A has taken on many variations, including some by Rainer herself such as *Trio A Pressured*, in which one person runs around attempting to catch the gaze of the performer who is dutifully following the choreographic instructions never to look at the audience. At one point I developed my own version (with permission from Rainer) called *Trio A Unplugged*, in which I perform the dance while speaking the names of the movements used by Rainer when learning it from her. I also had the opportunity of performing the dance alongside Rainer at the Hammer Museum in Los Angeles under the title we chose: *Trio A: Revisited and Reversed*, as part of the conference *Dancing with the Art World* (April 26 and 27, 2013). She performed a "revisited" version which she also personally referred to as the "geriatric version"[1] and I performed the dance starting on the opposite side, doing all the movements in a mirrored fashion to their original. This version consisted of changes to the original in which Rainer, instead of performing the handstand in the dance simply yelled out "handstand!" when the time came. In this way Rainer's and my versions of *Trio A* existed as individual entities in and of themselves while also passing across and overlapping each another as our individual adjustments and timings fluctuated and merged; each dancer suggesting a mirror-like image of the other and out of sync.

It is important to note here that the dance's pacing is based on the very first movement performed by the dancer. The swinging of the arms in the first move of the dance determines the pacing, or timing, of the movements being performed for that particular dancer and for the remainder of the dance. In other words, one should be able to track back to the original timing of that first move three minutes into the dance. In this way the dancers, when performed by two or more, will always fall out of sync and each carries the responsibility of holding their own timing, like an internal metronome. Imagine seeing the dance being done by its originator and one that recently learned it some forty-odd years later. Those overlaps and differences must have been intriguing for those interested in the lineage of a dance, the attempts at archiving it in the body and the slipperiness of holding a dance together over time, and of the living, breathing, dancing archive.[2] As one of the five transmitters now living in the UK (the others are based in the USA) I co-carry the task of maintaining this Post-Modern legacy of dance.

BECOMING A *TRIO A* TRANSMITTER

While earning my Masters of Fine Arts degree at the University of California, Los Angeles I told my professor, Susan Foster, of my then distaste for performing dance to the point of calling it perverse. Foster promptly responded saying that I should go study with Rainer and followed up with saying something to the effect that in her mid-thirties Rainer once felt the way I did. Without hesitation, I followed Foster's suggestion. That was in 2006 when Rainer had just moved to Los Angeles from New York City and was teaching a course called 'Approaches to Performance' in the Art Department at the University of California, Irvine. By this point in her career Rainer had come back to dance making after working as a filmmaker and was engaged in making new choreographies. To my surprise, what I thought would be my exit from an art form with which I had become disenchanted evolved into my own unexpected return to dancing, through studying with the woman who turned dance on its head. After completing the course with Rainer she agreed to work with me as an advisor on my Master of Fine Arts committee (advisory board). Over a period of five years our mentor/mentee relationship included lunches, walks in Downtown Los Angeles, sitting at her dining table in her Silverlake home talking, dinners out and seeing performances together. This is all to say that by the time I asked her over a lunch of bacon, lettuce and tomato sandwiches at a diner in Los Angeles if I could learn *Trio A* to teach it, I had established both a professional relationship and friendship with her. I knew that I wanted to embody, finally, a dance that I felt I had known conceptually for so long, to pass it on to others and to continue working with this legendary choreographer and, now, friend.

I was 'certified' by Rainer as a *Trio A* transmitter in 2010. At the time I was not aware that she had certified dancers to teach it. I do remember distinctly saying that I would be the fifth and last dancer to be certified by her. The term 'transmitter' emerged in a conversation we had, much later, when I showed her a graduation certificate of my grandmother's. It was from her elementary school completion and was nearly the size of a dining room table. I was prompting a discussion about what 'certified' might mean in the context of *Trio A* and asked her, if there was a paper document, what it would say. She replied without hesitation, "Transmitter of *Trio A*". My guess is that 'transmission' is more suitable for someone, like Rainer, whose language is detailed and to the point. A word such as 'translate' might suggest too much allowance for misreading or interpretation.

While working with Rainer and learning the dance, one thing that struck me was the precise and consistent verbal language she uses to describe movements and intention. Her language references historic dance forms and choreographers such as, "allow the ballet arm"; and "the Martha Graham walk"; as well as metaphor, adjectives and imagery "like hammering a nail" and "like rocks on the end of a string". It is this kind of information that, for me as a dancer and now transmitter of the dance, provides the backbone of it. Rainer's language supports the correct delivery of the movements, points to what is important to her about her dance and how she wants it to be performed. I can only compare this astute approach to language used to teach movement to the ancient form of Iyengar yoga in which words are selected carefully in order to produce a certain quality or use of the body—for example, 'extend' is used, never 'stretch'.

In order to capture this language, in conjunction with the physical movements, I have created a set of approximately 100 index cards that contain hand-drawn illustrations and words in the form of quotes from Rainer and my own descriptions that accompany the illustrations. This personal notation system[3] also reflects an organization that consists of four tiers of information in the dance: the physical movements, the spacing, the gaze, and the pacing, each of which is addressed as a separate, but overlapping system. It is this obsessive note taking that can be helpful for taking a dance into the future. It is to assist in the memory of a dance over time and for the generations of people to whom I will transmit it (Fig. 7.2).

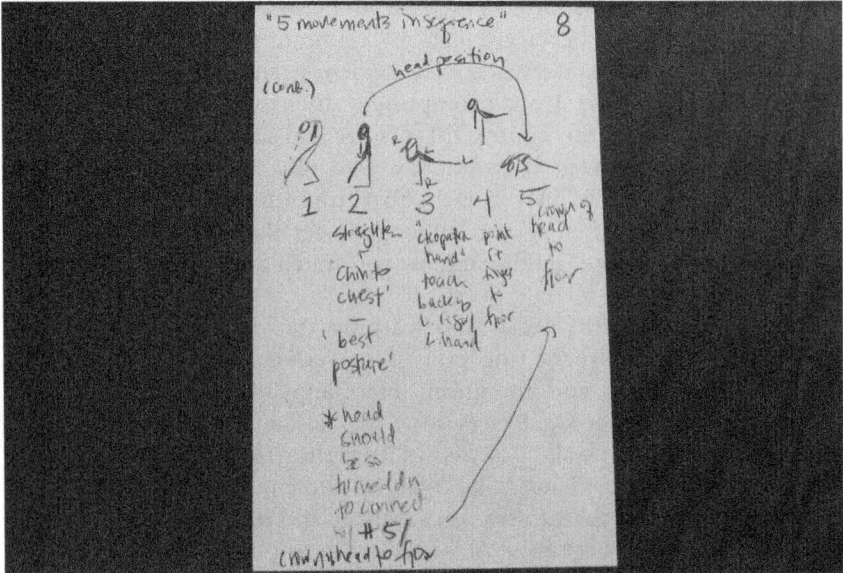

Fig. 7.2 Sara Wookey notation of *Trio A*

On Transmitting

There are currently three tools for transmitting *Trio A*, only two of which have Rainer's approval—the Labanotation score and the certified transmitters. As mentioned earlier, there is also the film of the dance directed by Sally Banes in 1978, twelve years after *Trio A* was first performed. Rainer has made it very clear to me that the film is not to be used as a tool for learning the dance because it contains several notable mistakes, such as more bending in the knees and slightly different uses of the hands and arms in particular places.

When I teach the dance, either to individuals or in a workshop setting, many participants express their interest in learning the dance in the way that I did. They want to embody a dance they have known conceptually for so long and that has been a large part of their own artistic education and influence on their practice. There is a difficult-to-describe sensation when learning, for the first time, the opening moves of *Trio A*. It can be best described as a surge of recognition that travels into the body. There is an 'a-ha' moment of getting something physically that has, for so long been understood only outside of the body, comparable, perhaps, to finally tasting a bite of enticing food that has been sitting in front of one for a very long time.

Each time I fly somewhere to transmit the dance I have this very poetic feeling of bringing information in my body, a dance embedded in my muscles and bones, a vessel carrying information, history and stories. My teaching of the dance is also enhanced with anecdotes from my time working with and befriending Rainer and of my own experiences of learning and transmitting this dance. A dance is not an isolated endeavor, it emerges from the choreographer's taste and approach to making. A dance also emanates from a personality, a subject, whose politics and ethics are real and embedded in their work. Rainer, for example, is straightforward, dependable and possesses a special kind of humour that appreciates the absurd in the mundane. I think these qualities can be seen and felt in her dance. The more I pass on *Trio A* to following generations of dancers and artists, the more I realize how intertwined the dance is to the subjectivity of its maker, my story of coming to be a transmitter of the dance and my relationship with its choreographer.

The anecdotes and stories that I share about working with an icon of Post-Modern dance are as valuable to the learning process as the transmitting of the dance movements. This is because of access to sharing what has not been written down—oral traditions that contribute to a whole experience and history that a dance is holding but cannot fully express. These personal experiences highlight the more personal connections that dancers and choreographers often have. As I evolve in my practice of carrying the dance forward my methods remain constant, yet the nuances of my approach become more visible, and include a lot of sharing and talking in between the dancing.

In her book, *The Mind is a Muscle* (2007) Catherine Wood describes the transmitting of *Trio A* as an "expandable person-to-person thread that can travel, via mind and body, through time" (2007, 93). Passing on a dance to different sets of dancers is like a role being passed down across generations of ballerinas by the older masters, a carrying of the torch in the name of dance's legacy. Perhaps it is a reminder that the arts can still be about mastering something, about putting in the labor, the rigor, and the time, and trusting the next generation of practitioners to carry the torch. Only out of that kind of dedication can one taste what it means to be a part of a process of mastery and of oral history, trust, tradition, and the living archive (Fig. 7.3).

Fig. 7.3 *Trio A* (1966) tune-up with Yvonne Rainer and Sara Wookey at FADO performance Art Centre. March 22, 2015. Photograph by Henry Chan

As part of that process, each dancer that engages with the dance belongs to the evolution of it. It is a celebration of doing together as a group, collective experience and being a part of dance's legacy. It is about passing down experience and knowledge as well as a sense of importance, value and weight. As one recent participant and dancer, Coral Montejano Cantoral (who took part in my *Transmitting Trio A* workshop at Greenwich Dance Agency in July, 2016), shares:

> I do feel in these days [of the workshop], "Wow, I am doing something really important." I feel this week is not like any other weeks in my life when I am learning [just] any phrases. I feel something is happening. I definitely feel it's important. I mean, I don't know how much I think about Yvonne [Rainer], because of course for me it's not like Sara [Wookey], she knows her and she is her friend, while I only know her from video, but I definitely feel that we are learning a dance that has a lot of value.[4]

Another perspective comes from dramaturge Martin Hargreaves, when he observes:

> I am thinking about *Trio A* as a thing that is not me at the moment, but is also not not me. I am in dialogue with this thing, which is outside of myself, and that's what I like. I am trying to make this thing happen. It's not coming from inside of me, it's already there. I am activating it, but I am definitely also encountering myself.[5]

Rainer's original insistence that the dance be available to anybody wishing to perform or to teach it—something which may pose some confusion for those who want to learn the dance today—sets up an awareness of *Trio A* as intended in 1966. Many are not aware that Rainer, at one point in her career, said that she saw a *Trio A* she did not recognize. In a more current concern for the legacy of her dance, she stands by the model of body-to-body transfer. The way to learn it is to engage one of the five transmitters to work in the studio together for between fifteen to thirty hours.[6] I sometimes face a group of performance and visual artists not trained in dance who are eager to learn *Trio A* but discover that it is incredibly hard to do, and their efforts may not be enough for them to be successful in performing it.[7] It is in these moments, as well, that talking within the social exchange of the studio becomes necessary.

One recent example was in Toronto, where I was working with a dedicated group of performance artists (and a few dancers) organized by FADO Performance Art Centre. Early on in the one-week process I consulted with Rainer by email. She was in New York City at the time but flying out to work with the group so that the artists had the chance to meet and rehearse with her before they performed the dance at The Art Gallery Ontario (AGO). I discussed the possibility of presenting, not a performance of *Trio A*, but a more process-based showing of the ongoing work of transmitting the dance, a rehearsal, per se, and title it *Transmitting Trio A*. I suggested this because the majority of artists in the group, despite their incredible efforts and will to learn the dance, would not be ready to present a cohesive *Trio A* for a public performance that was up to Rainer's standards.

What emerged from this challenging situation was a series of discussions between Rainer and myself, followed by the artists and myself, and, then, between Rainer and the artists. When Rainer arrived in the studio in Toronto the atmosphere was somewhat nervous and unknowing. There had been a series of conversations about what performing in AGO might mean and I had wanted, in this instance, to default to Rainer to help make the difficult decision of how to present dance in this context. Whether Rainer was aware of the mood in the room or not, she did something very socially intelligent in the first few moments: she turned to me and invited me to dance *Trio A* so that we could do, what she calls, one of our regular 'tune-ups'. This 'tune-up' is her way of checking in on the status of the dance by the transmitters who carry it forth. I had done several 'tune-ups' with her in the past but never in front of those to whom I was currently transmitting the dance, and this was a perfect way to make visible something I was trying to communicate in words: that I am also in a process of always locating the dance in my body, and that there is no means to an end. This experience of doing a 'tune-up' for the group achieved several other things:

i. It leveled the room and equalized experiences for I, too, was an ongoing student to this master dance. The only difference was that I had the support of my dance training knowledge and many, many hours of rehearsals of the dance behind me.
ii. It revealed the rigor and difficulties of what looks like an unspectacular and easy-to-do dance.

iii. It introduced Rainer as expert but one who also asks questions to her transmitters—as she did that day—to confirm particularities of the dance, claiming her own vulnerability to human memory and that this business of keeping a dance intact is to be done by a select few while it is also, to some extent, a collective action.

At the end of that day of rehearsing we all gathered for drinks around the table, Rainer in between the participants, engaged in convivial exchange with the group—artists talking with artists after a day of work. *Transmitting Trio A* went off as a well-received event at AGO and opened up new possibilities for sharing the dance through a pedagogical framework for a public.

PHYSICALLY PREPARING, EXCHANGE AND LIVENESS

As a transmitter I have come up with a rigorous, very physical starting movement practice based on repetition, spatial orientation and easy-to-remember movements that do not demand much in terms of memory but quickly and directly get the body warm, pliable and ready to move. The patterns of movement are influenced by the work of Irmgard Bartenieff and the practice starts with the dancer lying on the floor. It then moves those same physical patterns (upper-lower, side-to-side, and diagonal/cross lateral) into the vertical and through the space, repeating them across the floor in an ongoing manner as influenced by the Body Weather.[8] Having studied both Bartenieff at The Ohio State University and Body Weather with Katerina Bakatsaki and Frank van de Ven in Amsterdam, I find the combination of these techniques important for the orientation of one's own body, as well as through reperforming patterns known from one's early development. Only then do I feel that my own body and, I am guessing here, the bodies of the participants in the workshop can tackle the arduous learning experience of piecing together and remembering a dance of unfamiliar and heady sequences. In my experience *Trio A* asks for both an orientation internally, or how one body part relates to the other, to be able to execute different movements of different parts of the body at once and to relate to the space.

Then the passing on of the dance begins and has different stages of experience for the participants. The participants, in their newness to the work, begin to negotiate the challenges of learning the complex sequencing of the dance. They attempt to inhabit the moves, repeating and repeating them with the intent of similarity and with an approach of copying. They may question whether they are going to make it and show signs of slight discontent with the dance not being as easy to learn as they had anticipated. Then, around day three, I witness the individuals in the group begin to own the material. Not that they have ownership in the practical sense but that their bodies begin to settle into the material of the work and they begin to become more familiar and comfortable in it. There is a shift in their interest–they are determined to 'get it'. They want to digest as much as possible and then practice what they have learned. There is also an interest and an eagerness to reach the end of this dance that, although only four-and-a-half minutes (approximately) in length, takes a week, or longer, to learn.

When those learning it reach the end of the dance they often feel elated and there are spontaneous cheers, high-fives and clapping. This celebratory arrival has more to do with the sensation of having made it to the end of a very long and demanding journey, like a mountain climber upon reaching the summit after so many days of uphill, continuous action. More than that, and particularly for the generations of dancers I work with,[9] it is about engaging in a learning process that is both mentally and physically challenging. It is also that the dance belongs to another era of dance making, of craftsmanship, that they have witnessed in books, films and imagery but now embody and feel. They know the dance in a new way and, through my having transmitted it to them through physical and aural means, they also have a taste of the experience, albeit mediated, of working with Rainer.

To return to an earlier point, for me, it is the collaborative mix of movements, memory and anecdotes that make up an exchange across generations and keeps dances alive. My role as transmitter moves beyond the transfer of physical memory and knowledge and onto a platform of exchange that includes my experiences with Rainer as dancer, choreographer and friend. It moves us beyond nostalgia for the final dance product and into the realm of subjectivity, narrative and interpersonal exchange, of the dance's sociality, or a way of connecting through a common interest and want for dancing and lived experience.

This view may open up possibilities not only for the exchanges between the unique relationships between dancer and choreographer but also offer insight into the world of an artist who lived and worked during a different socio-economic time. This might tell us what making dance means at different periods; how different historic moments allow or hinder dance making and how dance reflects the times. In order to talk about Judson, for example, it seems appropriate to also talk about the socio-economic conditions that existed during that period that allowed the work that was being made by the Judson artists. This includes the low cost of living in New York City at that time. To engage those narratives in my role as transmitter and with the participants makes possible new spaces for social and political understanding through a process of learning a dance (Fig. 7.4).

One of Wood's main arguments is that *Trio A* is a dance of social interactions. Wood claims that Rainer created certain forms of social relations and by doing so reimagined social ways of being alone while together. Rainer, according to Wood, does this by structuring acts of labor within her choreographies wherein dancers may be dancing together yet there are no instructions to interact, make eye contact or connect through temporal or spatial relations. Wood suggests that Rainer's *Trio A* "represented a new narrative script for relations between

Fig. 7.4 Sara Wookey co-teaching with Yvonne Rainer as part of *Trio A in 10 Easy Lessons* at University of California, Irvine. 2010. Photograph by Scott Klinger

people" (2007, 23). Wood talks about the literalness of the dance and believes that Rainer's work questions the very foundation of any true relationship through a consideration of authenticity and representation (ibid., 57). She discusses the social currency that dances such as *Trio A* have, situating that next to a discussion about more autonomous operations of art in order to make the claim that *Trio A*, through its "images of social relations", challenges other images as part of a consumerist agenda (94). According to Wood, Rainer considered the relations between image, social interaction and work and directed her dancers as workers. Wood suggests that *Trio A* is also a "fine art object" at the same time, "artistic practice can no longer revolve around the construction of objects to be consumed by a passive bystander" (11). Wood goes on to write, "Rainer made dances that she called 'objects' representing 'work', but—deliberately—did not make any salable product" (20).

Perhaps, as Wood suggests, there is a conflict between art as idea and art as object. I think this is particularly important when considering dance. As a transmitter of a dance that broke boundaries within the field as an idea, I may well be teaching the dance in an object-like way. I will try and unpack that thinking. However, first I want to say, in contrast, that when I transmit this dance—and as I have made claim—I am passing on the ideas behind the dance, the theory, and how those ideas impacted the trajectory of contemporary dance as well as more personal anecdotes and stories of my working with Rainer and who she is as a person, as a thinking, dancing being. At the same time, I am passing the dance from my body to others in a way one would pass an object. The object is a relic, a piece to be treated with care and consideration, one that holds value. It is also an idea, a dance, that brings people together in a conscious and very focused period of time. In that space is work/labor and care.[10] These ideas are also described by dance theorist Randy Martin, as referenced by Wood, when he discusses Rainer's work in Marxist-socialist terms concluding that, "[i]n the face of all-consuming market rationality, a movement that has no other purpose than to allow people to gather to reflect on what they can be together is perhaps the supreme figure of an ongoing desire for socialism" (Lepecki 2004, 62). Within the discussion of consumption and economy, Wood claims that *Trio A* is an "'editioned' artwork taught person-to-person as a kind of code" (2007, 93). She says that this passing of a dance from one to the other is an exchange that transcends a conventional economy. On one hand, Wood suggests that *Trio A* proposes new ways of being together by, on some level, not engaging and that it moves beyond the object-based market place art has become.

In getting back to the sociality of *Trio A* I suggest, while transmitting the dance to the participants, that they get on with the business of dancing while the audience gets on with the business of watching, and remind them that they just happen to be in the same space. This instruction, I believe, was passed down to me from Rainer and was part of her way of transmitting her ideas. I remember thinking at the time I was learning *Trio A* that my assumption of 'successful' relationships when seeing a couple at a restaurant, for example, was based on how much the two people interacted through talking and engaging. Now I think—after working with Rainer—that a couple at a restaurant not interacting but simply sitting quietly together and eating might signal 'success' in terms of togetherness, of just being together.

In my own research and writing[11] I aim to unpack where and how dance is situated in the museum and challenge the tension between how dance, such as *Trio A*, and as Wood argues, is an art form making available new modes of togetherness. At the same time Claire Bishop, in her book *Artificial Hells* (2012), suggests that dance may also repair the social bond even while potentially falling into the realm of art object coveted by the museum and consumed by its visitors. This tension underlies my research and will contribute to what are still gaps in the area of critical thinking about dance, performance, subjectivity, relations and art object.

I am interested in going back, now, to Wood's discussion of how dance might be intervening in an economy within the art market. She argues that "*Trio A*'s existence in material form (i.e. as dance) is also founded upon a network of relationships that enables its transmission. Rainer's insistence, however, on the importance of detailed one-to-one teaching prevents the work's acceleration to hyper-dissemination in any familiar technological sense" (Wood 2007, 100).

In my experiences of working with Rainer, I have come to believe that she is quite aware that by claiming *Trio A* is best learned by hiring one of the transmitters (and that the video is inadequate and also, to some extent, the Labanotation score[12] of the dance) there is a feeding back of work to dancers in the dance community. I earn money teaching her dances. I do not make my living doing this but it produces income that is part of what sustains me as a practicing artist. This feeding into the paying of live work for dancers in the field is important to note. Should the dance be learned by video on YouTube, transmitters would be out of work—and such a version would not be anything like Rainer's intention. Should an institution own the dance, the entire structure of how we, the five transmitters, operate and the negotiations[13] we each make individually with the organization and institutions we engage with would be highly mediated by that institution.

If this were to happen (thankfully, I do not see it as a possibility given Rainer's continued stance against it) questions around methodology, subjectivity and value would certainly emerge. The fact that Rainer's choice of who transmits her dances came out of one-to-one professional and personal relations she has with each of us speaks volumes to the value within dance of interpersonal connection. Let's not lose that in our attempts to preserve dance's past as we continue in the journey of dance making, transmitting and liveness.

NOTES

1. Rainer first performed a solo version of *Trio A* called *Trio A, subtitled Geriatric With Talking* at Judson Memorial Church in 2010.
2. A documentation of this performance can be seen at: https://hammer. ucla.edu/programs-events/2013/04/dancing-with-the-art-world-day-2/.
3. I created this set of note cards when initially working with Rainer in Los Angeles and completed them while I was her Teaching Assistant at the University of California, Irvine when co-teaching *Trio A* with her as part of her course *Trio A in 10 Easy Lessons*, taught as part of the curriculum in the Fine Art Department.
4. From an interview with Vanessa Michielon as part of my project *reDANCE*.
5. Ibid.
6. Rainer claims, based on the ten-week course *Trio A in 10 Easy Lessons*, that we co-taught at University of California, Irvine for two years when I was her assistant, that it takes approximately thirty hours to learn the basic movements and fifteen additional hours if the dance is to be rehearsed for performance.
7. Rainer only feels comfortable that a public presentation of the dance be done by those capable of fulfilling the dance's demands to a degree that renders it recognizable and does it justice.
8. A way of training and performing that was developed by Min Tanaka and investigates the intersections of bodies and their environments. I have been influenced by one component of the training called 'MB' (mind/body, muscles/bones). I borrow loosely from the training which I have adapted to my technique class and as a way to prepare the body for

dancing. I always aim to give credit to my teachers as I also make clear to my students that my class is inspired, in part, by the training (as well as other techniques) but is not representing Body Weather.

9. Most participants in my workshop are between the ages of 20 and 40.
10. The area of interest in caring for dance is the subject of my book *WHO CARES? Dance in the Gallery & Museum*. London: Siobhan Davies Dance, 2015.
11. http://sarawookey.com/blog/.
12. *Trio A* was Labanotated by Melanie Clark and Joukje Kolff at Greenwich Dance Agency in 2004.
13. Rainer leaves the transmitters to contract our own transmitting work via our network and make our own contracts and agreements. She has written up a contract that the participants learning *Trio A* sign and, should any money be charged for the performing of the dance, Rainer requires a minimal royalty fee from the venue.

BIBLIOGRAPHY

Banes, Sally. 1987. *Terpsichore in Sneakers*. Middletown, CT: Wesleyan University Press.

Bishop, Claire. 2012. *Artificial Hells*. London: Verso Books.

Dancing with the Art World. 2013. Hammer Museum. Los Angeles (April 26 & 27). https://www.youtube.com/watch?v=iUZwqB6P4Fc. Accessed 9 Aug 2017.

Lambert-Beatty, Carrie. 1999. Moving Still: Mediating Yvonne Rainer's 'Trio A'. *October* 89: 87–112.

Lepecki, André (ed.). 2004. *Of the Presence of the Body: Essays on Dance and Performance Theory*. Middletown, CT: Wesleyan University Press.

Rainer, Yvonne. 1974. *Work 1961–71*. Nova Scotia: Press of the Nova Scotia College of Art and Design.

———. 2006. *Feelings are Facts*. Boston, MA: MIT Press.

———. 2014. The Aching Body in Dance. *Performance Art Journal*, 3–6. Boston: MIT Press.

Wood, Catherine. 2007. *The Mind is a Muscle*. Boston, MA and London: Afterall Books.

Wookey, Sara (ed.). 2015. *WHO CARES? Dance in the Gallery & Museum*. London: Siobhan Davies Dance.

Interview

Vanessa Michielon in conversation with Coral Montejano Cantoral and Martin Hargreaves as part of *Transmitting Trio A*, a workshop at Greenwich Dance Agency in July 2016.

CHAPTER 8

Silent Transformations in Choreography— Making Over Time: Rosemary Butcher's Practice of 'Looking Back and Ahead'

Stefanie Sachsenmaier

Between 2014 and 2016,[1] British choreographer Rosemary Butcher actively engaged with the extensive archive of more than 40 years of her choreographic practices, including live works as well as films, which she presented in various formats, such as timed events or installations in performance spaces, galleries and alternative sites. But 'looking into the past' had already formed an important part of Butcher's creative processes. Choreography-making is a complex undertaking that may be understood as always involving aspects of past practice—not least in terms of the professional practitioner's past experience, including previously unresolved materials or abandoned ideas which can, in many instances, become an impulse for making a further 'new' work. Yet, as I proceed to demonstrate and discuss in this chapter, through carrying out research with Butcher for a decade, I was able to witness various ways in which engaging with past events—both her own past choreographic works as well as in one specific instance the work of another

S. Sachsenmaier (✉)
Middlesex University, London, UK
e-mail: S.Sachsenmaier@mdx.ac.uk

© The Author(s) 2017
L. Main (ed.), *Transmissions in Dance*,
https://doi.org/10.1007/978-3-319-64873-6_8

artist—informed the choreographer's thinking in the making of new work.

The focus on 'transmissions' in dance practice, with which the present publication is concerned, provides a curious perspective on Butcher's creative practice. The *Oxford English Dictionary* (OED online) lists the following definitions of the verb 'to transmit':

– Cause (something) to pass on from one person or place to another
– Allow (heat, light, sound, electricity, or other energy) to pass through a medium
– Communicate or be a medium for (an idea or emotion)

These definitions seem to me to resonate throughout Butcher's choreography-making and in this chapter I explore the complex ways in which Butcher engaged with the past in three selected creative processes between 2010 and 2015.

In the first instance, as part of a commission by the South Bank Centre for Butcher to 'reinvent' American artist Allan Kaprow's seminal first Happening—entitled *18 Happenings in 6 Parts*—Butcher engaged for the only time in her choreographic career in a creative process instigated through a direct engagement with another artist's completed work. Since the new work was described and framed as a reinvention of Kaprow's earlier work from 1959, the creative processes entailed did allow for this 'reinvention' to have unique and original characteristics—as one might have expected of the choice of Butcher to fulfill this commission. Kaprow died in 2006, which meant that Butcher could only access the different materials left in the artist's archive. In the event Butcher allowed for aspects of Kaprow's work to be 'passed on' into her own piece—*18 Happenings in 6 Parts 1959/2010*—which was performed in 2010 at the Clore Ballroom in London's Royal Festival Hall. Such a 'passing on' is a curious notion, to which I return in some detail below.

In a second act of transmission, and within a larger project of creating a retrospective of her works, Butcher engaged in processes that led—and would further lead—to presentations of works from her archive, alongside the creation of new choreographic works. In 2015 two retrospective exhibitions took place—a first one at the Bohunk Gallery in Nottingham, UK, as part of NottDance 2015, and a second, and larger event, at the Akademie der Künste (Academy of the Arts) in Berlin, Germany, as part of the *Tanz im August* Festival 2015. These featured materials from her extensive archive of choreographic works spanning several decades—including recorded film footage of live works, photographs, program notes, posters, cards, choreographic films and notebooks. Forming part of the retrospective event in Berlin, Butcher's *SCAN*, created in 1999 and subsequently further developed, was presented once again. In 2015 Butcher refrained from making changes to the work, and aimed to reassemble the original cast; apart from one dancer who was replaced, she was able to rehearse and present the work again some fifteen years after its first performance. Here the second definition of the verb 'to transmit', in describing a process of "[a]llow[ing] (heat, light, sound, electricity, or other energy) to pass through a medium" (OED online) seems to me to be curiously pertinent: the framing of the larger event focused on remembering past practice provided another framework for the work to be experienced anew.

In a third instance, I address Butcher's final[2] live choreographic work, entitled *The Test Pieces*. The third dictionary definition of 'to transmit' listed above—"Communicate or be a medium for (an idea or emotion)" (OED online)—is particularly pertinent. Butcher developed three versions of *The Test Pieces* with different casts, with the final version presented as part of the retrospective event in Berlin. In what follows I outline how the new work was created alongside her active engagement with her own archive, and how the past was addressed in Butcher's creative focus and through her interest in modern architectural ruins.

I further address the concept of transmission specifically in relation to Butcher's investment in times past through her consideration of what 'remains'—both in the form of past works, her wider archive and her interest in architectural ruins, as well as how what remains is processed and presented in the present. My concern throughout this chapter is Butcher's processes of choreography-making, rather than an interpretation of the public performances themselves, and the chapter includes materials from three different rehearsal processes. Crucially, Butcher's voice is represented throughout by the inclusion of fragments of her thoughts gathered at various stages of her creative work, stemming from interviews and recorded rehearsals. The discussion of her creative processes, however, is kept necessarily tight in this chapter whose wider focus is on the aspects of time, archive and memory that are at stake in her choreographic work. In this regard I draw on the areas of art history and philosophy, and specifically include the writings from American art historian George Kubler as well as French philosophers Jean-François Lyotard and Henri Bergson.

INTERMITTENT WORK OVER TIME

In *The Shape of Time: Remarks on the History of Things*, published in 1962, art historian George Kubler discusses the construction of time in the particular field of history making: "The historian composes a meaning from a tradition, while the antiquarian only re-creates, performs, or re-enacts an obscure portion of past time in already familiar shapes. Unless he is an annalist or a chronicler the historian communicates a pattern which was invisible to his subjects when they lived it, and unknown to his contemporaries before he detected it" (Kubler 1962, 13).

Patterns pertaining to the past as well as the activity of pattern making, according to Kubler, is what historians are concerned with in their work. In highlighting a distinction between the concerns of the antiquarian and historian, the latter's activity is here described as productive and creative in that it leads to new knowledge about past events. What emerges further from Kubler's conception of time is that there are patterns pertaining to the present, which however are invisible to the subject at the time of living: what is felt to be entirely new, in the present moment, is likely nonetheless to be already patterned by, and to 'carry' its past with it.[3]

What artists experience in (at least experimental) creative processes seems to be relevant here in that indeterminacy is at stake throughout a process with regard to a variety of parameters—often but not always implicit and/or tacit—which pertain both to the past and to the future. 'Dance'—and whatever we understand that classificatory term to mean at any time—is an established category of knowledge (and knowledge practices), and in this sense it is both historically determined and repeatedly redefined; and it is difficult, as a consequence, to avoid the suggestion that 'dance' is conventionally and institutionally determined, however it is experienced at the moment of making by the innovative practitioners involved. The past presents possibilities for connections and resonances of new works, the details of which tend to be discovered *after* the emergence of new work. Making sense of a process after its completion, and creating links between present, new works and previous undertakings and patterns in past practice is a widely shared concern for creative practitioners. The orientation towards the future in artistic practice does bring 'newness' into the frame but arguably also informs the established practice of restagings, where we see new ways of conceiving past works, providing new parameters for understanding the past.

On these sorts of bases I would argue that Kubler's discussion of the construction of time in history making offers insights into the ways we might understand relations to the past as well as patterns apparently at stake in creative practice. Plainly, however, the work of the art historian and the choreographer is not comparable as far as ways of working and the nature of insights are concerned: the first is discursively complex and critical-analytical in its agenda and tends to test different written accounts, one against the other, bringing new perspectives to bear upon already-existing accounts of the past; its processes and insights can cast light on the other, but not explicate the choreographic. The choreographic agenda and its processes are different and its capacity to critique quite different areas of knowledge is limited. This point is important in the context of the growing area of research into and through artistic practice: there is a need in this context to highlight the danger of a retrospective theorizing of creative practice, as though it were already theorized at its source and in its making. To retrospectively theorize may lead to distorted understandings of what is actually at stake for the practitioner at the time of making a work.[4] It is equally important to highlight a crucial difference between the critic and the artist him/herself in terms of how this looking at and 'making sense' of past events is exercised. A critic will tend to focus on the artistic outcome, while a practicing artist is driven by a channelled investment into his/her past work with a view to making further, new work. Susan Melrose has discussed in various publications[5] our need to acknowledge the constitutive differences between the work of the 'expert spectator' and her or his 'expert practices', on the one hand, and the work of the 'expert practitioner' who creates the work: differences in perspective, in temporal and spatial orientation, in process, in decision making and in the models of intelligibility and judgement that apply to these very different activities.[6]

In *The Shape of Time* Kubler further discusses various "shapes of time" and in this context highlights a specific criterion that he deems necessary to distinguish between historical time and biological time. While the latter is marked by "uninterrupted durations of statistically predictable lengths" (a 'life lived', for example), he ascribes to historical time the characteristic of being "intermittent and variable:" "Every action is more intermittent than it is continuous, and the intervals between actions are infinitely variable in duration and content. The end of an action and its beginning are indeterminate" (Kubler 1962, 13).

In the present context of Butcher's construction of her own history in choreographic practices, together with aspects of transmission of past key works into differently and present-timed contexts, my own interest was caught by the ways that Kubler describes historical time and specifically his use of the term 'intermittent' in its definition. Sharing the same Latin root as the verb 'to transmit'—'mittere' translates into English as 'to send', 'to let go'[7]—the verb 'to intermit' suggests an activity that takes place at irregular intervals, where something is 'let go' of, *at times*, but recurs or is taken up again and developed, in other instances. It crucially lacks the uninterrupted continuity that Kubler attributes to biological time, and it is here that I see a partial parallel with the creative practitioner who both develops and matures, and develops work *over time*. Kubler, from the perspective of an art historian aiming for adequately 'objective' accounts of the past, conceives certain periods as "clusters of actions" that occur "here and there" and "mark beginnings and endings" (Kubler 1962, 13), and are once again identified in hindsight. A conception of periods entailing 'clusters of action' occurring 'here and there' resonates with the work of professional practitioners in creative practice in that their processes do not tend to be straightforward and linear in time. Butcher's live performance *The Test Pieces*, by way of example and discussed further below, was developed in three different phases from 2014 to 2015, which led to three distinct performances in Munich, Nottingham and Berlin. In each of these phases, which might be seen as 'clusters of action' in Kubler's terms, Butcher investigated ways to abandon her preoccupation with 'form', 'testing' ways for the work to choreograph itself, actively embracing as a choreographer "not knowing what is happening" (Butcher in rehearsals, London 2015). In parts her dissatisfaction with earlier versions left something to be resolved and hence led to a continuing of her investigation and investment into the work in subsequent versions, with an entirely new group of dancers in Berlin in 2015.

Memory at Work

A transmission of something to 'another' implies a process that is not necessarily spatially marked but is crucially conditioned by time. A passage through a medium or from one person or place to another, as well as communication of an idea or emotion (see OED definitions of 'to transmit' above) takes time and is likely to deal with a prior event that is processed and formed at a later stage. Further, memory is involved when dealing with past events in the present, as in the creative process of an artist who addresses and presents a prior work again, or who develops previously unfinished or unresolved ideas in a further version of a given artwork, or a new artwork. Early twentieth-century French philosopher Henri Bergson, in his publication *Matter and Memory*,[8] explores two forms of memory—one pertaining to what Bergson calls imagination and the other to repetition (Bergson 1991). Suzanne Guerlac, in *Thinking in Time: An Introduction to Henri Bergson*, discusses Bergson's seminal publication and in this context provides her own (and in my view better) translation of a passage from the same book: "In concrete perception, memory functions in two important ways. First, it interweaves [*intercale*] the past into the present, such that memory is practically inseparable from perception. Second, it gathers together multiple moments of duration and contracts them into a single intuition" (Bergson in Guerlac 2006, 122).

Bergson's choice of terminology is crucial in allowing us to understand how the creative practitioner might arrive, through engagement with memory of past works made, at a 'single intuition', for a new work, where that single intuition brings together a multiplicity of temporal events. In the case of the creative practitioner's work, what motivates the activation of a memory in the making of a new work? The mature artist is likely to evaluate differently his/her (recall of) past work made, also in line with social and technological change that he/she has lived through.

Previous experience informs present undertakings through memories retained and worked through prior to their reexpression. Memories of past creative practice, in addition, are likely to entail both changing attitudes and judgment towards those past practices, shaped by processes of critical reflection on the works, both in terms of their emergence and their outcome. What is at work here is widely identified as a feedback loop, which suggests a continuous process of introspection, criticism—both personal and external—and reinterrogation. The 'multiple moments of duration' that are contracted 'into a single intuition' in Bergson's terms that constitute the formation of a memory crucially involve evaluative judgments which in turn inform present perceptions and future creative decision making.

In her publication *Relationscapes: Movement, Art, Philosophy*, Erin Manning discusses the ways that movement and thought are related in creative practices, focusing in particular on the concepts of intensity of movement and thought in motion. Manning addresses perception, stating that rather than the "thing as such", it is its "capacity for relation" that we perceive, which has the implication that perception pertains to the realm of an "event forming". In this context Manning refers to the role of memory in such processes and observes:

> A memory is not an unfolding of the bottled past in the neutral present. Remembering is the activation of a contrast that inflects the differential of experience unfolding such that the then is felt as an aspect of the nowness of experience. This is a relational event: it foregrounds the presentness through the past, emphasizing the quality of difference in their contrast. The event of the memory is how it takes form in the present, its hue activated through the contrast past-present, then-now. (Manning 2009, 80)

Memory is described here as a relational event, always taking place in the present, which also creates experience of contrast in relation to a past experience. In creative processes of professional artists, in which the transmission of something prior into the now is at stake, the aspect of relationality is foregrounded and examined, providing new insights not only into the present creation but also in terms of further conceptions of past events.

'Working Through' the Archive

In 1985 Jean-François Lyotard, together with design historian and theorist Thierry Chaput, curated a major exhibition at Centre Pompidou in Paris entitled *Les Immatériaux*.[9] The event sought to construct a history of exhibitions, crucially initiated by a philosopher. John Rajchman, who attended the event at the time, writes in 2009 that the exhibition event had "the distinction not simply of intersecting with philosophical questions, but actually of being the work of a philosopher, arguably even a work of philosophy, even if it was not recognised as such at the time" (Rajchman 2009).

Butcher's practices of choreography might now be understood as extending beyond the many dance works she created, live and in the medium of film, into a number of conceptual fields that encompass a range of ways of doing, seeing and understanding the visual arts. Indeed, a strong focus of Butcher's work in recent years was with how her choreographic practice might extend beyond 'dance', into writing, onto the page as well as into the creation of the exhibition events drawing on her own archive. During the preparation phase of her retrospective at the Academy of the Arts in Berlin, entitled *Rosemary Butcher: Memory in the Present*, Butcher observed: "This archive journey allowed me to undertake my own personal investigation, knitting together ideas of the past with a prospect for the future. For me this investigation is a continuous curiosity and questioning, not knowing where it will lead" (Butcher, exhibition catalogue 2015). In creating the exhibition, questions that needed to be addressed were concerned with the making of a history of contemporary dance in accessing and crucially *re*working materials that were created and presented in the past. For example, what is chosen from the archive and how is it processed? How is the past accessed in the present? Similar sorts of questions were at stake for Butcher in her reinvention process of Kaprow's *18 Happenings in 6 Parts* in 2010, a process that she often described as testing and difficult.

Lyotard identified two different forms of 'rewriting', which Hudek discusses in his chapter "The Affective Economy of the Lyotardian Archive" (Hudek 2016, 13). The French philosopher's focus in this context pertains to a discussion of postmodernity, which he did not conceive as a new age but rather a rewriting of certain aspects of modernity (Lyotard 1988, 202). On the one hand there is a rewriting of what is understood as 'original' material, a 'writing again', as Hudek notes in referring to Lyotard's "Réécrire la modernité". It is "repetitive, memorializing, a literal re-plying of material considered original and more authentic than what came later" (Hudek 2016, 13). On the other hand, however, Hudek refers to a mode of rewriting termed 'revenante' which is marked by the Freudian principle of *Durcharbeiten*, referred to by Lyotard in French as *perlaboration* and rendered in English as 'working through' (Hudek 2016, 13). Lyotard discusses this notion in the chapter "Obedience" in *The Inhuman: Reflections on Time* (Lyotard 1991, 173).

While Lyotard is concerned here with the sphere of writing, his considerations of readdressing past events in the present seem applicable to the wider area of performance making, and in particular in the present context of examining transmissions in terms of the definitions outlined above. As I have suggested, a process of transmitting involves a shift in terms of time as well as context, crucially producing change. Lyotard's distinction between approaches that are marked by repetition and those in which a *perlaboration* or 'working through' is involved, provides insights into qualitative differences in choreographic practice in which an aspect of the past is critically considered and informed by the feedback loop.

18 HAPPENINGS IN 6 PARTS 1959/2010—ENCOUNTER WITH A COMPLETED ARTWORK

Butcher was commissioned to 'reinvent' Allan Kaprow's first Happening as part of the larger exhibition entitled *Move: Choreographing You* at the South Bank Centre in London in 2010, which sought to explore the connections between contemporary dance and art since the 1960s. The event, curated by Stephanie Rosenthal, featured installations, sculptural works, live performances and further materials and activities by a range of artists including Anna Halprin, Trisha Brown, Simone Forti and Bruce Nauman (Rosenthal 2010 and South Bank Centre/Hayward Gallery).

In a public conversation between Butcher and Rosenthal during the event, Rosenthal highlighted the differing disciplinary art forms that were at stake in the reinvention process by a choreographer of the Happening, first created in 1959 by a visual artist in the Reuben Gallery in New York. Kaprow's work, at the time, challenged ready conceptions of art in the contemporary field in proposing a set of actions as an artwork (Meyer-Hermann et al. 2008). Rosenthal stated that Butcher's history of collaborations with visual artists as well as the presentation of her works in visual arts spaces, such as the Serpentine Gallery, Whitechapel Art Gallery and Tate Modern, were decisive parameters to the choice of the choreographer for the commission (Fig. 8.1).

As I previously explored in an article entitled "Reinventing the Past: Rosemary Butcher encounters Allan Kaprow's 18 Happenings in 6 Parts" (Sachsenmaier 2013), as a creative artist Butcher did not aim for a meticulous recreation of Kaprow's Happening. In my research collaboration with Butcher on Kaprow's archive, I observed her searching for points that might allow her to begin to undertake her own journey, rather than focusing on the Happening as it was presented in 1959. As part of the event in the late 1950s, visitors were invited to the Reuben Gallery in New York City's SoHo, and experienced six sets of activities in three different rooms, guided by instruction cards and the sound of a

Fig. 8.1 Rosemary Butcher during rehearsals for *18 Happenings in 6 Parts 1959/2010*, Clore Ballroom, Royal Festival Hall, London, 2010. Photograph by Rocco Redondo

bell to change spaces. Performers played instruments, somebody wound up a toy and set it off, a woman squeezed oranges into glasses and drank the juice, artists Red Grooms, Sam Francis and Jay Milder were painting.

The archive reveals that Kaprow's activities were rehearsed in great detail, to which his meticulous notes testify. The Happening is recognized as the first time that sets of actions became the artwork, while no art object as such was offered for sale.[10]

Butcher encountered a preoccupation, in Kaprow's archive, with the everyday as well as what the American artist termed 'activities', both aspects that caught her attention. In an interview in 2012, Butcher stated:

> What working on the Kaprow [reinvention] really forced me to do was to try and find out what an 'activity' was, to actually *really define* what an 'activity' was, as opposed to a 'dance movement' or an 'event'....[W]as it a combination of both, or was it that an 'activity' had to have a repetitive strain to it, or that it was functional, or that it belonged to another situation? I think that investigation was present during the Kaprow [reinvention] but probably [it] wasn't...necessarily fully achieved at that particular time under the umbrella of *18 Happenings in 6 Parts*. And there are probably many reasons for that. There was probably too much of a previous history to battle with. (Butcher in Sachsenmaier 2012, 272)

Butcher's investigation into working with activities in the way she understood them from her engagement with Kaprow's archive led to a rehearsal process that was markedly different from her established ways of working at the time. Previously, she created a specific aesthetic through her work with the dancers, and it was reinforced through working meticulously in modifying material. The Kaprow reinvention also marked a new beginning after a period of exclusively creating solo works with dancer Elena Giannotti (*Woman and Memory* (2005), *Episodes of Flight* (2008), *Lapped Translated Lines* (2010)). The detail of *18 Happenings in 6 Parts 1959/2010* was largely free of choreographic intervention on the level of detailed decisions of movement, leaving the dancers to create actions through spontaneous response to instructions distributed on cards by Butcher herself who sat in the performance space (mirroring Kaprow who also appeared in his 1959 Happening) (Fig. 8.2).

During the 2010 run Butcher observed that her concern was to "untidy" her aesthetic, exploring how "not to keep it very beautiful" (Rosemary Butcher in conversation with Stephanie Rosenthal 2010). As she explained five years after the event in an interview with Sigrid Gareis

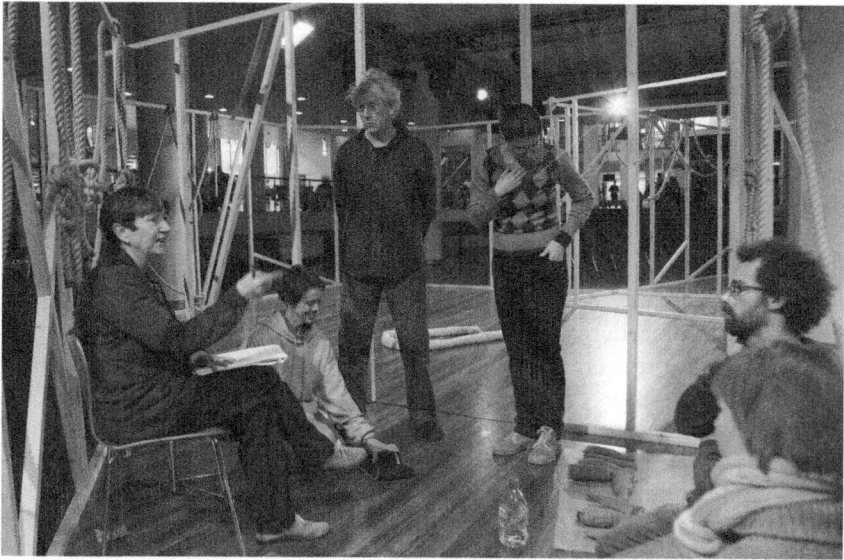

Fig. 8.2 Rosemary Butcher, *18 Happenings in 6 Parts 1959/2010*, Rehearsal Notes, Clore Ballroom, Royal Festival Hall, London, 2010. Photograph by Rocco Redondo

in 2015, she let go of "improving" the performance through identifying specific actions that "should happen":

> What I gained from that working process was that I could let go of some of the aesthetics I was controlling in my work—and that was good for me; it gave a different identity to what I was doing. Like Kaprow's contemporary Jackson Pollock, the energy was in the doing of the thing, not in the finished work. So I became interested in the doing of the movement rather than what it manifests.... Before Kaprow, my work needed to be totally resolved aesthetically in my mind. Now I'm more interested in the idea of things that just maintain their own identity as they are, and not necessarily building up to a completion. I got that from the study and the investment I made with Allan Kaprow. (Butcher in Gareis and Butcher 2016, 31)

If we return to the concept of transmission that constitutes the focus of this chapter, what seems interesting in Butcher's experience of taking on the task of reinventing the completed artwork of a different artist is the ways in which the creative process impacted on her own artistic signature (Melrose 2009) in the sense that she struggled to retain a specific aesthetic and way of working in her choreographic invention. However the idea that something was 'passed on' from one artist to another seems to miss something vital in the process that arguably led to a reinvention of Butcher's own choreography-making, because Butcher herself must be seen as the agent of this process. The use of the passive in 'passed on' does not render the active searching that Butcher undertook, nor does it suggest how certain aspects of Kaprow's practice that resonated for her in a constructive way were appropriated and actioned by her as a way of setting up rehearsals that was new to her at that particular time in her choreographic practice. Here Lyotard's conception of readdressing past events by a process of 'working through' provides useful insights on Butcher's approach to Kaprow's Happening, which was marked by a continual searching for new ways of working. Butcher captures this active search acutely in 2012, reflecting—in this clear example of the working of the feedback loop—that:

> [A]t the beginning, possibly, if you had asked about the reinvention and what I needed, I thought of a strategy to reinvent, but in fact it wasn't until I completed the actual reinvention that I began to understand more about how I could work with a more genuine aspect of reinvention in terms of my own work. And probably when I did the reinvention of Kaprow's work I moved away, too much away, from my own beliefs. And what I am learning now is that I should have stayed closer to my own beliefs. I didn't know what I was looking at, whereas I know that Kaprow knew what he was looking at. (quoted in Sachsenmaier 2012, 270)

The difficulties that Butcher describes here, retrospectively, in work on a choreographic approach characterized by her *not knowing* what she was 'looking at' mirror her struggle to process Kaprow's piece in ways that would allow her to retain her own beliefs. In terms of the brief discussion of memory above, the reinvention process put relationality at the core of the creative undertaking: the piece would bear almost the same title as Kaprow's Happening in 1959—modified slightly but also poignantly by the insertion of the dates 1959/2010, indicating the passage of time and highlighting changes that had occurred over this period. Yet the very idea of the commission set up a particular relationship between

Kaprow and Butcher. Crucially the ways Butcher would engage with Kaprow—and not vice versa—would inform the terms and the detail of Butcher's reinvention: she could not cast him off, for ethical as well as aesthetic reasons, bringing that issue of judgement back into the frame.

Intermittent Work Over Time *SCAN* 1999–2015

As part of the retrospective event at the *Tanz im August* festival, Butcher presented two live performances. In June 2015, alongside the development of *The Test Pieces*, Butcher also re-rehearsed *SCAN* (1999) with a cast that was mostly made up of the dancers who initially created and performed the pieces. Having first been created in 1999 and further developed in 2002, *SCAN* had a pivotal function in Butcher's career and is credited on her website as "[t]he work that was to launch Rosemary Butcher on the international touring circuit" (rosemarybutcher.com, accessed August 6, 2017).

In the making of the piece, Butcher worked with the idea of "looking at the inside of the body from the outside" (Butcher in Butcher and Melrose 2005, 200), inspired by Lisa Cartwright's publication *Screening the Body: Tracing Medicine's Visual Culture*, which deals with medical imaging and specifically x-rays. Susan Foster, writing in *Rosemary Butcher: Choreography, Collisions Collaborations* (Butcher and Melrose 2005), discusses the work as it was presented at the turn of the Millennium and explains that Butcher, during the rehearsal process, asked the dancers to create movement phrases in response to the medical images in Cartwright's publication. Further, Butcher asked the dancers to "mov[e] the bones from one location to another, presenting or connecting them", as well as "holding on to the skeleton" (114). She further observed that "all of the material came from the idea of rebuilding a body, through the joints and the bones. The sense was there that it was a photographic negative as opposed to a positive, which in fact is impossible with a live body" (200).

The choreography is set within a tight square, which is marked out by a lighting installation created by artist Vong Phaophanit. The dancers continually shift and change their orientation between the four viewing sides while carrying out fast-paced movement, marked by repetitious swinging, dropping, bending, circling. The proximity between the performance space and the audience arrangement makes the dancers' breath and effort tangible to audience members.

In 2015, as part of the retrospective event in which *SCAN* was presented again, Butcher described the work in the following way:

> For me *SCAN* was sort of the end of working with a certain language, which was much more technical. But it was also a highly collaborative piece with composer Cathy Lane and visual artist Vong Phaophanit, a Turner prize nominee. He used light to make an installation, and his collaboration is presented as visual art, not as lighting design. And I think that crossover was very important. Also I worked on shifting the space so that the audience was very close to the performance, on four sides. Generally, *SCAN* seems to have left a mark. (Butcher in Gareis and Butcher 2016, 27)

The performance of *SCAN* was directly followed by a film by Vong Phaophanit, which was projected onto the floor of the performance area, presenting fragments of moments that had been recorded during the rehearsal process, in a fast edit of close-ups. Feet move in and out of the camera frame, arms and torsos can be seen, sometimes faces, there are hands outlined by a bright light against a black background and we only get a fleeting glimpse of full bodies. Butcher can be heard giving instructions and feedback to the dancers, on and off, her phrases cut by the fragmented edit; we see glimpses of her sitting on a chair, watching intently. After the live choreography the film, which is presented as part of the work, added an element of "going backwards" (Butcher in Butcher and Melrose 2005, 200). Butcher further states in 2015, reflectively:

> It's about how you perceive yourself, about looking at yourself through an x-ray. It's connected to the interior of the body. So in that way it is quite visceral, very close to the audience. In order to really get the weight, and the sense of exhilaration, and the change in mood and atmosphere, the dancers are always in contact with someone else. There are no solos. Everything is instigated by another person. (Butcher in Jacobson 2015)

There is arguably little to say about the process of re-rehearsing the piece in 2015. Involved were dancers Lauren Potter, Charlie Morrissey, Henry Montes and Rahel Vonmoos, all of whom had been part of the earlier cast, with Jonathan Burrows replaced by Ben Ash, with whom Butcher previously worked in her reinvention of *18 Happenings in 6 Parts*. In rehearsals the dancers watched film recordings from 1999 and meticulously recreated the material. Butcher observed in a 2015 interview regarding the dancers' work: "They're getting it back together from their memory, from their notes and from video. We were rehearsing this week and they could still feel it in their bodies, which was amazing. It took me back in time. This was the last of a series of quite physical, vibrant, technical pieces, which I then moved away from. I do recognise that I made it, but I just can't remember quite how I put it together" (Butcher in Jacobson 2015).

The fast-paced choreography was rehearsed over and over again, and several times I witnessed Butcher giving instructions to the dancers during run-throughs, asking them to keep up the speed, or keeping the small performance space even tighter. Yet the piece was not intended to change in terms of its choreography. Already in 2005 Butcher had observed, reflectively that "there was a devised physicality that I would not now want to work with." Through a process of "looking back at the piece" she realized that it was still "dominated by the skills of the professional dancer," which subsequently she had attempted to "decrease... while using them" (Butcher in Butcher and Melrose 2005, 200).

SCAN, in other words, had been fully completed in the early 2000s. Returning to Kubler above, the creative process was marked by 'clusters of action' from 1999 to 2002, the time of its conception and development. In 2015 Butcher returned to it, not in ways that would further 'work through' (in the Lyotardian sense) the creative ideas that form the basis of *SCAN*. What was 'worked through', however, was the framework that the retrospective event provided. Its focus on memory, and specifically the creation of a history of Butcher's creative practice over several decades, provided a lens for *SCAN* to be experienced by an audience in Berlin some fifteen years after its creation (Fig. 8.3).

This frame of retrospection becomes about a second remembering—not only the remembering of the making of the work at a different time by Butcher as well as the dancers who still found 'traces' of the work in their (now older) bodies. It also creates a direct link to the archive exhibition within which the live work was placed, in which traces of the original *SCAN* could be found, such as a card and a poster designed by Why Not Associates, a company photograph by Marc Hoflack featuring Butcher with dancers Henry Montes, Rahel Vonmoos, Jonathan Burrows and Lauren Potter in 2000 in Vooruit, as well as Butcher's copy of Cartwright's book on screening the body, as mentioned above.

Fig. 8.3   Rosemary Butcher, *SCAN*, Tanz im August, Berlin, 2015. Photograph by Tanz im August—Vitali Wagner

'Working Through' What Remains—*The Test Pieces*

In 2014 Butcher accepted a commission by Joint Adventures and Städtische Galerie im Lenbachhaus in Munich to create a new live work with local dancers as part of a larger event entitled "Judson Dance and on and on and on."[11] The wider context provided a specific reflective frame with a historical focus on the events of the Judson Dance Theatre in New York City in the late 1960s and early 1970s, which is known to have shifted and loosened the boundaries between the disciplines of art and dance.

Butcher experienced the Judson Dance movement firsthand while spending time in New York City in the early 1970s. As she stated in an interview in Munich in 2014, the events influenced her own choreography-making in terms of a radicalism and an attention to less formalized movement. Further, she found great interest in the heightened subjectivity of the dancer and in experiencing dance to be—at least apparently—no longer to be bound to conventional structures with a hierarchical relationship between choreographer and dancer. She witnessed performances taking place in all sorts of spaces, indoors and outdoors, including exhibition spaces and galleries, and appreciated experiencing interconnections between dance and the visual arts—the latter of which Butcher was to further explore extensively over the following four decades in her own choreographic works. For Butcher there was "no way back" after these experiences in New York City and she felt she could no longer hold on to the conventions present in Modern Dance (Butcher in Trang 2014). In this sense, 'history' occupied her imagination thereafter.

For *New Work—Test Pieces*, as she initially called the work in 2014 in Munich, Butcher worked with four local dancers Sabine Glenz, Judith Hummel, Katrin Schafitel and Mey Sefan. The piece was to be performed at Kunstbau im Lenbachhaus in Munich, a subterranean art gallery that was converted in the 1990s from a disused space, which had been abandoned due to technical reasons when the underground station Königsplatz, located directly underneath, was built.[12] Butcher was given free use of the space which mirrors the shape of a long and narrow underground station. Dan Flavin's light installation *UNTITLED (FOR KSENIJA)* provided an environment for the work to be set within (Fig. 8.4).

At the time, besides creating the new work, Butcher actively engaged with her archive of works as well as the development of a methodology allowing her to sort, present and rework her archive materials. She practiced this meta-research engagement of looking into and 'working' the past, engaging with the concept of 'what remains' while anchoring the conceptual basis of the development of the live work in the field of architecture in a focus on physical remains in the form of ruins. In the preface to the edited collection *Ruins* by Brian Dillon—a publication that informed Butcher's creative process—the editor refers to the "relation of ruins to a future or futures": "Ruins embody a set of temporal and historical paradoxes. The ruined building is a remnant of, and portal into, the past; its decay is a concrete reminder of the passage of time. And yet by definition it survives, after a fashion: there must be a certain (perhaps indeterminate) amount of a built structure still standing for us to refer to it as a ruin and not merely as a heap of rubble" (Dillon 2011, 11).

Butcher commented on her interest in the gallery venue Kunstbau and specifically its history of abandonment as well as conversion (Butcher in Trang 2014). She found further fascination in the abandoned S-Bahn train station München Olympiastadion (Munich Olympic Stadium), which was built in the early 1970s and used during the 1972 Olympic Games that were marked by the notorious acts of terrorism, falling into

Fig. 8.4 Rosemary Butcher, *The Test Pieces*—Munich 2014; Nottingham 2015, Berlin 2015. Photographs top and mid by Sam Williams; lower by Tanz im August—Vitali Wagner

Fig. 8.5 München Olympiastadion Station, 2014. Photographs by Sam Williams

disuse in 1988. She visited the site near the Olympic Stadium with disused railway tracks, an abandoned ticket hall and platform, grown over with weeds, decaying over time (Fig. 8.5).

Butcher observed that these spaces—the Kunstbau gallery and München Olympiastadion station—interested her since they constitute modern ruins that tell a story and bear traces of past times and events, which directly links to her research and interest in time and history, as well as material and immaterial remains (Butcher in Trang 2014). She further explained in an interview with Sigrid Gareis in 2015: "*The Test Pieces* works with memory and site—the site being whatever was left behind after the demolition of a building. The performance is an exploration of how the site can be recorded and inscribed through a movement language resting in an empty space" (Butcher in Gareis and Butcher 2016, 28). As Dillon further notes, "radical potential" can be found in ruins, precisely due to their "fragmentary, unfinished nature" (Dillon 2011, 18): "Ruins are part of the long history of the fragment, but the ruin is a fragment with a future; it will live on after us despite the fact that it reminds us too for a lost wholeness or perfection" (ibid., 11). What Dillon observes here recalls aspects of Jacques Derrida's discussion in the publication *Archive Fever: A Freudian Impression* of the archive as not only pertaining to the past but also to the future, further making the point that no future is possible without repetition of something that has already occurred (Derrida 1996, 80).

In the making of *The Test Pieces* Butcher created a set-up that relied on the dancers' improvising and thus not referring to pre-fixed movement material, which meant a return for the choreographer to her ways of working from the 1970s and 1980s. For the first time the choreographer integrated an object into her work—the dancers were manipulating large ropes in using simple actions such as pulling, throwing, layering, carrying, picking up, adding to. Butcher commented that she pursued "a new direction" in the work, yet recognized a connection in particular to her earlier works *The Site* (1983) and *Body as Site* (1993) (Butcher in Gareis and Butcher 2016, 28).

After its initial performance in Munich in 2014, Butcher developed the piece in two further instances, once for Nottdance Festival 2015 with dancers Sabine Glenz, Judith Hummel, Katrin Schafitel who had worked with her in Munich, as well as Ana Mira, with whom Butcher had previously created solo and duet works, live and on film. She further developed the work with a new set of dancers for Tanz im August in Berlin 2015, all of whom she had a history of working with: Lauren Potter, Charlie Morrissey, Elena Giannotti and Ben Ash. In both instances of its performances in 2015, *The Test Pieces* was presented in relation to an exhibition from Butcher's archive, which further framed the focus of the choreography on processing remains from the past. Yet, drawing back on the third definition of 'to transmit' outlined at the beginning of this chapter, the piece in itself might be understood to 'communicate' the very 'idea' of remains from the past, both in terms of architectural as well as Butcher's choreographic remains in her own archive.

CONCLUDING THOUGHTS

These three choreographic works presented by Butcher from 2010 to 2015 deal in various ways with an active remembering of past events, crucially processed in the practice of choreography making. Butcher's reinvention of Kaprow's *18 Happenings in 6 Parts*, as noted above, was the only time that she attempted to address the artwork of another artist. In doing so, she set up a creative process that was marked by her own interpretation of Kaprow's concept of activities and his interest in the everyday. While Kaprow's Happening provoked a radical shift in the conception of an artwork in the late 1950s, Butcher experienced a radical shift in her own choreographic practice. It might be argued that something was 'passed on' from one artist to another, or from one artwork to another, yet as I indicated above, I prefer to understand this process in active terms—Butcher has 'taken over' aspects of Kaprow's thinking that she encountered in his archive.

Further, the presentation of Butcher's choreography *SCAN* from 1999 as part of the retrospective event *Rosemary Butcher: Memory in the Present Tense* in Berlin in 2015 created a specific focus on processes of remembering past works made. Butcher did not attempt to make any changes to the choreography itself, yet the framing of the event set up a specific lens focused on history and memory as such, within which *SCAN* was experienced.

Butcher's most recent choreography *The Test Pieces*, as I have sought to demonstrate, dealt in thematic as well as in structural terms with remains from the past, both in terms of a consideration of architectural ruins in the creative process, as well as in the wider sense of a focus on remembering the past. Linking back to Manning's account of memory, Butcher was also preoccupied with how to give form to memory in her choreographic invention.

As I discuss above, the creation of new work can always be understood in relation to its past, and hence is likely to provide new ways of seeing and understanding that past. In Butcher's own words, during her involvement in setting up the large retrospective event in Berlin in 2015: "It was important to me to look back as well as to go forward. I wanted to show selected older pieces and to present new work, whatever the risk. It was important to allow the older works to rest against what was present" (Butcher in Gareis and Butcher 2016, 27).

Overall these six years of Butcher's creative practice might be seen to be marked by a continual preoccupation with her own past as a choreographer whose history is bound up with Judson Dance. Each of the choreographic works discussed here, from the perspectives set up in this chapter, formed 'clusters of action' that informed her conception of her own past as well as her investment in the future—to making new work.

NOTES

1. Rosemary Butcher 1947–2016.
2. Butcher was not aware that this would be her final choreographic work. Indeed, still earlier in 2016 she had been planning rehearsals for a new solo work, on which however she was unable to embark.
3. Melrose (2009) points out that 'dance'—as institutionally-ratified conventions, patterns, ways of doing and knowing creatively—is always already present and actively engaged in new work, even when that new work is felt by the practitioner and by others to be radically different.
4. These issues have been debated within the wider field of practice-as-research within the arts.
5. See for example www.sfmelrose.org.uk.
6. Melrose (2005).
7. See *Oxford English Dictionary*.

8. Bergson (1991)—translation by Nancy Margaret Paul and W. Scott Palmer.
9. See Hudek (2009).
10. I further discuss Kaprow's event in Sachsenmaier 2013. Also see "Beyond Allan Kaprow: An Interview with Rosemary Butcher" for further information on Butcher's creative process and the implications the reinvention had in her choreographic practice (Sachsenmaier 2012). For a brief description of Kaprow's Happening see indicatively Aronson, Arnold (2000, 67) and Meyer-Hermann et al. (2008, 122).
11. See *Dance at Judson and on and on and on* event website: http://www.jointadventures.net/en/dance-at-judson-and-on-and-on-and-on.html. Accessed 31 October 2016.
12. For more details on the history of Kunstbau see http://www.lenbachhaus.de/the-museum/architecture/kunstbau/?L=1.

Acknowledgment I would like to thank Susan Melrose for providing detailed comments and suggestions for this chapter.

BIBLIOGRAPHY

Aronson, Arnold. 2000. *American Avant-Garde Theatre: A History*. London and New York: Routledge.

Bergson, Henri. 1991. *Matter and Memory*, trans. Nancy Margaret Paul and W. Scott Palmer. New York: Zone Books.

Butcher, Rosemary, and Susan Melrose (eds.). 2005. *Rosemary Butcher: Choreography, Collisions and Collaborations*. Enfield: Middlesex University Press.

Cartwright, Lisa. 1995. *Screening the Body: Tracing Medicine's Visual Culture*. Minneapolis and London: University of Minnesota Press.

Derrida, Jacques. 1996. *Archive Fever: A Freudian Impression*. Chicago and London: University of Chicago Press.

Dillon, Brian (ed.). 2011. *Ruins: Documents of Contemporary Art*. London: Whitechapel Gallery and Cambridge, MA: The MIT Press.

Guerlac, Suzanne. 2006. *Thinking in Time: An Introduction to Henri Bergson*. Ithaca, NY and London: Cornell University Press.

Hudek, Antony. 2009. From Over- to Sub-Exposure: The Anamnesis of Les Immatériaux. *Tate Papers* 12, Autumn. http://www.tate.org.uk/research/publications/tate-papers/12/from-over-to-sub-exposure-the-anamnesis-of-les-immateriaux. Accessed 25 Oct 2016.

———. 2016. The Affective Economy of the Lyotardian Archive. In *Rereading Jean-François Lyotard: Essays on His Later Works*, ed. Heidi Bickis and Rob Shields. London and New York: Routledge (first published by Ashgate Publishing, 2013).

Kubler, George. 1962. *The Shape of Time: Remarks on the History of Things.* New Haven, CT and London: Yale University Press.

Lyotard, Jean-François. 1988. Réécrire la modernité. *Cahiers de philosophie* 5: 205–213.

———. 1991. Obedience. In *The Inhuman: Reflections on Time*, trans. Geoffrey Bennington and Rachel Bowlby, 165–181. Stanford: Stanford University Press.

Manning, Erin. 2009. *Relationscapes: Movement, Art, Philosophy.* Cambridge, MA and London: The MIT Press.

Melrose, Susan. 2005. *...just intuitive....* http://www.sfmelrose.org.uk/justin-tuitive/. Accessed 4 Nov 2016.

———. 2009. Expert-intuitive Processing and the Logics of Production: Struggles in (the Wording of) Creative Decision-making in 'Dance'. In *Contemporary Choreography: A Critical Reader*, ed. Jo Butterworth and Liesbeth Wildschut, 23–37. London and New York: Routledge.

———. 2009. Rosemary Butcher: Jottings on Signature in the Presence of the Artist. Keynote Presentation at *Bodies of Thought*, Siobhan Davies Studio, London, 3 April. http://www.sfmelrose.org.uk. Accessed 4 Nov 2016.

Meyer-Hermann, Eva, Andrew Perchuk, and Stephanie Rosenthal (eds.). 2008. *Allan Kaprow—Art as Life.* London: Thames & Hudson.

Rajchman, John. 2009. *Les Immatériaux* or How to Construct the History of Exhibitions. *Tate Papers* 12, Autumn. http://www.tate.org.uk/research/publications/tate-papers/12/les-immateriaux-or-how-to-construct-the-history-of-exhibitions. Accessed 25 Oct 2016.

Rosenthal, Stephanie (ed.). 2010. *Move: Choreographing You Exhibition Catalogue.* London: Hayward Publishing.

Sachsenmaier, Stefanie. 2012. Beyond Allan Kaprow: An Interview with Rosemary Butcher. *Journal of Dance and Somatic Practices* 4 (2): 267–281.

Sachsenmaier, Stefanie. 2013. Reinventing the Past: Rosemary Butcher Encounters Allan Kaprow's 18 Happenings in 6 Parts. *Choreographic Practices* 4 (2): 223–244.

Interview

Butcher, Rosemary, and Sigrid Gareis. 2016. *All is Now: A Talk with Rosemary Butcher.* Interview with Sigrid Gareis in: Rosemary Butcher: Memory in the Present Tense. Catalogue Retrospective Rosemary Butcher, Tanz im August 2015, ed. Andrea Niederbuchner, Hebbel am Ufer.

Websites

Butcher, Rosemary. n.d. The Document Series. http://thedocumentseries. com/. Accessed 31 Oct 2016.

———. n.d. Rosemary Butcher—Dance & Visual Artist. http://rosemary-butcher.com/. Accessed 30 Oct 2016.

Ilmberger, Andy. 2015. Lost Place in München—der Geisterbahnhof München Olympiastadion. 20 February. http://xn--mnchenblen-9db.de/gscheng-und-gseng-in-muenchen/lost-place-in-muenchen-der-geisterbahnhof-muenchen-olympiastadion/. Accessed 31 Oct 2016.

Jacobson, Rebecca. 2015. Muscles and Memory. http://www.exberliner.com/ rosemary-butcher-interview/. Accessed 30 Oct 2016.

Joint Adventures. n.d. Dance at Judson and on and on and on. http://www. jointadventures.net/en/dance-at-judson-and-on-and-on-and-on.html. Accessed 31 Oct 2016.

Oxford English Dictionary. https://en.oxforddictionaries.com/definition/trans-mit. Accessed 28 Oct 2016.

South Bank Centre/Hayward Gallery. n.d. Move: Choreographing You. http:// move.southbankcentre.co.uk/microsite/. Accessed 30 Oct 2016.

Städtische Galerie im Lenbachhaus und Kunstbau München. n.d. Lenbachhaus: Das Museum. http://www.lenbachhaus.de/the-museum/architecture/ kunstbau/?L=1. Accessed 1 Nov 2016.

Vu Thyuy, Trang. 2014. Ein Interview mit Rosemary Butcher. http://www.len-bachhaus.de/blog/?p=3575. Accessed 30 Oct 2016.

CHAPTER 9

The Living Cultural Heritage of Robert Cohan

Paul R. W. Jackson

To be ignorant of what occurred before you were born is to remain always a child.
For what is the worth of human life, unless it is woven into the life of our ancestors by
the records of history? (Cicero, *The Orator.* 46 BC)

In his article 'The Body as Archive: Will to Re-enact and the Afterlives of Dances', André Lepecki writes "contemporary dancers and choreographers in the United States and Europe have in recent years been actively engaged in creating re-enactments of sometimes well-known, sometimes obscure, dance works of the twentieth century" (Lepecki 2010, 28). He goes on to list examples from Germany, the USA and Belgium, with the UK conspicuous by its absence. In the contemporary dance landscape of Britain it is an extremely rare occurrence to find dances of the distant or recent past revisited. Of the established contemporary companies (the repertoire of the ballet companies is of course based around their heritage) only Richard Alston and Rambert Dance Company revisit past work with any frequency; the push from funders and artists alike is to focus their energies on the new. In 2014, Theo Clinkard was funded by Arts

P. R. W. Jackson (✉)
Winchester University, Winchester, UK
e-mail: Prwj60@gmail.com

© The Author(s) 2017
L. Main (ed.), *Transmissions in Dance*,
https://doi.org/10.1007/978-3-319-64873-6_9

Council England to travel to New York City to learn and then tour and perform Trisha Brown's 1971 dance *Accumulation*, but this was a singular occurrence.

This attitude is perhaps surprising in a country that prides itself on preserving and promoting its heritage. There are many organizations in the UK dedicated to heritage: English Heritage, The Heritage Alliance, and National Heritage Lottery Fund whose website states that "[h]eritage provides the roots of our identities and enriches the quality of our lives" (NHLF 2016). The Royal Opera House Covent Garden received capital funding in the millions for its refurbishment in the 1990s and at the time of writing there are plans for the Palace of Westminster have upward of £4 billion spent on it. Here then is the crux. All of the projects cited are concerned with tangible cultural heritage as defined by the UNESCO 1972 *Convention Concerning the Protection of the World Cultural, Natural Heritage* (World Heritage Convention), being concerned with the preservation of buildings, monuments and sites. An enormously important declaration that has influenced the policies and practices of governments around the world in relation to the 'universal value' of heritage, it has however been criticized for fostering a view that looks too closely at a western perception of heritage (Byrne 1991; Pocock 1997; Cleere 2001). Since 2006 however, many practices, skills, arts and performing traditions, including dance, have been added to the UNESCO lists as a result of the approval in 2003 of the *Convention for the Safeguarding of Intangible cultural heritage* (ICH). The dance practices and forms that appear on the lists include Flamenco and Argentine tango, as well as many dances of indigenous peoples around the world.

The two UNESCO Conventions, which define rules to which member states must adhere in law (UNESCO n.d.), were the results of years of intense negotiations. The 1972 Convention states: "For the purpose of this Convention, the following shall be considered as 'cultural heritage': monuments...groups of buildings...of outstanding universal value from the point of view of history, art or science; sites...of outstanding universal value from the historical, aesthetic, ethnological or anthropological point of view" (UNESCO 1972, 2). This position was obviously skewed to western cultures that have frequently built large monuments and buildings at the expense of the heritage of cultures that do not. According to Isar (2011, 46–47), it was the arrival of the Japanese diplomat Kichuro Matsura as UNESCO Director General in 1999 that led ultimately to the 2003 convention.[1] It is interesting to note that while there were no votes against the Convention, some countries including Australia, Canada, the USA and the UK abstained (Smith and Akagawa 2008, 3).

Article 2 of the 2003 Convention states:

> The "intangible cultural heritage" means the practices, representations, expressions, knowledge, skills – as well as the instruments, objects, artefacts and cultural spaces associated therewith – that communities, groups and, in some cases, individuals recognize as part of their cultural heritage. This intangible cultural heritage, transmitted from generation to generation, is constantly recreated by communities and groups in response to their environment, their interaction with nature and their history, and provides them with a sense of identity and continuity, thus promoting respect for cultural diversity and human creativity.

It was significant that dance was included, as Bodo notes, "whilst in the former, decisions are made on what is worth preserving and transmitting to future generations, in the latter, this heritage is constantly questioned and rediscovered by individuals who breathe new life into it" (2012, 82). However Naguib (2008, 2013) argued that tangible and intangible are not separate entities but in fact closely bound together. This concern has been developed further by Kirshenblatt-Gimblett (2004) who worried that the 2003 Convention would result in another list as exclusive and excluding as the first.[2] She also registered her discomfit with UNESCO's parcelling of intangible and tangible into separate bundles because they do not reflect the real-life interactions of the two. For Ruggles and Silverman: "Place and performance are bound together through the human body... The dramatic shift in values implied in the IHC...represents a radical paradigm shift from the nature of material culture to the subjective experience of the human being" (2009, 1).

Iacono and Brown (2016), through a close analysis of the work of Merleau-Ponty ([1945] 1992), Bourdieu (1977) and Giddens (1984), have convincingly argued that the term 'living cultural heritage' should replace the in/tangible dualism. They propose that: "Living cultural heritage' is embodied by individuals, in connections with the artefacts they produce and use and the environment they interact with and it is expressed through practices, activities and performances...it is also 'constituted by the feelings and emotions of people and the way they relate to this heritage, including taste and perceptions. Heritage and human beings are indissolubly connected and continuously shape each other in an open ended fluid dialogue" (Iacono and Brown 2016, 90–91). This would seem in part to answer the concerns raised by Nas (2002), Amselle (2004), van Zanten (2004) and Airize (2004), who feared that the management of such a list as part of an ever-changing 'living culture' would result in the embalming or trivializing of such a heritage. Pietrobuno (2013) further posits the view that YouTube, as an unregulated and constantly updating repository of recorded material, has the possibility of countering "the fossilising of representations of national intangible heritage" outside the realm of sanctioned lists. The main purpose of the 2003 UNESCO convention was to ensure the survival of centuries-old practices which were in danger of being lost in the technological 'advances' of the twenty-first century. But it is not only long-established traditions that are in danger of being lost, it is more recent ones as well.

Under the terms described by Iacono and Brown above, Robert Cohan CBE can certainly be considered part of the 'living cultural heritage' of contemporary dance in Britain—the heritage of the last 40 years proving to be as fragile as that of the last 400. In the events leading up to two performances held at The Place, London to celebrate his ninetieth birthday on March 26, 2015, he was referred to in the press as the 'founding father' of British contemporary dance, a significant accolade. Cohan was born in New York City in 1925 and joined the Martha Graham Dance Company after active service in World War II. He soon became one of the significant figures in that organization, not only dancing many major roles for Graham but also becoming Assistant Artistic Director in 1963. A hiatus occurred after a disagreement with Graham and he left to follow personal projects from 1957 to 1962. During this period he danced in Cuba for Jack Cole but more importantly, he formed his own dance company and began to choreograph and to develop his own ideas on teaching. It was this managerial and artistic experience that convinced Robin Howard, the English businessman who created and financed the Contemporary Dance Trust in London, to invite him to become Artistic Director of the Trust and as such Cohan became the founding Artistic Director of The Place, London Contemporary Dance School and London Contemporary Dance Theatre (LCDT), which he directed for over 20 years. He created many works for LCDT in collaboration with leading composers and designers, including acknowledged masterworks such as *Cell, Stabat Mater, Forest* and *Nymphaeas*. Cohan, thus, had an enormous influence on the development of dance in Britain. Through his ground-breaking work in the teaching of contemporary dance technique and his pioneering development of dance residencies throughout the country, Cohan was central to the development of a sizeable new audience, not only for the repertoire of LCDT, but for many other British companies which followed. The list of artists who trained with Cohan is extensive and includes Robert North, Richard Alston, Siobhan Davies, Lloyd Newson, Rosemary Butcher, Darshan Singh Bhuller, and Anthony van Laast. Such a list is considerable and could go on to include choreographers and dancers in every part of the world. From 1980 to 1990, he acted as the Artistic Advisor to the BatSheva Dance Company and was instrumental in placing Ohad Naharin as Artistic Director. He was much in demand as a director of choreographic courses, notably the International Course for Professional Choreographers and Composers which he directed six times.

This is a significant list of achievements, but Cohan's work was largely forgotten until a number of events drew attention to him. The publication in 2013 of my biography, *The Last Guru, Robert Cohan's Life in Dance from Martha Graham to London Contemporary Dance Theatre*, coincided with his return to the UK after living in France for many years. Following the publication of my book, Yolande Yorke-Edgell asked Cohan to work with her company, Yorke Dance Project, firstly restaging and then creating new work. These all fed into the events centred around his ninetieth birthday in 2015 which included a series of seminars on choreography, dance training and music for dance held at The Place, and two gala performances at the Robin Howard Theatre which included new and classic choreography by Cohan as well as new dances inspired by his work. His significant body of work—whether one appreciates its artistic merits or not, it is undeniably significant—up to this point was sadly likely to be regarded in the same way as Lepecki described Martha Graham's: "completely outmoded, derided, and neglected by contemporary dance" (Lepecki 2010). Sanjoy Roy was correct when he wrote: "If you see a Robert Cohan piece—well, you're lucky. Once the mainstay of Britain's premier modern dance company, his works are now rarely seen" (Roy 2010). The dance culture in Britain, which Cohan did so much to create from 1967 onwards, has changed out of all recognition.[3] Long-time advocate for contemporary dance in Britain and founder of Swindon Dance, Marie McCluskey puts this down to the fact that the "the contemporary dance world is cannibalistic" and "has no respect for its past" (Jackson 2013, 320), whilst Janet Eilber, director of the Martha Graham Company, feels "[i]t's time for contemporary dance…to come to grips with the fact it has an important past" (Jackson 2013, 320).

TRANSMITTING COHAN'S STYLISTIC LEGACY

This chapter considers current efforts being made to preserve Cohan's work in both the educational and professional fields. The focus is primarily on the work of Anne (Went) Donnelly at Middlesex University and of Yolande Yorke-Edgell, director of the Yorke Dance Project. Between them, they have been remarkably successful in ensuring that Cohan's choreography has returned to the stage; but also that his technique (Cohan/Graham) has continued to be taught and, just as importantly, his words have been recorded in the form of interviews and videos. The work has been transmitted, translated and transformed by these artists working in close conjunction with Cohan and it is the voices of all three that I have tried to capture. The works considered are Donnelly's restaging of *Forest* (1977), the Yorke Dance Project's translation of *Canciones del Alma* (1978, 2013), the transformation of *Lingua Franca* (1984, 2014), and *Sigh* (2015), a wholly new work created for Liam Riddick of the Richard Alston Dance Company in which Cohan transmits his legacy to a new generation.

Cohan's work may not have been seen on the professional stage but his work has been kept alive within certain conservatoires and universities. Ross McKim, former student of and dancer with Cohan, taught Cohan/Graham technique at the Rambert School until his retirement in 2015 and would also stage Cohan's choreography for the students.[4] Likewise, Anne Donnelly, who as Anne Went danced with London Contemporary Dance Theatre, teaches and stages his work at Middlesex University in London. Donnelly (Went) attended the London Contemporary Dance School (LCDS) from 1977 to 1979, a period when its teachers were very much part of the 'living cultural heritage' of western theatre dance.[5] Her instructors in contemporary dance included Jane Dudley, Bill Louther and Noemi Lapzeson who had danced with Martha Graham, and Danny Lewis who had danced with José Limón. Molly Lake (ballet) had danced with Diaghilev, and Nina Fonaroff (choreography) had also danced with Martha Graham but was the principal assistant of Louis Horst. Emilyn Claid, who briefly demonstrated for the arthritic Dudley in 1973, observed her "urgent desire to transfer knowledge" (Claid 2006, 49), a telling phrase that could be applied to all the teachers at LCDS. Between them, they embodied a wide range of the dance heritage of the twentieth century and Donnelly "instinctively knew that these people knew what they were talking about and you just absorbed it" (Donnelly 2016, interview). Donnelly was invited to become an apprentice in the company in her third year at LCDS, becoming a full member in 1980. She remained with LCDT until 1990, creating many roles and learning as many existing roles from the extensive repertoire. Cohan was the primary teacher for the company and since she retired from performing, Donnelly has become a leading teacher of Cohan/Graham technique, working closely with Cohan on preserving his methods and restaging his works for her students, clearly demonstrating Iacono and Brown's ideals of 'living cultural heritage'.

When Donnelly joined the company, the use of video recording was limited and material was learned in the traditional way, either from dancers who had previously performed the role or from Moshe Romano, the rehearsal director. Romano was himself a part of the living heritage of contemporary dance, having been a founder member of the BatSheva Dance Company, working closely with the likes of Martha Graham, Anna Sokolow and John Cranko. Romano also performed in *Celebrants* (1965), Cohan's first work for Batsheva. He seemed to have the entire repertoire in his body, but what was more important was his ability to transmit the material in a supportive environment that encouraged deep learning. The company was not hierarchical in the sense of a traditional ballet company but there were roles that new members would learn before moving on to some of the more demanding ones. On reflection, Donnelly viewed this process of learning different roles within those works as invaluable in remembering the works in a more in-depth way. In *Class* (1975) she recalls learning first the triplet steps in the female sextet then moving onto the female quartet and, finally, the female solo originally created on Sally Estep. In *Stabat Mater* (1975) the new members of the company would learn 'back line' parts before moving forward as their experience grew. Rehearsals with Romano were to learn the movement, rehearsals with Cohan were to work on the subtleties of performance. He being very concerned with the sensation of the movement as well as ensuring that the intention of the work was passed on.

Time spent with Cohan was, for Donnelly, precious and unique. When Cohan entered the room "the space changed" (Donnelly 2016, interview). The studio ceased to be simply a studio; it did not become a theatre but he brought with him some of the electricity found in a performance space. Donnelly felt then, and still does, that "in his presence there is a charge in the air" (ibid.). This sensation was particularly noticeable with regard to a new work, when Cohan would enter the studio and seem "almost magnetically charged" (ibid.). He would have listened to the music intently, he would know who would be dancing with whom and as the artistic process unfolded, he would give clear direction or perhaps an evocative image and the dancers would work with that through an exchange of physical artistic skill. Sometimes, serendipitously, out of what may have seemed a mistake, perhaps a lift that did not quite go to plan, something new would emerge and he would craft that. His intuitive awareness of structure, form and design is that of a master craftsman; with this consummate skill, he seemed prepared for any eventualities. In restaging a role that was created on somebody else, if the original movement was not working because of either physical differences or technical differences, Cohan would work with the dancer and offer a range of possibilities that might change the original movement in order that the choreographic essence was not lost. This adaptability obviously creates a plethora of issues for someone attempting to stage the work at a later date if they do not have an authoritative and integral understanding of the piece. This is not the case, however, with seasoned artist practitioners such as McKim and Donnelly.

From the mid-1970s onwards, all of the dancers in LCDT came from the school and were trained in Graham-based work (Jackson 2013). Once in the company, Cohan taught his very specific development of Graham's technique as company class. In addition, the younger dancers could see the work being danced every day by performers who were themselves a living archive of its development. Now, in the twenty-first century, none of Donnelly's students have had the opportunity of seeing Cohan's larger works performed live, nor are they able to see (apart from herself and the very occasional guest teacher) what a Cohan-trained dancer looks like. There are only four professional recordings of Cohan's work[6] that appear in university library collections and that show his company at their peak. These, as I discuss later, are useful for garnering the shape but not the execution of the movement. Other videos, often of very poor quality, circulate 'underground' and are of limited use.[7] Donnelly, therefore, becomes what Cohan calls the 'witness teacher', the one person who has to give her students all the information needed for their development. She must teach them how to contract and release, fall and rise, jump and land. She must teach them the movement material of the dances and how to execute these movements; how to enter and exit and how to transition from one phrase to the next. Most importantly, she must ensure that this is not in any way a mechanical exercise but fully embodied and stylistically correct.

Along with Cunningham, Limón and various styles of ballet, Graham-based work is often described as a codified system, and wrongly considered to stand in opposition to somatic practices (Claid 2006, 80). Somatic practices and release-based techniques are however, believed to "free the dancer from rigid holding patterns or other constraints that bind thought, feeling, and action" (Batson 2009, 248). Some current thinking places Graham-based technique as the type of training that is goal-oriented because it evolved from the "stylistic preferences of its inventor" (Batson 2009, 248). Graham, then, is characterized as a non-somatic technique, designed to mold the dancer to a specific set of neuromuscular patterns the dancer has to make look 'right' or execute the movements involved 'correctly' (Bannerman 2010). But Cohan's development of the technique places it very much in the somatic camp. Emilyn Claid, describing the X6 Collective's reimagining of a ballet class, writes: "Stripped of its external affectations and ways of learning, ballet, with its technical strategies, provides a balanced, intelligent way to train the body" (Claid 2006, 82), and the same could be said of Cohan/Graham. As long ago as 1958, Gus Solomons Jr, who trained with Cohan in Boston, was able to observe that Cohan was rediscovering Graham for himself and that he had jettisoned the emotional base for so much of the movement to rediscover the physical truth of the technique (Jackson 2013, 198). In the coming years, Cohan honed and refined his ideas on technique so that what he was teaching LCDT in the 1980s was far removed from the accepted understanding of Graham technique, and it was something that was barely known outside of the dancers in the company. It was very much a somatic way of working, emphasizing the inner workings of the anatomical structures of the body but also the spirit's relation to them.

Romano, who died in 2014, wrote a letter to Donnelly in 2009 outlining his analysis of Cohan's technique:

> Bob's teaching method was not a class or movements for choreography but simply aimed to train the dancer's body, which is his instrument. He taught class like a physician. He knew how to make the dancers work on

each organ, on each muscle and tendon. He taught the class like a scientist who used the space in many different ways as a means to move around. He taught the class like an archaeologist teaching the dancers how to excavate into the body and into the floor, so much that you felt the body spring from the floor. He could teach a major part of the class without moving from a single spot... Bob in his method of teaching was tuning the dancers' bodies like musicians tuning their instruments, but altogether they played the score or danced the choreography with great strength of harmony and beauty. (Romano 2009)

It is the essence of this work that Donnelly has to pass onto her students before they begin to work on the repertoire. She wants her students "to understand the fascination and experience the depth of understanding I experienced with the company" (Donnelly 2016, interview).

FOREST (1977)

Donnelly has restaged Cohan's *Forest* a number of times because for her, it "shows clearly the way Bob articulated the movement of the spine and the pelvis, but without necessarily being dramatic. It was really physicalizing the body so the audience was drawn into what we were doing and I think that was fundamental. As opposed to a piece that was going, 'Look at me'" (Donnelly 2016, interview). Over the years *Forest*, has come to be regarded as one of Cohan's greatest creations and was warmly welcomed when Darshan Singh Bhuller restaged the work on Phoenix Dance Theatre to celebrate Cohan's eightieth birthday in 2005. Yet, at its early performances, its silent rituals puzzled a number of critics such as Noel Goodwin in *The Daily Express*, who found it "limited in contrast of dynamics and pace" (Goodwin 1977) or James Kennedy who in *The Guardian* thought it "a piece which is no more than an exercise for the majority of his talented group, and which lacks shape and conviction" (Kennedy 1977). But for those, as Charles Ives might have said, 'with eyes to see and ears to listen' such as Clement Crisp, it was "fluent, highly imaginative and gratifying" in which a "richness of movement imagination suffice to hold our attention completely" (Crisp 1977). Richard Davies told his readers: "The work is so self-contained and really splendid. It ratifies Cohan's position in the pantheon of modern dance choreographers" and that it was "a remarkable composition, not merely because it rendered the audience blissfully cough less, but because of its totally restful atmosphere" (Davies 1977).

Cohan shaped the material for *Forest* around his memories of childhood visits to Camp Raleigh in the Catskill Mountains of upstate New York. From those early years he remembered the sensation of the stillness and calm of being on his own in the forest where "a twig breaking would startle and you would look quickly to see what was there; the wind, the sound of the leaves falling from the trees, tinkling all around and an awareness of being" (Jackson 2013, 221). For him "that is what *Forest* is about and the dancers have to be in that state of awareness that I was in as a kid alone in the forest. That's all there is to it, if you can do that and keep it all together then it works" (Jackson 2013, 223).

Forest is, however, an extremely difficult piece to perform because there is nothing for the dancers to rely on except the exposing painted costumes and some natural sounds. It is filled with difficult balances, particularly for the women, but the men also have long sustained phrases and balances and there are many difficult strenuous lifts and sustained positions. Cohan calls the movement 'sensuous', the dancer has to feel the physical movement itself and its relationship to its environment. Just as he, as a child, was aware of all of the living forest so the dancer has to be aware of that entire environment, sensation, mood, smell, temperature, recreated on stage. In this work more than any other, the dancers have to be so skilled at performing so that they can forget the audience, forget everything except the sensation of the movement. If they can do that and can enjoy their own sensation of movement and maintain that sensation in their body "then the audience will become mesmerised... they won't know why but they will watch" (Jackson 2013, 217).

In performance, the music, an electronic score by Brian Hodgson follows the dancers. Cohan wanted them to take as long as they needed to fill the movement: "they need to feel each other, if they are together on the stage or if they are alone and they need to take time and be aware (of each other and the space)" (Cohan 2015, interview). The music, therefore, is open ended and could last anywhere between 22 and 40 minutes, though in practice the work usually lasted 25 minutes. There is no pulse or rhythm to the music and the dancers have to learn to recognize certain sounds, bird song, rain or wind in the music and in relation to these, shape the performance.

It was, therefore a brave choice for Donnelly to stage, but a sensible one. This is one of the few works by Cohan to have been professionally recorded for broadcast by the BBC in the early 1980s and to be readily available. There is also a good quality video of Phoenix Dance Company

performing the work in 2005 and there exist a number of video recordings of the dance, from live performances by LCDT of varying quality. In addition Donnelly performed almost all of the female roles in
the dance and therefore brought an embodied knowledge of the work
honed over two decades. There are also reviews, an in-depth analysis by
Janet Adshead and Cohan's comments on the work (see *The Last Guru*,
2013). Donnelly and the dancers also had access to Cohan himself, who
attended the later rehearsals.

Donnelly feels the work coheres around the core tenets of Cohan's
technique—Centering, Breathing, Gravity, Balance, Posture, Gesture,
Rhythm, Moving in Space, and so for the dancers there is a clear connection from class work into performance and back again. There is,
therefore, what she calls a 'loop effect' in which class work feeds the
choreography and vice versa. By engaging with both, the students are
able to sculpt a physical moving body informed by Cohan's methodology of teaching and are able to appreciate the many layers of his choreography. The process was not entered into lightly and Donnelly began
preparations for the restaging a year in advance. Central to this was her
awareness that she would be working with dancers from varied technical backgrounds and would therefore need to find ways to embrace this
range of experience without compromising the essence of the work or
aim of what she wanted them to embody.

Lesley Main, in Chap. 5 of this book, draws attention to the role of
the director in restaging dance works. In the absence of the choreographer, a director necessarily makes the decisions in relation to staging
and execution of movement material. Here, Donnelly was undoubtedly
the director with years of corporeal and informed knowledge of the work
but one who also had access to the choreographer. Any changes she
made to the work would be seen by Cohan and ultimately approved or
not approved by him. Cohan's view on making changes is characteristi-
cally open; he believes that a director should have the option of changing material to suit their dancers because movement made on one body
may not fit another. The proviso is that as long as the director has a fully
informed understanding of the intention of the choreographer then what
is added or taken away will work within the context of the dance. Cohan
developed this outlook from his many years of dancing with Martha
Graham, who regularly changed material when a new dancer took over
a role and who encouraged her dancers not to be precious about movement, telling them that there was an abundance of movement in the

world but that finding the right one for the right context was what mattered (Jackson 2013, 40). Cohan's willingness to change and adapt his material or to trust others to do so is what makes the work so interesting for the performers. They feel, and indeed are, part of a living tradition (heritage) that is secure in itself but malleable enough to change over time.

In Donnelly's staging this willingness to adapt has been essential. While the dancers in LCDT were of various shapes and sizes, they were not as diverse as her student dancers. At "Transmission: A Performance Symposium,"[8] held at Middlesex University in 2014, she showed a photograph of one of her casts which outlined the great variance in height and shape. The lead male dancer was smaller than his female partner and few resembled the bodies on which the work had been created. As a consequence, various sections of material had to be changed to accommodate the physical differences between the cast members. Body image was also something Donnelly and the dancers had to contend with. Cohan's dancers in LCDT worked consistently to develop the muscled bodies of highly trained athletes and many of his works were costumed in body-fitting unitards or for the men, simple tights,[9] and *Forest* is no exception. When the student dancers first saw the costumes (all-in-one shiny Lycra for the women and tights and bare chests for the men), Donnelly remembers there was a palpable feeling of dismay, the dancers never before having been asked to expose their bodies on stage. The costumes are very much part of the work and of Cohan's aesthetic and as part of the dancers' coaching Donnelly enlisted the help of John Cree, a lecturer in strength and body conditioning coach from the Sports Department. He observed rehearsals, paying particular attention to the lifts, and devised a gym training regime to aid with the dancers' physical development. For some of the dancers, working in the gym was a new experience, but with careful coaching, in which they were encouraged to view the weights not as dead objects but as physical bodies, the dancers quickly saw the benefits. As their bodies began to change so did their outlook on the costumes and one day Donnelly walked into the studio to see the men were dressed in shorts and bare chest and the women in tight fitting unitards and "we smiled—they obviously wanted to show me their bodies were physically changing in order to grasp more accurately the movement required" (Donnelly 2016, interview).

Reference was made earlier to the importance of filmed versions of the work being available. Phelan (1993) and Auslander (2006) both argue that recordings of performances are objects in themselves, separate from the performance and with their own authenticity. As Donnelly actually appears in some of the recordings she consulted, she was able to mediate between these documents and her 'lived experience' of performing, and more importantly of rehearsing the work many times with different casts, rehearsal directors and with the choreographer. This 'lived experience' of performance enabled her to view various video recordings and question why something may have been changed. Was it whim, accident or human error, or was it an intentional change by the choreographer? Even with an original cast, every time they dance the piece, it is going to be slightly different because it is a living and thus, fluid, art form. Therefore, the older VHS video recordings of LCDT and other companies performing the piece are, realistically, only a snapshot of a moment, and the deciphering requires a skilled experienced director who understands the whole process and can elicit the essential quality of the work—someone who can understand the sensation and physical authenticity of the movement. It is only through this understanding of and ability to translate the physical inner quality of the movement that the work lives again and the knowledge/signature held within it is passed on. Without this 'signature' explicitly evident, both Donnelly and Cohan agree that what the audience sees is only "an outward shape or a shell" (Donnelly 2016, interview) (Fig. 9.1).

In addition to choreographic changes, Donnelly in discussion with Cohan decided to adapt the lighting. Cohan himself in his alter ego of 'Charter' had designed the original lighting plan but now was happy to create a new environment on stage using contemporary projection techniques and LED lighting technology. Cohan designed the new projection and lighting in conjunction with Mikkel Svak and Zak Hein, Middlesex University lighting technicians. This new technology allowed images to be projected onto the floor of the stage which picked up some aspects of the sound score including the use of water droplets in the 'storm section'. So successful does Cohan feel these effects are that he would like them to be incorporated in any future productions. The 'fluid dialogue' Iacono and Brown envisaged has here ensured the ongoing development of a masterwork of British dance.

This 'dialogue' had a profound influence on the students who took part in Donnelly's restaging, with one commenting: "Learning Cohan technique over the last few years has changed the way I view dance and the way I feel while dancing" (anon), whilst another felt that: "Being

Fig. 9.1 Darja Guzikova and Harshil Chauhan in *Forest*. Photograph by Andrew Lang

able to become completely immersed in Cohan's work over the past three years has drawn me in more and more. The connections that Middlesex University has with former Cohan dancers, Graham dancers, and of course Robert Cohan himself have been tremendously beneficial for making an older, established technique seem relevant and desirable to new generations of contemporary dancers like myself' (anon). These 'connections' between past and present and how these shape the future give authority to the importance of preserving Cohan's legacy for future generations.

CANCIONES DEL ALMA 1978/2013

If Cohan's work existed in the educational setting, where it was regarded by some as an essential part of the living dance heritage of the UK, it was all but invisible in the professional arena. From the time of his eightieth birthday celebrations at Sadler's Wells in 2005, there were no professional productions[10] of his dances until 2012, when Richard Alston's company restaged and briefly toured *In Memory* (1989) until Cohan's association with Yolande Yorke-Edgell began in 2013. Yorke-Edgell had an extensive performing career with Rambert Dance Company and Richard Alston and in America with Bella Lewitzky. She established Yorke Dance Project in 1998 as a repertory company to present work by herself and others, including restagings of works from the recent past. She had long wanted to include Cohan's work in the company repertoire and the publication of *The Last Guru* (Jackson 2013) provided the impetus for her, facilitated by the author, to contact Cohan and discuss the possibility of working together. The resulting project, funded in part by Arts Council England, saw Cohan acting as Yorke-Edgell's choreographic mentor and as her director for the restaging of the 1978 solo, *Canciones del Alma*.

Canciones del Alma was a solo made at the request of the Canadian dancer Susan Macpherson. Macpherson had studied with Cohan at the Graham School in New York City in the 1960s and along with fellow Canadian David Earle, had participated in the early work of the Contemporary Dance Trust in the UK, including the very first performance of the London Contemporary Dance Group, organized by Robin Howard at the Jeanette Cochrane Theatre in East Grinstead in 1967. Like Earle she had returned to Canada soon after and became a founder member of the Toronto Dance Theatre. In 1978, she participated as a dancer in the Canadian Dance Seminar, a choreographic course directed by Cohan. Cohan and his work had always impressed her and, like many people who worked closely with him, she was greatly in awe of him but at the end of the seminar she summoned up her courage to ask him to make a work for her as part of an evening of solos she was planning to tour. To her delight Cohan readily agreed but his response, "I always wondered what sort of solo I would make for you if you asked" (Jackson 2013, 228), took her by surprise because she had never considered that he had ever given thought to making a work on her.

The solo lasted almost fifteen minutes and was an extraordinarily taxing dance, both technically and emotionally, and stands as a testament to Cohan's high opinion of Macpherson's abilities. He had, in fact, given her two options for a dance, one would have been a comedy number, slightly shorter and easier, but she opted for the challenge of the darker, dramatic work. For music, Cohan chose Geoffrey Burgon's *Canciones del Alma* (1975) for two counter tenors and orchestra, and this would also become the title of the dance. This work is a setting of two poems and part of a longer poem by Juan de Ypes y Alvarez, the sixteenth century mystic known as St John of the Cross. The three songs are *Oh llama de amor viva*, (Oh Loving Flame of Love), *Tras de un amoroso lance*, (Full of hope I climbed the day) and, finally, the last five verses of *Canciones entre el alma y el esposo* (Song between the husband and wife).

Cohan had long been interested in the works of the Spanish mystic priest/poet, who in many of his fantastical works tried to reveal something of the mysteries of the universe. Like Cohan, the priest felt his work was sacramental, but while noting that it was impossible for man to express these mysteries in literal terms, he observed in his writings that "by means of figures, comparisons and similitudes, they allow something of that which they feel to overflow and utter secret mysteries from the abundance of the Spirit, rather than explain these things rationally" (Jackson 2013, 228). For St John, these 'figures, comparisons and similitudes' were his writings; for Cohan, they were his dances.

The shape of Burgon's songs closely follows that of the poems, and the colours and textures of the music are suggested by the successive images found in the verse. Alongside this Cohan draws a rather more homogenous line, the differences between the three poems drawn closer together with a vocabulary far more 'Grahamesque' than he had used with his own company for many years. The first song begins:

> O Love's living flame,
> Tenderly you wound
> My soul's deepest centre!
> Since you no longer evade me,
> Will you, please, at last conclude:
> Rend the veil of this sweet encounter!

It is formed around a cross-like floor pattern on which the dancer carves strong contracted shapes with cruciform arms and cupped hands.

The dancer returns to her starting position for the beginning of the second song:

> Full of hope I climbed the day
> while hunting the game of love,
> and soared so high, high above
> that I at last caught my prey.

This shows the dancer in various bird-like poses scurrying across the stage, 'the game of love' being a metaphor for the search for Christ.

The words for the final song come from a long conversation between a bride and her husband with the final verses spoken by the bride:

> Let us rejoice, O my Beloved!
> Let us go forth to see ourselves in Your beauty,
> To the mountain and the hill,
> Where the pure water flows:
> Let us enter into the heart of the thicket.

The sensuality of the verse is absent and the picture of 'serene night' painted in the verse not shown. Similar to Graham's *Errand Into The Maze* (1947), where the female dancer goes on a journey leading to a resolution, Cohan's dance seems intent on exploring the same idea without resolution and the effect is unsettling, although the three poems chosen by Burgon paint a journey to serene acceptance.

Cohan had not seen the dance in more than thirty years when I suggested that it would be a suitable work for Yorke-Edgell. In 2010, when I interviewed Macpherson for *The Last Guru*, she had given me a DVD that included three performances of the dance. Cohan felt one in particular was closest to his original intention and it was this version he used to restage the work. For Cohan: "There was no problem starting, accepting[sic] to do the piece with Yolande because I wanted to get back into the studio, because it was the place I always wanted to be and where I lived for years. My only question was could I make the work valid again because I like to work on the people, so when I create a work it is for that person" (McCormick 2014). In this comment, Cohan is in agreement with Andre Lepecki, who argues that in revisiting existing work (Lepecki calls it the "will to archive") there must be the possibility to "identify in a past work still non-exhausted creative fields of impalpable possibilities" (Lepecki 2010, 31), as referenced in Chap. 5 of this book. For Cohan, there were still many possibilities within this work and it manifests Walter Benjamin's idea of translatability. In Chap. 5 Main cites Benjamin's suggestion that some works have "a specific significance inherent in the original [which] manifests itself in its translatability" (Benjamin 1992a, 71). The search for "significance" was an important aspect of the work between Cohan and Yorke-Edgell in the studio. In relation to his work generally, Cohan will frequently speak of the "significance" of a work or a movement within a work and he is only interested in revisiting an old choreography if he can capture, for him, the significance of the material when he originally made it.

In the early stages of rehearsal it could be argued that Cohan was operating in the mode of 'translator' as defined by Benjamin: "The task of the translator consists in finding the intended effect [intention] upon the language into which he is translating which produces in it the echo of the original" (Benjamin 1992a, 77). The translation of the material from Macpherson's body to Yorke-Edgell's was of prime importance. It was not the steps themselves which concerned him but the intention— "once the dancer learns the steps then you have to put them in a certain relation to the music but it may be different [from the original] because they may move differently. The main thing is whether the movement they are doing is saying the same thing you thought of originally. You have to change the movement so that it is saying the same as the original" (Cohan 2015, interview). He may not have been familiar with the steps, not having seen the work for many years, but he is adamant that, for him at least, "when you choreograph something meaningful you can always recall the sensation when you made it, even if it was years later. Your body doesn't forget motivations" (Cohan 2015, interview).

Having admired Cohan for years and being aware of his unique place in the dance world, Yorke-Edgell admits to being "extremely nervous" (Yorke-Edgell 2015, email) in the first rehearsals, but Cohan was clear about what he wanted. He worked slowly on the dance, understanding that the vocabulary was not something her body was attuned to. In each rehearsal he would give enough information and criticism to be able to move forward and not saturate her with too much information. He seldom gave technical notes but worked on developing and shaping an understanding of the work in its entirety, one that would be real for her because "she has to believe what she is doing" (Cohan 2015, interview). This was all aided by Cohan's wonderful sense of humor, which meant that "there was never any tension in the room, just a strong focus and intention about the work" (Yorke-Edgell 2015, email). The differing and highly personal vocabularies of each of the artists here came together to convey "the form and meaning of the original as accurately as possible" (Benjamin 1992b, 73).

Cohan's coaching was often in itself poetic, as when he said to Yorke-Edgell: "You dance in your dreams? So there is a sequence of narration in the dream but your body is lying in the bed, so now it is showing the body so it is the same thing, the dream inside that has to come out. There are no steps; there are internal movements which produce steps. Especially in this dance which is like a meditation, the steps are of course there but it has to be what the body tells you to do or the dream tells

the body what to do and that way it will create a mood for you to perform" (McCormick 2015). It was in this slow, careful building up of an
understanding of the entirety of the work that the rehearsals progressed.
Very little of the actual movement was changed, although emphasis on
certain aspects was. Macpherson is very tall, her legs are longer than
Yorke-Edgell's and for her, the extension of the legs was important.
For Yorke-Edgell, Cohan placed less emphasis on the extension of the
leg and more on swift turns that worked better on Yorke-Edgell's body.
Further changes came in the use of the back since Macpherson, who
was rigorously trained in classic Graham technique, wanted a Graham-
based dance incorporating the isolation of the torso with the exaggerated
rounding of the back, the dropping of the chest, the bringing it back up
again in high release. This was not embedded in Yorke-Edgell or Cohan
who admits, "I have come a long way from that myself," but he was
happy to make alterations to bridge "the gap between the movement and
the person" (Cohan 2015, interview).

Near the end of the rehearsal process a team from BBC Radio 4
recorded material for an edition of the arts program, *Front Row*. For part
of the recording Yorke-Edgell danced and Cohan talked, about where
she was going, what she was feeling, why she stood still. When it was finished, it had lasted only a minute or so and the team said "But you never
talked about the movement only the quality" to which Cohan replied,
"[S]he knows the movement, the most important thing is the quality"
(Cohan 2015, interview).

Cohan worried about how the dance would read to a twenty-first-
century audience, but the work in the studio paid off. Audience and
critical response was enthusiastic as Luke Jennings' 5-star review in *The
Guardian* shows:

> Performed by Yorke-Edgell, the piece describes the journey of the soul
> through the *noche obscura*, the dark night, to final union with the Creator,
> whom the poet presents in the form of a lover. But a lover within the self,
> as Cohan's choreography makes clear. This is no simple walk into the
> light. As Yorke-Edgell first resists – body language quivering and fretful,
> arms pushing fearfully away – and then surrenders herself to ecstasy, you
> have the sense of an almost sexual capitulation. And, in the angularity and
> anguish of the physical vocabulary, a real sense of that dark night and the
> abyss it conceals. This is the mysticism of old Europe, presented not as
> the high baroque of Bernini's swooning St Teresa, but with spare, almost

austere, gravity. Yorke-Edgell's self-containment and authority as a performer count for everything here; she radiates outwards even as she draws
inwards. (Jennings 2014)

Cohan had achieved, to use Benjamin's phrase, a "real translation" of the
work, one which "does not cover the original, does not block its light,
but allows the pure language, as though reinforced by its own medium"
(Benjamin 1992a, 79). Macpherson saw Yorke-Edgell perform the dance
at the Cohan Gala at the Place in 2015 and felt that 'her' work had disappeared, 'lost in translation' so to speak. In her recorded performances,
the gentle eroticism of the poetry is largely missing and she paints a
picture of an obsessive, possibly neurotic woman, earthbound in her
movements and continually searching for something she does not find.
Translated by Cohan for the twenty-first century, the figure is altogether
more human, frail and feminine, a more identifiable figure than the strident figure he drew from Macpherson. For Yorke-Edgell, the journey has
been a remarkable one (Fig. 9.2):

> When I first learned the solo it was quite raw, it is technically difficult
> and so there was a lot to deal with, as I needed to be able to be in the
> work without thinking about the steps. What has been a gift is that I have
> had time to develop my relationship with it, I keep finding new ways of
> approaching moments in the work and find something new every time
> I perform or rehearse it. It is the most important work to me person-
> ally I have been involved in as I can put the whole of myself into it. It
> has become a sort of out of body experience when I perform it now. It is
> physically challenging when I rehearse it but when I perform it there is no
> effort. It is a 15-minute solo that feels like a minute during performance.
> It is a very emotional journey that I take and at the end there is a sense of
> having lived through something quite extraordinary. (Yorke-Edgell 2015,
> email)

LINGUA FRANCA (2014)

Cohan and Yorke-Edgell enjoyed working together and, following the
positive reviews for *Canciones del Alma*, she asked him if he would like
to make a new work for her company. The proposition interested Cohan
because he had been impressed by the calibre of dancers her company
attracted. He was also somewhat nervous since at his advanced age he
wondered whether he would have the energy and stamina to work on a

Fig. 9.2 Yolande Yorke-Edgell in *Canciones del Alma*. Photograph by Pari Naderi

group dance with dancers he had not himself trained. A decisive moment in his decision to make a new work happened when he and the Yorke Dance Project were visiting the University of Winchester and during a break Cohan saw dancer Jonathan Goddard practicing. Cohan has seen dancers rehearse many, many times but what struck him as new in this instance was that Goddard would stare intently at his laptop then stand up, move, sit down, look and stand and move again. Cohan was fascinated by the impact of technology on the rehearsal process of dance, which was so different from his own past experience of daily rehearsal and creation. The possibility that material could be worked on in a studio, recorded and then viewed at a different time fascinated him because he could see that he would be able to pace himself physically, spending less time in the studio and more time at home, yet with recorded material that he could work on. As recently as 2003, Helen Thomas could write: "As a consequence of the lack of dance literacy, the majority of dancers, unlike their counterparts in music, cannot take their parts home to learn and come in prepared to work with the director or choreographer to generate a performance" (Thomas 2003, 130). The tremendous advances in mobile phone and other recording technology, however, mean that dancers now use such recordings as standard practice to continue work outside of the studio, an opportunity that was once unthinkable. Despite all of this, Cohan was still nervous at the prospect of starting a new group work from scratch but, serendipitously, he found a video of the first section from *Agora*, a work from 1984 made for LCDT, and decided this would be a useful starting point.

Cohan originally made *Agora* as a three-section work, with titles, "Intimations," "Chasm" and "Hymn" for LCDT, who performed it after an intensive rehearsal period at the Grand Theatre in Leeds on February 16, 1984. The idea for the work first manifested itself in the 1960s, whilst Cohan was visiting Athens. He was fascinated by and made a number of visits to the Parthenon which was then open to visitors at any time of the day or night. On one occasion, Cohan found himself in the ruins very late at night when he had "the impression that there were ghosts coming up from subterranean passages and living their lives again. The feeling stayed and gave me the idea" (Jackson 2013, 261). On another occasion, he went with some close friends who knew each other well and were able to sit in close proximity to one another in quiet contemplation of the beauty of the space and its mystery, not speaking a word but still and in the silence aware of their connection and relationship. These two ideas of connections of individuals through silence and communication with something barely perceived formed the basis for the work.

'Agora', the Greek for 'place of assembly' or 'meeting place', was translated in Cohan's vision as a meeting place of ghosts. He devised the idea that there were four people who were there at night, just as he had been, as the ghosts appeared. His regular collaborator Norberto Chiesa made an effectively simple set in which the ruins were laid on stage but covered by a black cloth making little hills. When the cloth was removed, the ruins were revealed as a sort of Parthenon.

Each of the sections of *Agora* had poetic quotes in the program notes. "Intimations" was prefaced with a quote from Heraclitus: "The Lord whose oracle is at Delphi neither speaks nor conceals. He gives signs." Set to J.S. Bach's great *Chaconne in D minor* from the *Partita No 2* for solo violin, Cohan created a quartet for the human characters. They enter one by one, each solo yielding to the next as the group assemble and as a community they watch each other, occasionally adding a small broken phrase like a friendly comment on the newcomer's movements. Once the whole group is assembled, the solos, which seem to highlight the differences of each member, come together and the two men and two women dance together, exploring a myriad of human relationships in an attempt to achieve self-consciousness. It was an unusual dance for Cohan in that there was little contact between the dancers; rather each phrase was picked up and passed—transmitted between each member until at the end they were all moving as a single harmoniously connected group. Cohan added touches of everyday movement into his classic vocabulary, slight leanings of a supported head, or casual sitting down, or a hand casually placed on the hip. He did not feel that he had been entirely successful in merging the two styles and this was one of the reasons he was keen to return to the work.

In revisiting the work in 2014, Cohan also revisited the music. The 1984 version used the original solo violin version of the Bach *Chaconne in D minor*. I suggested to Cohan that he try listening to Ferucio Busoni's arrangement of the work for solo piano, since I felt that the greater tonal and harmonic range of the piano version would provide a greater support for the dancers and the structure of the dance as a whole. He listened to many performances of the work by many great pianists, rejecting most as too virtuosic and Romantic in approach. Eventually he settled on a little known recording by the Italian pianist Maria Tipo, feeling that it had enough flexibility in tempo without becoming wayward, and a wonderful clarity in exposing the different layers of Busoni's sound world, which are a substantive extension of the harmonic progressions only hinted at in the Bach original.

Rehearsals began in August 2014 with a company consisting of Yolande Yorke-Edgell, Laurel Dalley-Smith, Jonathan Goddard and Kieran Stoneley. Each of the dancers had been sent a copy of the film to study before the rehearsal period and a particular part to learn. In reality the bulk of the material was learned together in the studio watching the video, which was of poor grainy quality and four heads were better than one in deciphering the material. Cohan would join the rehearsal in the afternoons, to go over what they had done and begin to fit the movement to the piano recording, which in many if not all of the timing aspects was very different from the violin version used on the video.

In the first rehearsals Cohan introduced the work, discussing the original *Agora* and in particular this section, although without using the Greek quotes which went with the original performances as he now considered these a distraction. He explained that each dancer was thinking about where they were and that they had individual personal relationships and thoughts about each other but that they were all different and they only came together at certain moments—a formal four-way conversation without words. He made it very personal, that they had to be in their own worlds and yet together; they had to look at each other and try to see what the other person was saying and react to it, but stay in their own place.

With LCDT, Cohan had trained all of the dancers and knew how they moved. Here, the dancers came from different backgrounds and experiences: Yorke-Edgell from London Studio Centre, Goddard from the Rambert School, Dalley-Smith from Central School of Ballet and Stoneley from the Royal Ballet School. The company did have regular classes in Cohan/Graham, given by Anne Donnelly or Paul Liburd, and while the mix of experience excited Cohan, it also proved to be a challenge. With the original cast, if one dancer moved while someone else moved and even though they performed a different movement, "the texture was similar and you could see the two forms of movement at the same time doing different things or even if all four moved at the same time but they would have the same quality" (Cohan 2015). With the 2015 dancers he found it a struggle, all the way through the process, "to not make them match up to each other, but to find the right way for each of them to do the movement at the same time" (ibid.). If he was working on Yorke-Edgell, he had to think of her personal way of moving while at the same time taking into consideration how the others moved

Fig. 9.3 Yorke Dance Project (Yolande Yorke-Edgell, Laurel Dalley-Smith, Kieran Stoneley, Jonathan Goddard) in *Lingua Franca*. Photograph by Pari Naderi

or looked in relation to her. With the LCDT dancers, the connectivity was automatic and a given. Here, with dancers who did not have years of working together, it took time and effort. It was from this approach that the title *Lingua Franca* appeared and, one could argue, confirms Benjamin's view that "[l]anguages are not strangers to one another, but are, a priori and apart from all historical relationships, interrelated in what they want to express" (Benjamin 1992b, 73) (Fig. 9.3).

Cohan's approach to this work was very different from that for *Canciones del Alma*. With the solo, his aim was to stay as close as possible to the original work, translating it onto a new body. With *Lingua Franca*, he wanted to use the original material from *Agora* as a starting point for a new work. The studio was like a cocoon and the rehearsal process was like a form of metamorphosis. Metamorphic variation is quite common in music, with the term finding its way into a number of musical titles, Strauss' *Metamorphosen for 23 Solo Strings* (1945), Bliss' *Metamorphic Variations* for orchestra (1973) and Philip Glass' *Metamorphosis* (1988). The form can be seen at its clearest in the first movement of Bernstein's *Second Symphony* (1949), in which each variation is a development of the preceding one rather than of the original theme. This is the form Cohan follows in *Lingua Franca*, the material organically reshaped on the bodies of the dancers in the 'hothouse' of the studio. Each day Cohan would take a video of the work home and study it; the next day he would come back with minute corrections to each part—a raised arm here, a bent wrist there, a hold of a shape, a slight adjustment of weight or spacing. These tiny changes saw the work grow organically on the bodies of the dancers moving further and further from the original until a new work emerged. As Goddard recalls, "Bob is a wonderful teacher and his involvement in that way transforms the work, he creates an atmosphere of growth and reflection that keeps the process alive and the movement relevant" (Goddard 2015, email).

The major changes were in the men's roles. Jonathan Goddard had learned a part originally danced by Christopher Bannerman and the material was made to suit his body and performance style. Cohan took great effort to ensure that Goddard, who Cohan feels is a gifted and unique dancer, was able to shape the material to his own body. Stoneley had learned a part which was originally Darshan Singh Bhuller's role. Singh Bhuller had a slender but flexible body and Cohan had to work hard in shaping that material to Stoneley who, although extraordinarily flexible, was firmly trained in ballet and the somatic interchanges needed for Cohan's work were alien to him. There were more changes when, after the work was completed, Stoneley decided to leave the company and take up another contract. His replacement, Philip Sanger, had a different body type again, tall, slim and very flexible, and the material was, after an intensive rehearsal period, metamorphosed onto his body.

Cohan believes that "spatial awareness is vital to a dance work," that "a dance will work if the space is absolutely right for that movement; where they are on the stage, how far forward, how far back, angle, everything has to be considered and I want the dancer to be comfortable in the place I have put them" (Cohan 2015, interview). He spent a great deal of time working on the spatial relationships in this work which he sees as being very much about proxemics. He wanted to extend to the extreme the personal space of each dancer, to a point where they would almost, but not quite, lose contact. The varying sizes of the stages at each performance venue challenged the spacing, even though Cohan designed the lighting to create the optimal dimensions.

As the work progressed and Cohan watched the dancers rehearse together and alone with their computers, he became interested in extending the work by adding an opening section which would begin with the dancers slowly assembling and rehearsing. The dancer and video artist David McCormick made a film for this section which included images of the dancers working and with fragments of Cohan giving directions in rehearsal. As the rehearsals continued, it was decided that for some performances at least, there would be live music to accompany the dance and so Cohan approached his former music director, the pianist and composer Eleanor Alberga to perform the Bach/Busoni. It seemed natural, therefore, to ask her to write and perform a score for this new section. Taking material from the Bach score, Alberga created a new composition which in performance would precede and then lead straight into the *Chaconne*. So *Lingua Franca* moved from a 15-minute exploration of the original dance to a 25-minute work which also explored the use of technology in the rehearsal process. Still later, in some performances, the opening began before the music and the audience entered to see the dancers warming up on stage in silence before the music began. Indeed, Alberga also had a staged entrance and a physical warm-up before she began to play. In this version, the amount of action became rather unwieldy and distracted somewhat from the work as a whole.

In reviews of *Lingua Franca* much was made of it being based on *Agora*, and some critics who remembered that work could not get away from comparing this new piece to that one and these dancers to the originals (Parry 2015). This is one of the blights of the dance world, where critics or older dancers, instead of seeing what is being done to keep dances alive, often bemoan what has been 'lost' in technique or performance quality, whether it be from Balanchine, Ashton, Graham or Cohan.[11] As with *Canciones del Alma*, Cohan has transformed the original for a modern audience. Here is the Theseus Paradox: in rehearsal, much of *Agora* had been 'taken away' and replaced with new material, so was this a new piece or a reconstruction? The dancers see it as a new work, with Dalley-Smith feeling, "it is a new piece in its own right, however its core has come from *Agora*, like a sibling or relative that has the same mannerisms or expressions, it is still its own person" (Dalley-Smith 2015, email), and Goddard observing, "for me the bones of the original text are there, but the flesh around the steps is new" (Goddard 2015, email). In his approach here Cohan has moved on from Benjamin's concepts of translatability and reproduction to more align himself with Mark Franko (1993) who, as Thomas (2003) discusses, believes that revisiting the past should not be about trying to recapture the impossible but reevaluating it and thus avoiding any form of nostalgia.

Sigh (2015)

Robert Cohan and Richard Alston have known each other for more than forty years, Alston being one of the first students in the LCDS, and receiving his first opportunities as a choreographer from Cohan. Following the closure of LCDT in 1994, the Richard Alston Dance Company became the resident company at The Place. Alston subsequently 'loaned' some of his dancers to the Cohan eightieth birthday celebration in 2005, and in 2012 the company restaged Cohan's *In Memory* (1989). It is not surprising, therefore, that Alston invited Cohan to make a new work on his company as part of the celebrations for the choreographer's ninetieth birthday. Cohan accepted and agreed to make a solo on Liam Riddick, who had impressed Cohan by his dancing in *In Memory*.

Cohan gave a great deal of thought as to what type of work he might make for Riddick. One of the problems of getting older is that one's body slows down, the joints get stiffer, the muscles less elastic. For Cohan, this has been a frustrating process but he says, "I dance in my dreams and it's wonderful. Then I wake up and have to work out how to get out of bed" (Cohan 2015, interview). This 'dream dancing' led Cohan to think about his life as a dancer and he had a clear idea for a work that would reference his career, a step from this dance, a phrase from that one, all reimagined through the mind and body of a dancer approaching ninety; a summing up of his life, swansong even.

He was still at this point on the day of the first rehearsal. He had no music, but had been thinking of using Barber's *Adagio for Strings*, which a number of people had told him to avoid because of its overuse in popular culture. Alston suggested Edward Elgar's *Sospiri*, Op. 70 which is a five-minute adagio for string orchestra, harp (or piano), and organ (or harmonium) written in 1914. Elgar had originally intended the composition to be scored for violin and piano, as a companion piece to his popular *Salut d'amour*, and was going to call it *Soupir d'amour* (Sigh of Love). While composing it, however, he realized that he was writing something more intense and so chose an Italian word, *sospiri*, meaning 'sighs'. The work was first performed on August 15, 1914 in Queen's Hall in London, conducted by Sir Henry Wood. Alston found a version online that Cohan listened to and after thirty seconds, asked Alston where the climax was. When he said "in the middle," Cohan said "yes" and went off to the studio with Riddick, not having heard the whole piece.

Once in the studio with Riddick all thoughts he had of summing up his life's work by referencing older repertoire disappeared and he did what he does best, worked with what was in front of him. Cohan believes that "you may get into the studio and have a goal which you cannot explain at all; the goal is the feeling of the whole piece. What it is going to feel like to the audience when it is performed, what is the emotional quality, the colour of it, the feeling of what you just saw without naming it. That feeling has to persist throughout the whole work. Feeling means sensation, emotion, thinking, everything; but it has to be nameless it has to be a qualitative feeling you have in your whole body before you start" (Cohan 2015).

As soon as he had heard the music he had an image of Riddick running, and once they got into the studio and he asked him to run in a circle, he could see the whole dance: "I knew everything" (ibid.). Cohan had been with Martha Graham when he heard her say, "I am the witness to my work", much like Stravinsky saying, "I am the vessel through which Le Sacre passed" (Stravinsky and Craft 1981, 147–148). This has happened to Cohan in the past, most notably with his *Stabat Mater* (1975) in which the movement flowed effortlessly from him to the dancers; and so it did here: "I told him exactly what I wanted and he responded; we were in tune totally" (Cohan 2015, interview).

So quickly did the movement come that it was a bit of a shock to Riddick who was used to working with Alston, who choreographs in the space and then gives the dancer their own time to work on the material before he will add more. "With Bob it was very much a memory challenge. He would start and carry on and carry on and carry on which at first threw me a bit because I wasn't used to having to remember so much so fast! But after a while it was familiar and easier, once I figured out how he worked" (Riddick 2015, email). The speed at which Cohan worked was not the only surprise for Riddick, who, understandably, thought Cohan would be seated the whole time. But, this was not the case, the movement flowed and Cohan was active in moving around the space and lifting a leg or an arm or demonstrating a contraction. There is a considerable amount of floor work in the dance and while Riddick would be on the floor Cohan would use the mirror as the floor and his arms and legs would move, free of weight so he could be clear about what he wanted. The running step which is such a feature of the work, the relaxed poses on the floor or when Riddick on his back would pedal the air are for Cohan memories of his childhood in rural Brooklyn, when he would cycle off to the beach without a care in the world and enjoy nature, free from the distractions of teenage life. Although the work was no longer going to be based on earlier dances, Cohan did reference some earlier material. There is a side-stepping phrase with the arms stretched to the side which comes from a solo Merce Cunningham had performed in Martha Graham's *Deaths and Entrances* (1943) and which was one of the earliest steps Cohan had learned when he joined her company. He also referenced the 'American Document Step', a classic Graham phrase in which an opposite arm leg in parallel are forcibly thrust forward before opening to opposite sides. From its original appearance in *American Document* (1938) it entered class technique, though Cohan recalls it more from the role of Jason in *Cave of the Heart* (1946) with which he was particularly associated.

The dance utilizes a relaxed Cohan vocabulary. Since Riddick is a graduate of LCDS he had never studied Graham-based technique, and his only previous encounter with Cohan's material was in the cast of *In Memory*. Through the techniques mentioned above, however, Cohan was able to be very clear about what he wanted, and Riddick found it easy to adapt the material to his body while, at the same time, Cohan was adapting his material to Riddick: "His input was being him and I designed it around his body" (Cohan 2015, interview). Cohan would push Riddick with information and directions, almost going past the point of limitation. But Riddick thrived on it, finding: "It was a physical and mental test for me and something that kept me on my toes and challenged me every time I performed it" (Riddick 2015, email).

The spark between the two proved fruitful and they had a finished dance at the end of the first three-hour rehearsal; certainly it was rough but there was structure. As Riddick recalls: "He didn't choreograph it to music, it was made in silence. It was a magical moment when we had finished and said 'Shall we try it with some music?' He played the track and I began the piece and everything as I was going through it just fell into place. I finish by running in two large circles around the stage and then exit and as I got to the top corner of the studio the music just faded away. It was perfect!" (Riddick 2015, email). There was a further rehearsal with Cohan and then Riddick rehearsed independently and with Alston while on tour and in the studio. There was a great deal for

Fig. 9.4   Liam Riddick in *Sigh*. Photograph by Camilla Greenwell

the young dancer to piece together at the beginning because the move-ment was unfamiliar and challenging and, in addition there was Cohan's insistence on attention to the intention of the material. But as Yorke-Edgell found, once the two came together, the work was ready for per-formance (Fig. 9.4).

In performance at the "Cohan at 90" Gala at The Place Theatre, London, the dance puzzled critics who tried to read many interpreta-tions into it—"*Sigh* involves a young man undergoing an existential search, running in circles in between being cast down to the ground, striving to rise again" (Parry 2015). Graham Watts felt that because the music was written in the lead-up to World War I then this was "perhaps a nod by Cohan to the origins of The Place as being formerly the drill hall of the Artists' Rifles Regiment, which lost so many lives in that conflict" (Watts 2015). Judith Mackrell highlighted the importance of Cohan continuing to work: "This simple elegiac piece closes with Riddick run-ning in steadily widening circles round the stage—an image that perfectly embodies the spirit of Cohan at 90, as the baton of inspiration is passed from one generation to the next" (Mackrell 2015). As the work grows over the years and is performed in other programs alongside other new work and not in a celebratory gala, it will be seen as a work of its time not of the past. It is a work by a master choreographer with 70 years' experience in dance, but living very much in the present and keen to continue, as he says: "I think that if you make a work fresh, if the person you are choreographing for is of today then it works" (Cohan 2015, interview).

There is no question, as Mackrell suggests, that the baton has been handed on. After 70 years of working in dance Cohan has a unique perspective on the art of dancing and it is a testament to the dance world in Britain that he did so much to create that he is still able in his tenth decade to share his knowledge with a whole new generation—a generation who never saw him dance with Martha Graham and never saw his work with the LCDT. As Lepecki says: "Dance is the passing around and the coming around of corporeal formations and transformations.... Thanks to transformative exchanges of steps and sweat, thanks to ongoing transmissions of images and resonances, choreography allows dancers to turn and return on their tracks in order to dance via ex and incorporations" (Lepecki, 2010, 39). Cohan is still part of this vortex of transformation and exchange that is the dance world and still able to change lives. Jonathan Goddard is eloquent about this unique experience: "I want to be in a studio with Bob because he is something I have not come across before—a guru. It is a strange and affecting experience to be around someone who speaks wisely, effectively and economically and invests in teaching at such a fundamental level. I am sure being around him changes me but I don't know how" (Goddard 2015, email).

The British love celebrating anniversaries, but with the very act of those celebrations they are happy to feel that the job has been done and they can move on and forget. Had Cohan's eightieth birthday in 2005 marked the end of his career, it is highly likely that his legacy would have been lost and he would have become merely a footnote in dance history texts. His work was not being performed professionally, his technical work was scarcely taught and there was scant documentation of his oral legacy. This lack of interest in the recent past was compounded by the attitude of the contemporary dance world, which at the urging of funding bodies, was focused on a very narrow definition of the word 'contemporary' at the expense of the art form's 'living cultural heritage'. The Mali people have a saying that "when an old man dies, a library burns to the ground,"[12] but Cohan did not die, neither metaphorically nor literally, and by the efforts of an array of artist practitioners and writers including Donnelly, Bannerman, Yorke-Edgell, McKim, Liburd and the author, his heritage is once again living. His technique is being taught at Middlesex University, the Rambert School, London Studio Centre, and the students of the first two are performing his work. Middlesex University has gone to great lengths to document his teaching and for them he has taught master classes in Beijing which were recorded.[13] Yorke Dance Project continues to perform his dances and added *Hunter of Angels* (1962) to their repertoire in 2015, and he has created a completely new work *Lacrymosa* (2015) for the company. In workshops and in public interviews, a new generation of dancers is being exposed to his knowledge of dance, accumulated over 70 years. The majority of these talks have been documented, either in audio or video format and a number are available on YouTube.

In addition, in 2015 Yorke Dance Project in collaboration with Middlesex University created the Cohan Collective, an annual two-week summer course for choreographers and composers. Based on the international courses Cohan taught from the 1970s to the 1990s, the course brings together selected choreographers and composers who, with a group of dancers and musicians, work intensively to experiment and create work without the pressure of public performance, and are mentored through the process by Cohan and Eleanor Alberga. The work has not been limited to the UK and Cohan has taught master classes on the West Coast of America where Yorke Dance Project in conjunction with John Pennington Dance Group have held residencies, including a one-week version of the Cohan Collective led by Cohan in Los Angeles in January 2017.

Archaeologists in the 1980s and 1990s became very interested in what could be called the "archaeology of the contemporary past" (Benton 2010, 286). In this period, there was an increased interest in oral histories and study in great detail of recent events in order to gain a greater understanding of contemporary societies (Buchli and Lucas 2001; Harrison and Schofield, 2010). The recent work in restoring the 'living cultural heritage' of Robert Cohan shows how it is possible for the contemporary dance field in the UK to engage with its recent past. The fluid dialogue between past and present, heritage and human beings has shown how it is possible to engage with the roots of our identities and enrich the quality of our lives.

NOTES

1. For further detail, see Aikawa-Faure, Noriko. 2008. From the Proclamation of Masterpieces to the Convention for the Safeguarding of Intangible Cultural Heritage in ed Smith, Laurajane and Natsuko Akagawa. *Intangible Heritage*. UK: Taylor and Francis.
2. The current lists can be found at http://www.unesco.org/culture/ich/en/lists.
3. For differing views as to why this may be so, see Adshead-Lansdale in McKim (2011: 65–89), McKim, Ross. 2011. *The Essential Inheritance of the London Contemporary Dance Theatre*. London: Dance Books and Jackson (2013: 286–310).
4. At the Rambert School this has now passed to Paul Liburd a former dancer with LCDT.
5. Before her studies at LCDS she had studied ballet with Cleo Nordi (1900–1983) a protégé of Nicolas Legat and a former dancer in Pavlova's company.
6. All directed by Bob Lockyer for the BBC in the early 1980s: Cell, Forest, *Stabat Mater*, and *Waterless Method of Swimming Instruction*.
7. Middlesex University via its research centre has documented some of Cohan's teaching, http://www.rescen.net/rctp/#.WCccW_mLSM8.
8. "Transmission—A performance Symposium" took place at Middlesex University, London on Saturday, December 13, 2014. The program included performances of *Two Ecstatic Themes* and Martha Graham's 'lost' solo, *Imperial Gesture* (1935) alongside work by Robert Cohan—see full details on http://www.transmissionperformancesymposium.wordpress.com.
9. Indeed many works prior to the late 1980s were so costumed. Since then the exposure of the dancer's body through costume has become a rare occurrence in British dance. They have occasionally been used in recent work by Richard Alston, Rambert Dance Company and Michael Clark, but these have been the exception not the rule.
10. The exception was a four-minute solo that Cohan choreographed for Darshan Singh Bhuller entitled *Study*, which was performed in the White Christmas season at the Robin Howard Theatre. Although it appeared in *The Observer* as part of Jan Parry's Top Ten Dance List 2005, and was set to be developed further, Singh Bhuller sustained an injury which put an end to his performing career and the Arts Council were not prepared to fund the project without him.
11. This theme came up a number of times at "Following Sir Fred's Steps: a Conference celebrating Ashton's work", held at Roehampton University in 1994. See Jordan Stephanie and Andreé Grau. 1996. 'Following Sir Fred's steps: Ashton's legacy: proceedings of the Ashton conference',

Roehampton Institute, London, 12–13 November 1994. London: Dance Books.

12. This is a phrase has entered the *Lingua Franca* but is attributed to Amadou Hampâté Bâ (1901–1991), a Malian writer and ethnologist, who is credited for saying before UNESCO in 1960: "En Afrique, quand un vieillard meurt, c'est une bibliothèque qui brûle" ("In Africa, when an old man dies, it's a library burning").

13. This can be found at http://www.rescen.net/rctp/#.WLVXpk9XXcs.

Bibliography

Batson, Glenna. 2009. Somatic Studies. From https://www.iadms.org/page/248. Accessed 2 Sept 2016.

Benjamin, Walter. 1992a. The Task of the Translator. In *Illuminations*, 70–82. London, UK: Fontana Press.

Benjamin, Walter. 1992b. The Work of Art in the Age of Mechanical Reproduction. In *Illuminations*, 211–245. London, UK: Fontana Press.

Benton, Tim (ed.). 2010. *Understanding Heritage and Memory*. Manchester, UK: Manchester University Press.

Bodo, Simona. 2012. Museums as Intercultural Spaces. In *Museums, Equality and Social Justice (Museum Meanings)*, ed. Richard Sandell, and Eithne Nightingale, 181–191. London: Routledge.

Burt, Ramsay. 2014. Memory, Repetition and Critical Intervention. *Performance Research: A Journal of The Performing Arts* 8:2, online, 34–41. Accessed 2 Sept 2015.

Butterworth, Jo. 2012. *Dance Studies—The Basics*. London and New York: Routledge.

Claid, Emilyn. 2006. *Yes? No! Maybe... Seductive Ambiguity in Dance*. London and New York: Routledge.

Collins English Dictionary. n.d. Definition of Intangible. Available at http://www.collinsdictionary.com/dictionary/english/intangible. Accessed 7 July 2016.

Connerton, Paul. 1989. *How Societies Remember*. Cambridge: University Press.

Crisp, Clement. 1977. Review for London Contemporary Dance Theatre. *The Financial Times*, April 17.

Elderkin, Rachel. 2015. Cohan at 90. http://downstagecentre.com/the-dsc-team/rachel-elderkin/cohan-at-90-the-gala/. Accessed 2 Sept 2015.

Goodwin, Noel. 1977. Review for London Contemporary Dance Theatre. *Daily Express*, April 6.

Harrison, Rodney, and John Schofield. 2010. *After Modernity, Archaeological Approaches to the Contemporary Past*. Oxford: Oxford University Press.

Jackson, Paul R.W. 2013. *The Last Guru; Robert Cohan's Life in Dance from Martha Graham to London Contemporary Dance Theatre*. London: Dance Books.

Jennings, Luke. 2014. Yorke Dance Project. http://www.theguardian.com/stage/2014/mar/09/yorke-dance-project-review-sadlers-wells-charlotte-emonds. Accessed 2 Sept 2015.

Kennedy, James. 1977. Review for London Contemporary Dance Theatre. *The Guardian*, April 17.

Kirshenblatt-Gimblett, Barbara. 2004. Intangible Heritage as Metacultural Production. *Museum International* 56 (1–2): 52–64. doi:10.1111/j.1350-0775.2004.00458.x.

Lepecki, André. 2015. The Body as Archive: Will to Re-enact and the Afterlives of Dances. *Dance Research Journal* 42/2. Accessed 2 Sept 2015.

Liber, Vera. 2015. Robert Cohan at 90. http://www.britishtheatreguide.info/reviews/robert-cohan-at-the-place-londo-11365. Accessed 2 Sept 2015.

McCormick, David. 2013. *Canciones del Alma* (film). https://www.youtube.com/watch?v=Q2M9rPZnJ7Y. Accessed 2 Sept 2015.

Mackrell, Judith. 2015. Robert Cohan at 90. http://www.theguardian.com/stage/2015/mar/27/robert-cohan-at-90-review. Accessed 2 Sept 2015.

Main, Lesley. 1995. Preserved and Illuminated. *Dance Theatre Journal* 12 (2): 14–15.

Main, Lesley. 2017. The Transmission-Translation-Transformation of Doris Humphrey's *Two Ecstatic Themes* (1931). In *Transmissions in Dance: Contemporary Staging Practices*, ed. Lesley Main. London and New York: Palgrave Macmillan.

Norman, Neil. 2015. Robert Cohan at 90. https://www.thestage.co.uk/reviews/2015/robert-cohan-90/. Accessed 2 Sept 2015.

Oxford Dictionaries. n.d. Definition of Intangible. Available at http://www.oxforddictionaries.com/definition/english/intangible. Accessed 6 June 2016.

Parry, Jan. 2015. Robert Cohan at 90. http://dancetabs.com/2015/03/robert-cohan-at-90-gala-evening-at-the-place-london/. Accessed 2 Sept 2015.

Phelan, Peggy. 1993. *Unmarked. The Politics of Performance*. Abingdon: Routledge.

Pietrobruno, Sheenagh. 2014. Between Narrative and Lists: Performing Digital Intangible Heritage Through Global Media. *International Journal of Heritage Studies* 20, Nos 7–8, 742–759. 10.1080/13527258..2013.807398.

Preston-Dunlop, Valerie, and Ana Sanchez-Colberg. 2002. *Dance and the Performative: A Choreological Perspective-Laban and Beyond*. London: Verve.

Roy, Sanjoy. 2010. Step by Step Guide to Dance: Robert Cohan. http://www.theguardian.com/stage/2010/may/18/dance-robert-cohan. Accessed 2 Sept 2015.

Ruggles, D.Fairchild, and Helaine Silverman. 2009. *Intangible Heritage Embodied*. Dordrecht: Springer.

Schmitt, Thomas M. 2008. The UNESCO Concept of Safeguarding Intangible Cultural Heritage: Its Background and Marrakchi Roots. *International Journal of Heritage Studies* 14 (2): 95–111. doi:10.1080/13527250701844019.

Smith, Laurajane. 2006. *Uses of Heritage*. New York: Routledge.

Smith, Laurajane, and Natsuko Akagawa. 2008. Intangible Heritage–Introduction. In *Intangible Heritage*, ed. Laurajane Smith and Natsuko Akagawa, 1–9. Abingdon: Taylor & Francis.

Stravinsky, Igor, and Robert Craft. 1981. *Expositions and Developments*. Berkeley, USA: University of California Press.

Sweeney, Stewart. 2015. Robert Cohan at 90. http://www.criticaldance.org/2015/04/04/robert-cohan-at-90/. Accessed 2 Sept 2015.

Thomas, Helen. 2003. *The Body, Dance and Cultural Theory*. New York: Palgrave Macmillan.

UNESCO. 1972. *Convention Concerning the Protection of the World Cultural and Natural Heritage*. Available at http://whc.unesco.org/archive/conventionen.pdf. 6 July 2016.

UNESCO. 2003. *Text of the Convention for the Safeguarding of Intangible Cultural Heritage*. Available at http://www.unesco.org/culture/ich/en/convention. Accessed 6 July 2016.

UNESCO. 2014. *Lists of Intangible Cultural Heritage and Register of Best Safeguarding Practices*. Available at http://www.unesco.org/culture/ich/index.php?lg=en&pg=00559. Accessed 9 July 2016.

UNESCO. (n. d.). *General Introduction to The Standard-Setting Instruments of UNESCO*. Available at http://portal.unesco.org/en/ev.php-URL_ID=23772&URL_DO=DO_TOPIC&URL_SECTION=201.html. Accessed 8 Aug 2016.

Watts, Graham. 2015. Robert Cohan gala. http://londondance.com/articles/reviews/robert-cohan-at-90-gala-performance-the-place/. Accessed 2 Sept 2015.

Williams, Peter. 1967. Contemporary Breakout. *Dance and Dancers*, December 1967, 20–22.

Zhang, Zhiping. 2007. Cultural Resurrection in Beijing. *Review*, 2.

Interviews/Communications

Robert Cohan—Interview. June 27, 2015.

Laurel Dalley-Smith—Email Communication. July 14, 2015.

Anne Donnelly—Interview. August 26, 2016.

Jonathan Goddard—Email Communication. July 17, 2015.

Liam Riddick—Email Communication. July 10, 2015.

Moshe Romano—Letter to Anne Donnelly. February 2009.

Yolande Yorke-Edgell—Email Communication. July 11, 2015.

INDEX

A

Agora, 211–214, 216

Air for the G String, 86

Alberga, Eleanor, 216, 222

Alston, Richard, 7, 189, 193, 194, 203, 204, 217–219, 223

'Arc between Two Deaths', 96, 105

Archive
   archival, 3, 4, 7, 12, 13, 15, 17, 20, 30–32, 38, 43, 61, 63, 65, 66, 69, 70, 74, 77, 79–81, 91, 93, 163–165, 170–172, 174, 179, 181, 183, 184, 189, 196, 206

Arke Compagnia d'Arte, Turin, 131

Ash, Ben, 178, 184

Atkinson, Madge, 1, 3, 4, 64–69, 73, 74, 76–78, 80, 81

Ausdruckstanz, 4, 20, 37, 38, 40, 41, 44, 46–48, 50, 51, 53, 55, 57

B

Banes, Sally, 143, 147, 151

Bannerman, Christopher, 197, 215, 222

Barba, Fabian, 8, 44, 52, 55–57, 91, 93, 94

Bartenieff, Irmgard, 155

BatSheva Dance Company, 193, 195

Benjamin, Walter, 5, 92, 93, 206, 207, 209, 214, 216

Brown, Trisha, 144, 172, 190–192, 195, 202

Burrows, Jonathan, 178, 179

Butcher, Rosemary, 1, 3, 6, 7, 163–165, 168, 170–186, 193

Butler, Ethel, 122

C

Cage, John, 144, 145

The Call/Breath of Fire, 88, 97–99

Canciones del Alma, 7, 194, 203, 204, 209, 210, 214, 216

Capucilli, Terese, 5, 122–124, 128, 129

Cell, 192, 223

Childs, Lucinda, 99, 144

Choreutics, 14, 15, 22–24

© The Editor(s) (if applicable) and The Author(s) 2017
L. Main (ed.), *Transmissions in Dance*,
https://doi.org/10.1007/978-3-319-64873-6

Chronicle, 5, 109, 110, 112–115, 117–119, 121–124, 128–134, 136–138
Circular Descent, 85–87, 96, 99–103
Cohan, Robert, 1–3, 7, 9, 105, 192–223
Cohen, Selma Jeanne, 89
Construction, 18, 39, 56
Corbin, Gail, 96, 97, 100, 105
Creative process, 6, 7, 15, 17–18, 164, 169, 176, 179, 181, 184–186
Cultural heritage, 7, 190–192, 194, 195, 221, 222
Cunningham, Merce, 145, 197, 219
Curtis-Jones, Alison, 3, 7, 8

D
Dalcroze, 14, 18–21, 23, 25, 41, 50, 73
Dalley-Smith, Laurel, 213, 214, 216
Dance Notation Bureau, 86
Dancing Drumstick, 1, 3, 11, 12, 14–16, 18, 20, 22, 25, 33
Davies, Siobhan, 161, 193, 198
Deep Song, 110, 112, 134
Denishawn, 85, 101, 105
Derrida, Jacques, 65, 92, 93
Donnelly, Anne, 7, 194–202, 213, 222
Drumstick, 3, 11, 25, 27–30, 33
Dudley, Jane, 122, 194
Dunn, Douglas, 144

E
Effort, 13–15, 22, 24, 26, 31
18 *Happenings in 6 Parts 1959/2010*, 6, 164, 172
Embodied, 12, 13, 15, 17, 18, 22, 23, 26, 28, 31, 38, 40, 48, 50, 55, 62, 66–70, 72, 78, 79, 88, 90, 121, 122, 124, 130, 134, 136, 137, 191, 195, 197, 200
Embodiment, 61, 63, 69, 70, 79
Episodes of Flight, 174
Estep, Sally, 195

F
Fall and Recovery, 85, 86, 94, 96, 104
Federal Theatre Project, 133
Ferguson, Jacqueline, 67–70, 72, 74, 78, 79, 81
Fine, Vivian, 90, 101, 106, 138, 148, 149
Forest, 7, 192, 194, 198, 199, 201, 203, 223
Forti, Simone, 144, 172
Franko, Mark, 13, 18, 50, 121, 216

G
Giannotti, Elena, 174, 184
Goddard, Jonathan, 210, 211, 213–216, 221
Goodman, Deborah, 124, 125, 129
Gordon, David, 144
Graff, Ellen, 115, 116, 118
Graham, Martha, 1–3, 5, 9, 43, 91, 93, 98, 99, 105, 109–126, 128–131, 133–139, 145, 146, 149, 192–197, 200, 203, 204, 206, 208, 213, 216, 218–221, 223
Gray, Diane, 124
Green Clowns, 15, 30, 32

H
Halprin, Anna, 144–145, 172
Hill, Penelope, 96, 97
Horst, Louis, 101, 120, 194
Howard, Robin, 192, 193, 204, 223

Humphrey, Doris, 1, 3, 5, 17, 43, 85–91, 94, 96, 97, 99–103, 105, 106, 109, 116, 126, 127, 131
Hunter of Angels, 222
Hyper-historian, 4, 62, 63, 69

I

Imperial Gesture, 111, 114, 116, 120, 121, 124, 134, 135, 137, 139, 223
Imperial Society of Teachers of Dancing ISTD, 65, 80, 81
Intention, 13, 16, 17, 20–23, 30, 46, 50, 55, 67, 71, 74, 79, 87, 92, 95, 102, 109, 115, 119, 131, 134, 136, 138, 195, 200, 206, 207, 220
Interpretation, 3, 12–14, 16–18, 23, 30, 31, 65, 74, 91, 94, 101, 117, 119, 124, 137, 149, 165
Ishtar's Journey into Hades, 20, 30, 33

J

Jackson, Paul R.W., 7–9, 194, 196, 197, 199, 201, 204, 205, 211, 223
Jones, Kim, 120
Jowitt, Deborah, 99
Judson Dance Theater, 144, 146

K

Kaprow, Allan, 6, 172, 174–177, 184
Kaufmann, Sandra, 96, 98–100, 105
Kelsey, Louise, 91, 102

L

Laban, Rudolf, 1, 3, 11–16, 18–33

Labanotation, 89, 90, 151, 159
Lacrymosa, 222
Lamentation, 110, 114
Lang, Pearl, 122
Lapped Translated Lines, 174
Larsen, Lone Kjaer, 126, 138
Lepecki, Andre, 5, 12, 13, 15, 31, 91, 189, 193, 206, 221
Liburd, Paul, 213, 222, 223
Limón, Jose, 43, 197
Limón Dance Company Limón Company, 86
Lingua Franca, 2, 7, 194, 209, 214–216, 224
Linke, Susanne, 38, 93
Lloyd, Margaret, 86, 89
London Contemporary Dance Theatre LCDT, 7, 9, 192–194

M

Main, Lesley, 17, 18, 109, 200
Malipiero, G. Francesco, 85, 101
Martin, John, 86, 89, 114, 119, 120
Maslow, Sophie, 122–124
Maxwell, Carla, 86
McCormick, David, 206, 208, 216
McKim, Ross, 194, 196, 222, 223
Medtner, Nicholas, 85, 101
Melrose, Susan, 167, 176–179
Memory, 6, 7, 43, 54, 63, 65, 67–69, 76, 81, 120, 143, 150, 155, 156, 165, 168–170, 176, 179, 183, 185, 217–219
Mestizaje, 4, 37, 39, 56
Mindlin, Naomi, 99, 100
Minimal, 74, 76, 145, 146, 161
Mira, Ana, 184
Montes, Henry, 178, 179
Morgan, Barbara, 120, 122–124
Morrissey, Charlie, 178, 184
Move, Richard, 91, 93, 94, 99

N

Nacht, 15, 30–32
Naharin, Ohad, 193
Natural Movement, 1, 4, 64, 65, 67–69, 72, 74, 76–81
Newson, Lloyd, 193
North, Robert, 110, 133, 137, 139, 193
Nymphaeas, 193

O

Orihara, Miki, 126, 129, 138, 139

P

Panorama, 110, 114, 125, 134
Passacaglia, 88, 102
Paxton, Steve, 144
Performance
    performing, 2–5, 7, 8, 37, 38, 40, 48, 55, 61–70, 72, 74, 76, 78–81, 87, 89, 91–93, 97, 99, 100, 105, 109, 110, 118–121, 130, 134–137, 139, 147–149, 152–154, 159, 160, 163, 165, 168, 171, 174, 175, 177–179, 183, 184, 191, 195, 196, 199–202, 204, 209, 211, 215, 216, 220, 222, 223
Perrottet, Suzanne, 14, 20
Phaophanit, Vong, 177, 178
Phoenix Dance Theatre, 198
Pico, Wilson, 41–44, 49, 50, 57
The Place, London, 192
Pointed Ascent, 85–87, 96, 97, 99, 101–103
Pospisil, Miroslava, 99
Potter, Lauren, 178, 179, 184
"Prelude to Action", 118, 122–124, 128, 129

Preston-Dunlop, Valerie, 14–16, 18–20, 24, 31–33
Primitive Mysteries, 138
Prosperi, Alessandra, 125, 129, 130

R

Rainer, Yvonne, 1, 3, 6, 143–161
Rambert Dance Company, 189, 204, 223
Rauschenberg, Robert, 145
Reconstruction
    reconstructed, 2, 5, 88, 109, 110, 112, 121–124, 126, 128, 129, 133–135, 137, 138, 216
Recreation, 1, 2, 5, 86, 88, 90, 96, 114, 172
Reenactment, 1, 2, 4, 37, 39, 45, 88, 91, 93
Reimagining
    reimagine, 1–3, 5, 88, 110–112, 120, 121, 123, 126, 127, 134–137, 139, 197
Repertoire
    repertory, 4, 61, 63, 65, 69, 70, 76, 78, 79, 86, 114, 128, 137, 139, 189, 193, 195, 198, 204, 218, 222
Richard Alston Dance Company, 7, 194, 203, 217
Riddick, Liam, 7, 194, 217–220
Riegger, Wallingford, 118, 126, 127, 136
Romano, Moshe, 195, 197, 198

S

Sachsenmaier, Stefanie, 6, 7, 172, 174, 176
Sadler's Wells, 118, 203
Salgado Llopis, Maria, 4
Sanger, Philip, 215

Sayers, Lesley-Anne, 14–16
SCAN, 6, 165, 177–179, 184
Sehnert, Katharine, 4, 38, 46
The Shakers, 88
Sieben, Irene, 4, 38, 46
Sigh, 1, 7, 194, 217, 220
Singh Bhuller, Darshan, 198, 215, 223
Space Harmony, 13, 21, 23
Spiral curve, 89, 90, 100, 102, 103
Stabat Mater, 192, 195, 218, 223
"Steps in the Street", 110, 112, 119,
    122, 124–131, 138
Stodelle, Ernestine, 86–90, 94–97, 99,
    101, 103
Stoneley, Kieran, 213–215
Successional movement, 96, 104
Summit Dance Company, 3
Sussman, Stanley, 122, 124, 126, 127

T
Tamiris, Helen, 116, 133
Taylor, Paul, 62, 67, 69, 70, 111, 137
Technique, 110, 115, 124, 129,
    130, 134, 136, 143, 146, 160,
    193–197, 200, 202, 203, 208,
    216, 219, 222
The Test Pieces, 7, 165, 168, 177, 180,
    183–185
Topaz, Murirel, 86, 94
Tracer, 111, 120
Transformation, 1, 3, 5–7, 53, 54, 89,
    92, 100, 194, 221
Translation, 1, 3, 5, 7, 12, 13, 18, 30,
    41, 44, 89, 92, 93, 100, 169,
    194, 207, 209
Transmission, 1–9, 12, 27, 39, 40, 45,
    48, 55, 62, 63, 65, 67, 69, 70,
    72, 76, 78, 79, 87–89, 91, 92,
    100–102, 105, 109, 110, 112,

128, 130, 137, 164, 165, 168,
    170, 175
Trio A, 6
Two Ecstatic Themes, 3, 5, 85–89,
    94–97, 99, 100, 102, 104, 105,
    223

V
Van Laast, Anthony, 193
Viera, Kléver, 43, 44, 49, 50, 53–55,
    57
Vonmoos, Rahel, 178, 179

W
Water Study, 88, 102
Watt, Nina, 86, 87
Wigman, Mary, 1–4, 9, 37–41, 44–53,
    55, 56, 91, 93, 94
Wind Tossed, 4, 62–73, 76, 78–81
Witch Dance, 20
Woman and Memory, 174
Wood, Catherine, 158
Wookey, Sara, 5, 6, 8, 144, 145, 150,
    152, 153, 157, 161

Y
Yasko, Jeanne, 96, 97, 100, 105
Yorke Dance Project, 7, 193, 194,
    204, 210, 214, 222
Yorke-Edgell, Yolande, 7, 193, 194,
    204, 206–209, 213, 214, 220,
    222
Yuriko, 5, 122, 124–127, 129, 138